Lecture Notes in Artificial Intelligence   **9068**

Subseries of Lecture Notes in Computer Science

LNAI Series Editors

Randy Goebel
  University of Alberta, Edmonton, Canada
Yuzuru Tanaka
  Hokkaido University, Sapporo, Japan
Wolfgang Wahlster
  DFKI and Saarland University, Saarbrücken, Germany

LNAI Founding Series Editor

Joerg Siekmann
  DFKI and Saarland University, Saarbrücken, Germany

More information about this series at http://www.springer.com/series/1244

Danny Weyns · Fabien Michel (Eds.)

Agent Environments for Multi-Agent Systems IV

4th International Workshop, E4MAS 2014 - 10 Years Later
Paris, France, May 6, 2014
Revised Selected and Invited Papers

 Springer

Editors
Danny Weyns
Department of Computer Science
Linnaeus University
Växjö
Sweden

Fabien Michel
LIRMM UMR 5506
Université Montpellier
Montpellier
France

ISSN 0302-9743   ISSN 1611-3349 (electronic)
Lecture Notes in Artificial Intelligence
ISBN 978-3-319-23849-4   ISBN 978-3-319-23850-0 (eBook)
DOI 10.1007/978-3-319-23850-0

Library of Congress Control Number: 2015948703

LNCS Sublibrary: SL7 – Artificial Intelligence

Springer Cham Heidelberg New York Dordrecht London

Printed on acid-free paper

Springer International Publishing AG Switzerland is part of Springer Science+Business Media
(www.springer.com)

Preface

Ten years ago, researchers in multi-agent systems became more and more aware that agent systems consist of more than only agents. The series of workshops on Environments for Multi-Agent Systems (E4MAS 2004-2006) emerged from this awareness. One of the primary outcomes of this endeavor was a principled understanding that the agent environment should be considered as a primary design abstraction, equally important as the agents.

At AAMAS 2014 in Paris, researchers in the E4MAS domain organized a workshop on *E4MAS – 10 Years Later* with the following aims: (1) to reflect on the past 10 years of research and engineering on agent environments for multi-agent systems; (2) to investigate to what extent the challenges identified a decade ago have been tackled; (3) to outline challenges for future research on a short and longer term.

This book reports the results of the workshop and subsequent efforts. We start with a roadmap paper that consolidates knowledge from past research and from these insights defines a path for future research in the field. The roadmap focusses on three particularly relevant topics of modern software intensive systems from the viewpoint of agent environments for multi-agent systems: the large scale of systems, the openness of systems to deal with parts that enter and leave the system dynamically, and humans in the loop that interact with the system.

After the roadmap follow 13 contributions that span a wide variety of topics grouped in four parts. The first part presents three papers on the connection between agents, environments, and humans. The second part contains a set of interesting papers on environments for complex and stigmergic systems. The third part presents four papers on virtual and simulated environments. Finally, the fourth part concludes with two papers on open agent environments and interoperability. All papers presented in this volume were carefully reviewed.

We are grateful to all those who contributed to the successful organization of E4MAS 2014, in particular, the Program Committee, the AAMAS Committee, and the local organizers. We hope that the papers of this volume will stimulate further research in agent environments for multi-agent systems and contribute to enhancing engineering practice.

July 2015

Danny Weyns
Fabien Michel

Organization

Agent Environments for Multi-Agent Systems - 10 Years Later was organized in conjunction with AAMAS on May 6, 2014 in Paris, France.

Program Co-chairs

Danny Weyns — Linnaeus University, Sweden
Fabien Michel — Université de Montpellier, France
Van Parunak — ABC Research, Ann Arbor, MI, USA
Olivier Boissier — ENS Mines Saint-Etienne, France
Michael I. Schumacher — University of Applied Sciences Western Switzerland
Alessandro Ricci — Università di Bologna, Italy

Program Committee

Julien Saunier — LITIS, INSA-Rouen, France
Eugenio Oliveira — University of Porto, Portugal
Franziska Kluegl — Orebro University, Sweden
Flavien Balbo — ENS Mines Saint-Etienne, France
Pablo Noriega — IIIA-CSIC, Spain
Tom Holvoet — KU Leuven, Belgium
Ana De-Melo — University of Sao Paulo, Brazil
Kostas Stathis — University of London, UK
Gildas Morvan — Université d'Artois, France
Vincent Hilaire — UTBM/IRTES-SET, France
Juan A. Rodriguez — IIIA-CSIC, Spain
Eric Platon — Cirius Technologies, Inc. Japan
Mirko Viroli — Università di Bologna, Italy
Jacques Ferber — Université de Montpellier, France
Karl Tuyls — Liverpool University, UK
Luca Tummolini — ISTC-CNR, Italy
Olivier Simonin — INSA de Lyon, France
Franco Zambonelli — Università of Modena and Reggio Emilia, Italy
Lars Braubach — University of Hamburg, Germany
Rafael H. Bordini — FACIN-PUCRS, Brazil
Marco Mamei — Università di Modena e Reggio Emilia, Italy
Alexis Drogoul — IRD, Vietnam
Stefano Bromuri — University of Applied Sciences Western Switzerland
Giuseppe Vizzari — University of Milan-Bicocca, Italy
Andrea Omicini — Università di Bologna, Italy
Federico Bergenti — Università degli Studi di Parma, Italy
Sven Brueckner — Jacobs Technology Inc., USA

Jean-Pierre Muller	CIRAD, France
Shinichi Honiden	National Institute of Informatics, Japan
Ambra Molesini	Università di Bologna, Italy

Website

http://homepage.lnu.se/staff/daweaa/events/E4MAS/2014.htm

Contents

Roadmap

Agent Environments for Multi-agent Systems – A Research Roadmap

Danny Weyns[1,2(✉)], Fabien Michel[3], H. Van Dyke Parunak,
Olivier Boissier, Michael Schumacher, Alessandro Ricci
(Organizers E4MAS – 10 Years Later)
Anarosa Brandao, Carlos Carrascosa, Oguz Dikenelli,
Stépane Galland, Ander Pijoan, Patrick Simo Kanmeugne,
Juan A. Rodriguez-Aguilar, Julien Saunier,
Visara Urovi, and Franco Zambonelli
(Section Coordinators)

[1] Linnaeus University, Vaxjo, Sweden
[2] KU Leuven, Leuven, Belgium
danny.weyns@cs.kuleuven.be
[3] Université de Montpellier, Montpellier, France
fmichel@lirmm.fr

Abstract. Ten years ago, researchers in multi-agent systems became more and more aware that agent systems consist of more than only agents. The series of workshops on Environments for Multi-Agent Systems (E4MAS 2004-2006) emerged from this awareness. One of the primary outcomes of this endeavor was a principled understanding that the agent environment should be considered as a primary design abstraction, equally important as the agents. A special issue in JAAMAS 2007 contributed a set of influential papers that define the role of agent environments, describe their engineering, and outline challenges in the field that have been the drivers for numerous follow up research efforts. The goal of this paper is to wrap up what has been achieved in the past 10 years and identify challenges for future research on agent environments. Instead of taking a broad perspective, we focus on three particularly relevant topics of modern software intensive systems: large scale, openness, and humans in the loop. For each topic, we reflect on the challenges outlined 10 years ago, present an example application that highlights the current trends, and from that outline challenges for the future. We conclude with a roadmap on how the different challenges could be tackled.

Keywords: Agent environment · Multi-agent systems · Middleware · Large-Scale Systems · Open systems · Human in the loop

1 Introduction

Ten years ago, the awareness grew among researchers in the multi-agent systems community that agent systems consist of more than only agents. The Environments for Multi-Agent System workshop (E4MAS [1]) that was organized in conjunction with

© Springer International Publishing Switzerland 2015
D. Weyns and F. Michel (Eds.): E4MAS 2014 – 10 years later, LNAI 9068, pp. 3–21, 2015.
DOI: 10.1007/978-3-319-23850-0_1

AAMAS 2004 emerged from this awareness. The driver for E4MAS 2004 was the following statement:

There is a general agreement in the research community that agent environments are essential for multi-agent systems, yet researchers neglect to integrate the agent environment as a primary abstraction in their models and tools for multi-agent systems.

During three successful editions of the E4MAS workshop [1, 2, 3] and various additional activities, a substantial group of researchers worked intensively on the subject of agent environments. One of the primary outcomes of this endeavor was a principled understanding that the agent environment should be considered as a primary design abstraction, equally important as the agents. Different models and architectures have been proposed to design agent environments, and these designs have been validated in a variety of application domains. A special issue devoted to agent environments in multi-agent systems in the Journal on Autonomous Agents and Multi-Agent Systems in 2007 [4] included a set of influential papers that define the role of agent environments, describe their engineering, and outline challenges in the field that have driven numerous follow-up research efforts [6–10].

At AAMAS 2014 in Paris, researchers in the E4MAS domain organized a workshop on "E4MAS—10 Years Later," and this paper builds upon discussions at that workshop. The goal of this paper is:

- To reflect on the past 10 years of research and engineering on agent environments for multi-agent systems;
- To investigate to what extent the challenges identified a decade ago have been tackled;
- To outline challenges for future research on a short and longer term.

Instead of taking a broad perspective, we focus on three particularly relevant topics of modern software intensive systems: the large scale of systems, the openness of systems to deal with parts that enter and leave the system dynamically, and humans in the loop that interact with the system. Evidently, we focus on these topics from the viewpoint of agent environments for multi-agent systems. For each topic, we explain the topic and highlight challenges outlined 10 years ago, we present an example application illustrating the current trends, and then we outline challenges for the future. We conclude the paper with a roadmap to tackle the different challenges.

The remainder of this paper is structured as follows. Section 2 focuses on the impact on agent environments for large-scale multi-agent systems. Section 3 zooms in on open agent environments for multi-agent systems. Section 4 discusses the impact of humans in the loop on agent environments. Finally, Sect. 5 outlines a possible roadmap for future research in this important field.

2   Agent Environments for Large-Scale Multi-agent Systems

Many real world problems are of high dimension (lots of interacting features), large in size and often stochastic by nature [20]. Such Large-Scale Systems (LSSs) are intricately multifarious, with multiple objectives that can lead to conflicts among the multiple decision makers present in these systems. A system can be considered as an LSS if one (or both) of the following perspectives holds [21]: *(i)* It can be decomposed into a number of interconnected subsystems, either for practical reasons (design) or because computation needs to be distributed (performance); (ii) Its high dimensionality leads to a combinatorial explosion in its space of possible behaviors, so that the usual methods for modeling analyzing, controlling or designing cannot find a solution in a reasonable amount of time. As a result, these systems require that the control of the data and/or computation be decentralized over the subsystems. The engineering of LSSs has been subject of extensive research, including approaches proposed for dealing with complexity within the field of multi-agent systems.

In particular, MASs are a natural approach for modeling and implementing LSSs because they rely on decentralized loci of control by means of agents [20]. A Large Scale MAS (LSMAS) is a MAS that is hard to (i) *engineer* (e.g. coordination among thousands of agents) or (ii) *deploy* (e.g., real-time interaction may no longer hold due to the computational requirements). Bottlenecks in an LSMAS are usually related to the size of the system in terms of the number of agents and the amount of data in the system. Indeed, regardless of the application domain, each additional agent requires some computational resources. Moreover, the MAS should be able to accept new agents without compromising its functioning. This section discusses the crucial role of agent environments for an LSMAS, i.e., a MAS with a large number of agents evolving in application environments that potentially involve a huge amount of data.

2.1 Large Scale and Agent Environments

The agent environment is now broadly recognized as a first class abstraction for building a MAS, especially because it mediates interactions between agents and their access to resources [6]. In an LSMAS, the number of interactions and resources could be very large, hence the design of the agent environment is even more crucial because it directly impacts scaling issues and plays an important role in managing potential bottlenecks. We put forward four requirements that are central to engineering agent environments for LSMAS:

1. *Scalable Structure:* refers to distributing the computation and state of the agent environment. The agent environment may have different structures: multi-level or hierarchical, multi-stage or dynamic. For example, the agent environment may be structured in segments, each representing a local view on the physical environment; segments may be connected via a P2P network.
2. *Access to Resources:* Typically, LSMASs are composed of heterogeneous agents deployed in an agent environment, which defines laws that regulate access to resources. At a large scale, monitoring, trust, and security aspects are to be carefully designed so that the cost induced by managing access to resources does not become a bottleneck.
3. *Scalable Communication:* When coordination among thousands of entities is required, the agent environment should provide means for communication between agents that do not involve any central point of access or control.
4. *Interaction model:* to achieve scalable agent environments, it is important to provide agents with efficient means for perceptions, actions, and interactions. Central

here are suitable abstractions, e.g., the agent environment should offer high-level primitives to agents for perception, coordination etc., that support efficient processing by the agents.

2.2 Challenges on Large Scale Agent Environments in Retrospect

While scalability was not a prominent topic in the past E4MAS efforts, the four requirements mentioned in the previous section have been partly identified or addressed in different contexts during the period 2004-2007.

Scalable Structure and Access to Resources. Several researchers showed that the structural scalability of the agent environment is strongly related to the ability to achieve decentralized control over the environmental data and dynamics, so that one can move easily from a monolithic structure to a distributed one. In [22], the agent environment is decomposed into independent *interaction spaces,* each of which defines explicitly local environmental rules. In the domain of large-scale traffic simulation, [23] applies a holonic modeling of the agent environment so that the environmental processes apply only locally. These examples show that decentralizing the structure of the agent environment and managing access to resources based on the principle of locality are already identified as key principles for achieving scalability of agent environments.

Scalable Communication and Interaction Model. A decade ago, considering dynamics in the agent environment as a efficient means for achieving communication and coordination in an (LS)MAS was already a topic of interest in the E4MAS community. Especially, nature-inspired mechanisms supporting indirect communications through the agent environment, such as digital pheromones and force fields, were considered to scale better than direct message exchanges (see e.g. [24–27]), thus providing scalable interaction models for achieving coordination among numerous agents using stigmergic principles. Nevertheless, it is interesting to note that the mechanisms for engineering the agent environment discussed in [7] do not consider explicitly scalability as a main feature of interest. Since then, the dramatic evolution of the technological context, especially with respect to the exponential increase of smart mobile devices, has put scalability on the agenda as a major topic. Nowadays, scalability is no longer an option, but a requirement for many MAS applications.

2.3 Example Application

We illustrate a recent effort on agent environments for LSMASs in the context of *Personalized Health Systems* (PHSs). PHSs are systems that support patient-centered healthcare by assisting patients in self-managing their medical conditions. Using a PHS, patients and caregivers are connected so that health data are accessible independently from their geographical location. Since the patient's data is generated in a distributed setting, these systems require reliable, scalable and interoperable models of information flow. For example, [28] models the discovery and exchange of health records with a dynamic interoperable MAS network. A high-level model of this system is illustrated in Fig. 1.

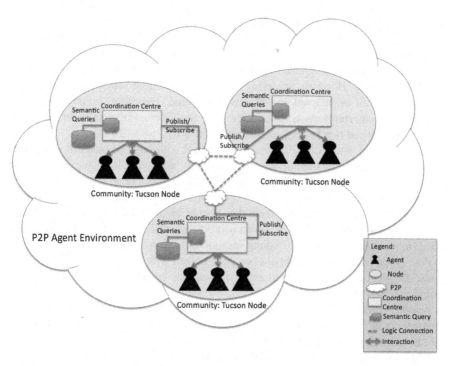

Fig. 1. SemHealthCoord: An agent-based LSMAS model for health data exchange

Different health communities (i.e. hospitals) store the patient's data. A Peer-to-Peer (P2P) architecture connects these communities dynamically and at large scale. Figure 1 shows how the agent environment is organized. Health communities are connected as *Nodes* in a *P2P* network. A set of coordination rules *(Coordination Center)* defines how agents can find patients' data and how they can propagate updates in the network of communities. Since the data in different communities may be organized differently, the querying of data follows a semantic knowledge base *(Semantic Queries)*. In this model, the agents specialize on performing specific tasks (i.e. finding the data about a patient) while the agent environment itself defines how the interactions can take place across communities. More specifically, the *Coordination Center* specifies how data can be queried in a distributed level and how new data can be propagated to different communities. The *Agent Environment* uses the TuCSoN coordination model [29] where agents retract, write or read (called *in-out* or *rd primitives*) data in the *Coordination Center* using specific tuple templates. These actions trigger reactions that coordinate the tasks of different agents, despite these agents may not share the same space, may not know each other's reference, and may not be synchronized.

2.4 Challenges Ahead

Realizing the requirements of LSMASs outlined in Sect. 2.1, namely: (1) making the structure scalable, (2) ensuring efficient access to resources, providing (3) scalable communication means and (4) interaction models, are still major challenges. In this respect, previous research emphasizes the crucial role of locality and decentralization when engineering the agent environment's structure and mechanisms. Not addressing these aspects puts more responsibility on the agents, which leads to complex agents and hampers scalability. However, achieving locality and decentralization is not sufficient if the system cannot be adapted and evolved over time. Therefore, future research on scalable agent environments is about addressing the different aspects in an integrated manner. We outline two key aspects for future efforts.

As we move toward LSMASs that have to deal with huge amounts of data, elaborating efficient structures and dynamics is not only a solution for achieving scalable communication and interaction, but also a key to more effective processing of data and information. To that end, we see two important challenges that agent environments have to address: *(i)* Preprocessing data: data should be modeled and structured so that they can be easily managed and evolved using large scale dynamics compliant to the underlying environment (e.g., by taking inspiration from map reduce approaches), and *(ii)* Post-processing data: data should be synchronized with the agents' needs. In other words, the agent environment could anticipate requests by processing data accordingly, through internal dynamics.

Another central challenge lies in designing agent environment structures and dynamics in an integrated way; e.g., design agent environment dynamics so that they accommodate the underlying physical infrastructure [2, 8]. Considering this aspect, one can take inspiration from the General-Purpose computing on Graphics Processing Units (GPGPU) community (High Performance Computing). In this context, computation and data models are explicitly considered so that they can benefit from the underlying physical infrastructure of the GPU (a massively parallel architecture). Performance and scalability are directly influenced by how the data model accommodates the underlying hardware. So, it is possible to design scalable agent environment dynamics very efficiently because they are modeled matching the physical infrastructure. One recent example is the use of digital pheromones in LSMAS simulations [30].

3   Open Agent Environments for Multi-agent Systems

Living in an environment, perceiving it, and being affected by it intrinsically imply openness. Software systems are no longer isolated, but become permeable sub- systems, whose boundaries permit reciprocal side effects. The reciprocal influence between system and environment is often extreme and complex, making it difficult to identify clear boundaries between the system and its environment.

In several cases, to achieve their objectives, software systems must interact with external software components, either to provide services and data, or to acquire them. More generally, different software systems, independently designed and modeled, are likely to "live" in the same environment and interact explicitly with each other. These open interactions call for common ontologies, communication protocols, and suitable broker and coordination infrastructures to enable interoperability.

A major advance in engineering multi-agent systems has been the recognition of the importance of the agent environment in which the agents are situated, and through which they interact, as a first-class abstraction. However, current environment-based multi-agent systems rely on a fixed, a priori definition of the agent environment, and only agents that conform to that definition can exploit it. A powerful next step is the notion of an open agent environment, one that adapts in response to the agents that inhabit it.

This section explores the theme of open agent environments for multi-agent systems. We start by explaining the viewpoint we take on openness of agent environments in this paper. Then we look at challenges of open agent environments that have been identified earlier and reflect on these. We continue by illustrating a typical existing approach to deal with openness in multi-agent systems. Finally, we reflect and outline challenges ahead.

3.1 What Is Openness?

The concept of openness of software systems is not well defined in the literature. [11] refers to open software systems as systems that are specifically built to allow for extensions. [12] considers openness as a property of software systems that are subject to decentralized management and can dynamically change their structure. [16] refers to openness as the system's ability to deal with entities leaving and entering the system. [13] refers to openness of a MAS as "the ability of introducing additional agents into the system in excess to the agents that comprise it initially." He categorizes openness in three levels: (1) off-line openness, which allows addition of new agents only off-line, e.g., by halting the system, adding agents, updating some connection information, and re-starting the system, (2) static openness where agents can be added to the system without re-starting it, but all of the agents either are notified of such an addition, or they hold in advance a list of prospective additional agents, and (3) dynamic openness that allows agents to leave or enter the system dynamically, during run time, without explicit global notification.

Our particular interest here is in dynamic openness, which enables a system to adjust itself dynamically to uncertainty in the environment, tasks, and availability of resources. As outlined by numerous researchers, this type of uncertainty is particularly relevant for systems that are deployed in environments with high levels of dynamicity and change, which are nowadays the rule rather than the exception [13, 14, 15].

3.2 Challenges on Openness of Agent Environments in Retrospect

In the period 2004 to 2007, several researchers pointed out challenges on the openness of agent environments. [1] poses the following question:

What responsibilities does the agent environment have and what services can it provide to increase its openness to heterogeneous agents?

Openness of agent environments was primarily seen as an engineering challenge. For example, [6] identifies the need for suitable software architectures for the agent environment, while [17] argues for suitable abstractions and infrastructures to support agent environment design. [18] stresses the need of suitable mechanisms for the agent environment to support social interactions. On a more concrete level, [16] poses the question whether electronic institutions can be further exploited to handle openness. The emphasis on openness of agent environments has been primarily on the need for architectures and infrastructures that allow different agents to join or leave a multi-agent system at will. The uncertainty in the deployment context, tasks, the availability of resources and changing system requirements, and its impact on the openness of multi-agent systems was not of primary concern a decade ago. This is not surprising, as the dramatic change of operating conditions in which software intensive systems are expected to operate has only become clear over the years.

3.3   Example Application

We illustrate the efforts on openness in engineering agent environments with an example in the domain of supply chain management. Modern supply chain management requires the collaboration of distributed and heterogeneous systems of multiple companies, which naturally maps to open multi-agent systems. However, developing such collaborative applications and building the supporting information systems poses several engineering challenges. [19] presents Macodo, an architectural approach that aims to address the problem of managing the design complexity of collaborative applications.

Central to Macodo are five abstractions: actor, collaboration, role, behavior, and interaction. Macodo offers a middleware infrastructure that supports these abstractions at the levels of design and implementation. An *actor* is an entity that has access to the collaboration environment and is capable of participating in collaborations by playing roles. In a concrete system, actors can be business entities, software agents, services, or even people. A *collaboration* is a controlled process, taking place in the collaboration environment, of a group of actors working together towards a set of goals. A collaboration consists of a set of roles, representing the different actors and their responsibilities in the collaboration, and a set of interactions among the actors of these roles. Collaborations are reusable and can be created and destroyed by the manager of the collaboration. A *role* is the embodiment of the participation of an actor in a collaboration that defines the actor's responsibilities in that participation. When an actor enters a collaboration, a new role instance is created. When the actor leaves the collaboration, the corresponding role instance is destroyed. The distinction between role and role instance is similar as in [51] that distinguishes between role types and role instances. Within the context of a role, an actor can execute behaviors and participate in interactions with other actors in the collaboration. A *behavior* is a coherent unit of reusable functionality that is executed in the context of a role. A behavior is typically application-specific and can encapsulate the execution of a task or the participation in an interaction. Finally, an *interaction* is a controlled exchange of information between the actors of a set of roles in a collaboration. An interaction can have an application-specific protocol.

Macodo offers a set of architecture views that support engineers in modeling applications using these abstractions. The *Collaboration View* models collaborations as reusable modules and shows how they are decomposed into reusable submodules (i.e., roles, interactions, and behaviors). The Collaboration View is used to describe the collaborations in a system in terms of implementation units. The *Collaboration & Actor View* models the actors in a system and the concrete collaboration instances among them. In this view, actors are represented as components, and collaborations as connectors. The Collaboration & Actor View is used to describe the runtime architecture of a system in terms of actors and the collaborations between them, assigning responsibilities to actors, while making abstraction of collaboration details. The *Role & Interaction View* models the internal runtime architecture of a collaboration in detail. This view allows documenting the concrete role and interaction instances in a collaboration, the active behaviors of roles, and how roles delegate the participation in interactions to behaviors. A behavior is executed in the context of a role, giving the actor of the role access to the interfaces of the behavior.

The Macodo abstractions and architectural views allow the modeling and documentation of collaborative applications. The Macodo middleware provides an agent environment to design and implement collaborative applications that are modeled in the Macodo architectural views. The platform supports the Macodo abstractions as programming abstractions by mapping them to concrete technology. Figure 2 shows the primary elements of the Macodo middleware.

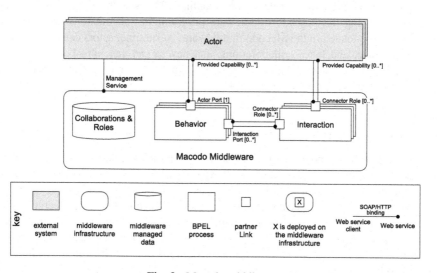

Fig. 2. Macodo middleware

[19] Presents a concrete realization of the Macodo middleware using Web Services technology. Once specified, collaboration modules can be loaded in the Macodo middleware. The management service of the middleware can then be used to register actors and to manage the life-cycle of concrete collaboration and role instances. After a role has been assigned to an actor, the actor can 'play' the role. To play a role, an actor uses interactions and behaviors. The information flow between the actors, interactions, and

behaviors is mediated by the middleware, which routes messages to the correct inter-actions, behaviors, and actors. Messages between the middleware and actors contain additional Macodo data, which uniquely identifies the role to which a message belongs. By decoupling actors from the roles they play, the Macodo middleware offers an open agent environment where different agents can join and leave collaborations at will.

In a concrete supply chain, the supply chain partners are the actors that can play the roles of vendor, warehouse, retailer, and transporter. Each supply chain network can be modeled as a collaboration. For example, in a vendor-managed inventory (VMI), the vendor is responsible for managing the inventory. Products in the inventory, kept in an intermediate warehouse, remain property of the vendor until consumed, or called-off, by the retailer. The warehouse regularly reports inventory levels to the vendor. Based on these inventory levels, the vendor replenishes the warehouse. The retailer can call-off products from the warehouse, after which it reports the consumption to the vendor. To model these collaborations, we can define roles, behaviors, and interactions. For example, we can define an Inventory Reporting Behavior for the Warehouse role to collect inventory levels and pass it to another role using an Inventory Reporting Interaction (send inventory levels to interested parties).

The architecture views then support modeling concrete applications. For example, with the Role & Interaction View can be used to model runtime qualities, such as throughput of interactions or robustness of behaviors. We can, for example, specify that the Call-Off Fulfillment Behavior should always reply to a Call-Off Interaction, even if the actor of the Warehouse role is not reacting. The specifications can then be implemented using the Macodo middleware programming abstractions and concrete instanced can be loaded in the Macodo middleware. At runtime, actors can dynamically enter, participate, and leave collaborations, and new actors can join. For example, a new transporter can enter a collaboration and supply chain partners may switch the transport service dynamically taking into account ongoing agreements.

3.4   Challenges Ahead

In previous research, openness of agent environments has primarily been approached from an engineering perspective, emphasizing the ability of different agents to join or leave a multi-agent system at will. As illustrated with the example above, the main focus has been on identifying suitable modeling abstractions, architectures and infrastructures to support open agent environments. However, the ever-growing com-plexity of software systems introduces a variety of uncertainties that need to be handled at runtime, including dynamics in operating conditions that are difficult to predict and the need to handle changing system requirements that may not be anticipated at design time. Several researchers have pointed out that traditional engineering approaches may not be sufficient to deal with these uncertainties, and call for new engineering solutions. To support openness, we see the following key challenges for the next generation of agent environments:

- Handling uncertainty as a first-class citizen to deal with the inherent dynamics of the context in which multi-agent systems are deployed.

- Reducing seamless integration of online runtime adaptation and offline evolution.
- Support for agents to form sustainable ecosystems (e.g., infrastructure that enables integration of mobile applications developed by different vendors).
- Efficient integration of a wide spectrum of services, from integrating 'things' to supporting intelligent cooperation between and among agents and humans.

4 Agent Environments and Humans in the Loop

Emerging technologies such as wireless sensor networks, Internet of Things (IoT), and smart and wearable devices, provide the basis for new types of applications where the physical world can be accessed or modified by computational systems. Examples of such systems are energy management, health care, and traffic systems. These applications are characterized by *humans in the loop*, i.e., humans are an essential part of the realization of the rich functionalities of such systems. Humans can have the role of users of the system, where they are in continuous interaction with the system through computational devices (PC, tablet, smartphones, etc.), or with the physical environment itself, as in IoT. Humans can also have a role as being integral parts of the system itself, i.e., socio-technical systems. Examples include incorporating users to perform security-critical functions, and incorporating activity models in smart homes to improve the independence of elderly people.

Multi-agent systems are an effective approach for modeling and designing systems with humans in the loop, given their characteristics of autonomy and sociality. In particular, the notion of agent environment can play a crucial role, since the environment is a natural place to model the shared distributed physical and social world with which systems and people interact, and it offers rich forms of communication, either explicit or implicit, temporary or persistent, with manageable levels of coupling.

In this section, we explore the role of the agent environment in the design of multi-agent systems with humans in the loop. We start by outlining the position of humans in the loop in computing systems. Then we look at challenges that have been identified earlier and reflect on these. We provide a recent example application that shows how humans are integrated in the loop in a multi-agent system, and conclude with challenges ahead in this promising area for future research.

4.1 Humans in the Loop

Based on a cursory review of the literature we identified several levels of involvement of humans in the loop in computing systems. We noticed a particular interest for humans-in-the-loop systems in the control systems community; see for example [31, 32, 34]. Example efforts in the context of MAS are [36–39, 45].

1. Humans-in-the-loop monitoring. This level is characterized by a system that monitors humans and takes appropriate actions when needed. An example is AlarmNet [33], which is a smart home health care application that monitors

activities of daily living by using environmental and wearable sensors and creates a continuous medical history. Authorized health care providers are allowed to monitor activity patterns to determine if the residents need immediate attention or new healthcare services.

2. Humans-in-the-loop interaction. This level is characterized by humans that are in continuous interaction with the system through computational devices. An example is a mobile application that supports users to find each other based on particular criteria such as locality, preferences, social contacts etc.

3. Minimizing human intervention. This level is characterized by a system that only invokes a human operator when necessary, and does so in a minimally intervening manner. An example is a human who is responsible for security-related configuration decisions and enacting particular policies [35]. Such tasks require knowledge that may be very hard to codify.

4. Humans-in-the-loop supervisory control. This level is characterized by intermittent human operator interaction with a remote, automated system in order to manage a controlled process or task environment. Examples include air traffic control, military and space command and control, crises response management, and unmanned vehicle operations.

Our interest in this section is on the different levels of human involvement in the loop in multi-agent systems.

4.2 Challenges on Humans in the Loop in Retrospect

In the period 2004 to 2007, humans-in-the-loop in the context of agent environments has not been explored very well in E4MAS research. [6] distinguishes between three levels of support provided by the agent environment in MAS:

1. Providing support to agents for accessing the deployment context. Agents have low-level knowledge to directly access hardware and software resources.

2. Providing agents an abstraction level to the deployment context. The abstraction level bridges the conceptual gap between the agent abstraction and low-level details of the deployment context.

3. Providing support to agents for interaction-mediation. The interaction-mediation level offers support to regulate the access to shared resources, ensure restrictions are met and mediate interaction between agents.

The three levels of support of the agent environment represent different degrees of functionality that agents can use to achieve their goals. The obvious question in the context of this section is: where are humans situated in this three level reference model? Given the different levels of involvement of humans in the loop in MAS, bringing humans in this picture is not a simple task. Straightforward modeling of humans as either part of the deployment context or "special agents" will not be satisfactory for the different responsibilities of humans in the loop in MAS. The key point is to understand how the agent environment as first-class abstraction can support different levels of involvements of humans in the loop in MAS.

4.3   Example Application

We illustrate current research on humans in the loop in MAS with an example application from the domain of pervasive and ubiquitous computing that is called a *sociotechnical superorganism* [40]. Pervasive and ubiquitous computing is a well-known and obvious case where humans are in the loop. In these kinds of systems, the infrastructure is used ubiquitously to access and deploy new services for interacting with the surrounding physical world and with the social activities occurring in it.

A sociotechnical superorganism comprises networks of entities – ICT devices and citizens – that continuously and seamlessly cooperate in highly decentralized activities. Entities can be involved in participatory sensing activities, and the results of real-time sharing of knowledge at city scale enables a shared understanding, via machine-based computing and humans-based reasoning, of urban issues of interest and their dynamics. This in turn makes it possible to plan and direct responses or fix problems with collective actions. Consequently, intelligent, coordinated responses to city-scale problems emerge from a closed feedback loop involving collective sensing activities, understanding and sharing of ideas, and collaborative actions.

In the SAPERE approach [41] pervasive service environments are modeled and architected as a non-layered spatial substrate, laid above the actual pervasive network infrastructure, on top of which human users act as prosumers continuously producing and consuming data. Figure 3 shows the SAPERE Reference Model. The agent environment (MAS Environment) abstractions support the design of agents' activities and interactions.

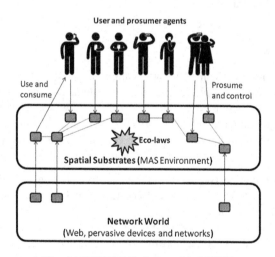

Fig. 3. SAPERE Reference Model [52]

The substrate embeds the basic eco-laws that rule the activities of the system. There, individuals of different species – agents/services, data, and devices – interact and combine with each other (in respect of the eco-laws and typically based on their spatial relationships), so as to serve their own individual needs as well as the sustainability of the overall ecology. In this data-centric approach, the agent environment supports human/agent interaction and coordination by providing an open distributed set of data spaces, hosting streams of tuples – generated by sensors, actuators, human actions and reactions – semantically combined, aggregated, manipulated, and diffused according to the eco-laws.

[52] proposes "In good company", a distributed application for the food court of a shopping mall, that is based on SAPERE, The application enables people to spend some time with friendly persons or anyhow sharing common affinities. A typical use case scenario is the following: (1) a user running the application on its mobile phone approaches the mall's food court willing to launch "in good company"; (2) user's request for friendly locations is shared between the displays associated to a food provider of the court; (3) for each given restaurant, the display takes care of polling its costumers (using the app) to provide a measure of friendship affinity towards the requesting user; (4) each display aggregates such measures and pushes back the answer to the requesting user; (5) given such information the user can decide in which restaurant to have lunch and which group of people to join.

For this application, a SAPERE node with the app code is running on users' smartphones and restaurants' display stands. Different agents running on different devices interact with one another by sharing data via the spatial structure (see Fig. 3). For example, the restaurant Agent propagates the affinity query (AQ) – with a gradient indicating the number of hops and decay time – to surrounding displays. The agent environment regulates the distribution of data through spread eco-laws and aggregation eco-laws. This example shows how the agent environment can provide support for humans-in-the-loop interaction.

4.4   Challenges Ahead

Bringing humans-in-the-loop in MAS applications through a supporting agent environment is an open research topic. These kinds of systems pose complex challenges for an agent environment such as to how model humans, how to design a humans-aware communication infrastructure, how to provide decision and co-ordination support, and how to implement regulation mechanisms. We conclude this section by listing some of the key challenges we see in this exciting research area:

- Obtaining a comprehensive understanding of the spectrum of different types of human-in-the-loop functions in MAS. The levels of human involvement in computing systems provide a starting point.
- Defining and incorporating human models into agent environments to support humans in the loop in MAS, incl. positioning these models into the levels of support of the agent environment [6], or revision or extending the levels.
- Defining agent environment mechanisms and effective means for enabling interaction, coordination, cooperation not only among agents, but among humans and agents too.
- Understand the engineering implications of bringing humans in the loop in agent environments. This challenge includes identifying methodologies for designing and

developing scalable agent environments for human-agent MAS, that integrate with the technology stack, e.g., Internet-of-Things and the cloud.

• Take an inter-disciplinary perspective, by bringing together researchers and expertise from both the human and the agent side, with the objective of designing mixed agent environments with agents and humans.

5 Roadmap

Figure 4 shows the typical progressing levels of maturity to solve problems of computing systems over time [42]. Software/system engineers typically start by solving specific problems in a specific way. When problems recur, the expertise is turned into reusable solutions, for example in the form of frameworks or libraries. In the next stage, engineers abstract from concrete realizations and document design knowledge in the form of architectural approaches to solve the problems, such as tactics, patterns and reference solutions. Then, the knowledge is often consolidated in stable middleware solutions, offering developers programming abstractions and supporting infrastructure. Finally, language support is developed that provides an integrated solution to software developers.

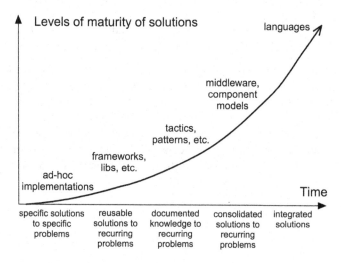

Fig. 4. Maturity levels of computing system solutions

In terms of Fig. 4, researchers and engineers have explored solutions for the different agent environment aspects we have discussed in this paper – large scale, openness, humans in the loop – at different levels. Most efforts have focused on solving specific problems with specific solutions, as testified in [1, 2, 3, 5]. Some of these solutions have been consolidated in reusable frameworks, e.g., [49, 50]. A few researchers have presented patterns to solve problems related to agent environment; examples are [43] with a set of patterns for self-organizing systems, and [44] presenting the results of a recent systematic survey of patterns applied in MAS. [48] presents an architecture framework for collective intelligence systems, comprising three viewpoints that support architects with designing agent environment for knowledge sharing platforms that are based on stigmergic principles. Different middleware solutions and a few component models have been developed. Prominent examples are electronic institutions [45] and coordination artifacts [46]. Recently, some initial efforts have been done on programming support for agent environments, e.g., [47].

A closer look at existing work shows that most efforts are at lower levels of solution maturity, in particular ad-hoc implementations and frameworks. This is a natural situation for research that has been in an explorative stage. However, we believe that the time has come to balance exploration with consolidation. In Sect. 4 we have presented a variety of opportunities for exploratory research on agent environments for MAS. We conclude with complementary opportunities to consolidate research efforts:

- Perform empirical research to validate the claims of existing solutions of agent environments for multi-agent systems.
- Consolidate existing knowledge on agent environments for multi-agent systems; one effective way to do so is by performing a systematic survey of the state of the art in the field;
- Consolidate existing know-how on agent environments for multi-agent systems by documenting recurring solutions in the form of patterns, reference models and reference architectures;
- Define model problems and exemplars to drive and communicate research advances, establish research agendas, and compare and contrast alternative approaches.

Computing systems are increasingly intertwined with the surrounding world in which they are deployed and used. Furthermore, the growing dynamics, integration, and expanding scale of software-intensive systems calls for decentralization. The agent environment lies at the intersection of these two evolutions and will be more relevant for future computing systems than ever before. We hope that both the opportunities for further exploration and suggestions for consolidation may be a stimulus to further study, development and maturation of the field of agent environments in multi-agent systems.

References

1. Weyns, D., Van Dyke Parunak, H., Michel, F. (eds.): Environments for Multi-Agent Systems I, E4MAS 2004. LNCS, vol. 3374. Springer, Heidelberg (2005)
2. Weyns, D., Van Dyke Parunak, H., Michel, F. (eds.): Environments for Multi-Agent Systems II, E4MAS 2005. LNCS, vol. 3830. Springer, Heidelberg (2006)
3. Weyns, D., Van Dyke Parunak, H., Michel, F. (eds.): Environments for Multi-Agent Systems III, E4MAS 2006. LNCS, vol. 4389. Springer, Heidelberg (2007)
4. Parunak, H.V.D., Weyns, D.: Guest editors' introduction, special issue on environments for multi-agent systems. Auton. Agent. Multi-Agent Syst. 14(1), 1–4 (2007)
5. Weyns, D., Omicini, A.: Special issue engineering environments in multi-agent systems. Multiagent Grid Syst. 5(1), 1–131 (2009)

6. Weyns, D., Omicini, A., Odell, J.: Environment as a first class abstraction in multiagent systems. Auton. Agent Multi-Agent Syst. **14**(1), 5–30 (2007)
7. Platon, E., Mamei, M., Sabouret, N., Honiden, S., Parunak, H.V.D.: Mechanisms for environments in multi-agent systems: survey and opportunities. Auton. Agents Multi-Agent Syst. **14**(1), 31–47 (2007)
8. Viroli, M., Holvoet, T., Ricci, A., Schelfthout, K., Zambonelli, F.: Infrastructures for the environment of multiagent systems. Auton. Agent Multi-Agent Syst. **14**(1), 49–60 (2007)
9. Valckenaers, P., Sauter, J.A., Sierra, C., Rodrıguez-Aguilar, J.A.: Applications and environments for multi-agent systems. Auton. Agent Multi-Agent Syst. **14**(1), 61–85 (2007)
10. Helleboogh, A., Vizzari, G., Uhrmacher, A., Michel, F.: Modeling dynamic environments in multi-agent simulation. Auton. Agent. Multi-Agent Syst. **14**(1), 87–116 (2007)
11. Buckley, J., Mens, T., Zenger, M., Rashid, A., Kniesel, G.: Towards a taxonomy of software change. J. Softw. Maintenance Evol. Res. Pract. **17**(5), 309–332 (2005)
12. Zambonelli, F., Van Dyke Parunak, H.: Signs of a Revolution in Computer Science and Software Engineering. In: Petta, P., Tolksdorf, R., Zambonelli, F. (eds.) ESAW 2002. LNCS (LNAI), vol. 2577, pp. 13–28. Springer, Heidelberg (2003)
13. Shehory, O.: Software architecture attributes of multi-agent systems. In: Proceedings of Agent Oriented Software Engineering, pp 77–90 (2000)
14. Weyns, D.: Architecture-Based Design of Multi-Agent Systems. Springer, Heidelberg (2010)
15. Cheng, B.H., de Lemos, R., Giese, H., Inverardi, P., Magee, J., Andersson, J., Becker, B., Bencomo, N., Brun, Y., Cukic, B., Di Marzo Serugendo, G., Dustdar, S., Finkelstein, A., Gacek, C., Geihs, K., Grassi, V., Karsai, G., Kienle, H.M., Kramer, J., Litoiu, M., Malek, S., Mirandola, R., Müller, H.A., Park, S., Shaw, M., Tichy, M., Tivoli, M., Weyns, D., Whittle, J.: Software engineering for self-adaptive systems: a research roadmap. In: Cheng, B.H., de Lemos, R., Giese, H., Inverardi, P., Magee, J. (eds.) Software Engineering for Self-Adaptive Systems. LNCS, vol. 5525, pp. 1–26. Springer, Heidelberg (2009)
16. Valckenaers, P., Sauter, J., Sierra, C., Rodriguez-Aguilar, J.A.: Applications and environments for multi-agent systems. Int. J. Auton. Agents Multi-Agent Syst. **14**(1), 61–85 (2007)
17. Viroli, M., Holvoet, T., Ricci, A., Schelfthout, K., Zambonelli, F.: Infrastructures for the environment of multiagent system. Int. J. Auton. Agents Multi-Agent Syst. **14**(1), 49–60 (2007)
18. Platon, E., Mamei, M., Sabouret, N., Honiden, S., Van Dyke Parunak, H.: Mechanisms for environments in multi-agent systems: survey and opportunities. Int. J. Auton. Agents Multi-Agent Syst. **14**(1), 31–47 (2007)
19. Haesevoets, R., Weyns, D., Holvoet, T.: Architecture-centric support for adaptive service collaborations. ACM Trans. Softw. Eng. Methodol. (TOSEM) **23**(1), 2:1–2:40 (2014)
20. Scerri, P., Vincent, R., Mailler, R.: Comparing three approaches to large-scale coordination. In: Scerri, P., Vincent, R., Mailler, R. (eds.) Coordination of Large-Scale Multiagent Systems. Springer, New York (2006)
21. Jamshidi, M.: Large-Scale Systems: Modeling and Control. North-Holland Series in System Science and Engineering. North-Holland, Amsterdam (1983)
22. Gouaïch, A., Michel, F., Guiraud, Y.: MIC*: a deployment environment for autonomous agents. In: Weyns, D., Van Dyke Parunak, H., Michel, F. (eds.) E4MAS 2004. LNCS (LNAI), vol. 3374, pp. 109–126. Springer, Heidelberg (2005)
23. Rodriguez, S., Hilaire, V., Koukam, A.: Holonic modeling of environments for situated multi-agent systems. In: Weyns, D., Van Dyke Parunak, H., Michel, F. (eds.) E4MAS 2005. LNCS (LNAI), vol. 3830, pp. 18–31. Springer, Heidelberg (2006)

24. Weyns, D., Schelfthout, K., Holvoet, T.: Exploiting a virtual environment in a real-world application. In: Weyns, D., Van Dyke Parunak, H., Michel, F. (eds.) E4MAS 2005. LNCS (LNAI), vol. 3830, pp. 218–234. Springer, Heidelberg (2006)

25. Van Dyke Parunak, H.: A survey of environments and mechanisms for human-human stigmergy. In: Weyns, D., Van Dyke Parunak, H., Michel, F. (eds.) E4MAS 2005. LNCS (LNAI), vol. 3830, pp. 163–186. Springer, Heidelberg (2006)

26. Mamei, M., Zambonelli, F.: Motion coordination in the Quake 3 arena environment: a field-based approach. In: Weyns, D., Van Dyke Parunak, H., Michel, F. (eds.) E4MAS 2004. LNCS (LNAI), vol. 3374, pp. 264–278. Springer, Heidelberg (2005)

27. Van Dyke Parunak, H., Brueckner, S.A., Sauter, J.: Digital pheromones for coordination of unmanned vehicles. In: Weyns, D., Van Dyke Parunak, H., Michel, F. (eds.) E4MAS 2004. LNCS (LNAI), vol. 3374, pp. 246–263. Springer, Heidelberg (2005)

28. Urovi, V., Olivieri, A.C., Bromuri, S., Fornara, N., Schumacher, M.I.: Secure P2P cross-community health record exchange in IHE compatible systems. Int. J. Artif. Intell. Tools IJAIT **23**, 1440006 (2013)

29. Omicini, A., Denti, E.: From tuple spaces to tuple centres. Sci. Comput. Program. **41**(3), 277–294 (2001)

30. Michel, F.: Translating agent perception computations into environmental processes in multi-agent-based simulations: a means for integrating graphics processing unit programming within usual agent-based simulation platforms. Syst. Res. Behav. Sci. **30**(6), 703–715 (2013)

31. Munir, S., Stankovic, J., Liang, C.M., Lin, S.: Cyber physical system challenges for humans-in-the-loop control. In: 8th International Workshop on Feedback Computing (2013)

32. Cumming, M.: Supervising automation: humans on the loop. Aero-Astro, MIT Aeronautics and Astronautics Department, Massachusetts Institute of Technology (2008)

33. Wood, A., Stankovic, J., Virone, G., Selavo, L., He, Z., Cao, Q., Doan, T., Wu, Y., Fang, L., Stoleru, R.: Context-aware wireless sensor networks for assisted living and residential monitoring. IEEE Network **22**, 4 (2008)

34. Li, W., Sadigh, D., Sastry, S., Seshia, S.A.: Synthesis for human-in-the-loop control systems. In: Ábrahám, E., Havelund, K. (eds.) TACAS 2014 (ETAPS). LNCS, vol. 8413, pp. 470–484. Springer, Heidelberg (2014)

35. Cranor, L.F.: A framework for reasoning about the human in the loop. In: Conference on Usability, Psychology, and Security, UPSEC (2008)

36. Lancelot, F., Causse, M., Schneider, N., Mongeau, M.: Human-in-the-loop multi-agent approach for airport taxiing operations. In: Bajo, J., Hernández, J.Z., Mathieu, P., Campbell, A., Fernández-Caballero, A., Moreno, M.N., Julián, V., Alonso-Betanzos, A., Jiménez-López, M.D., Botti, V. (eds.) Trends in Practical Applications of Agents, Multi-Agent Systems and Sustainability. Advances in Intelligent Systems and Computing, vol. 372, pp. 235–236. Springer, Heidelberg (2015)

37. Claes, R., Holvoet, T., Weyns, D.: A decentralized approach for anticipatory vehicle routing using delegate multiagent systems. IEEE Trans. Intell. Transp. Syst. **12**(2), 364–373 (2011)

38. Schurr, N., Marecki, J., Tambe, M., Scerri, P.: The Future of disaster response: humans working with multiagent teams using DEFACTO. In: AAAI Spring Symposium on AI Technologies for Homeland Security (2005)

39. Bradshaw, J.M., Feltovich, P., Johnson, M.: Humans-agent interaction. In: The Handbook of Humans-Machine Interaction: A Humans-Centered Design Approach (2011)

40. Zambonelli, F.: Toward sociotechnical urban superorganisms. IEEE Comput. **45**(8), 76–78 (2012)

41. Zambonelli, F., Castelli, G., Ferrari, L., Mamei, M., Rosi, A., Di Marzo, G., Risoldi, M., Tchao, A., Dobson, S., Stevenson, G., Ye, J., Nardini, E., Omicini, A., Montagna, S., Viroli, M., Ferscha, A., Maschek, S., Wally, B.: Self-aware pervasive service ecosystems. Procedia Comput. Sci. **7**, 197–199 (2011)

42. Weyns, D., Caporuscio, M., Vogel, B., Kurti, A.: Design for sustainability = runtime adaptation U evolution. In: Proceeding of the Sustainable Architecture: Global collaboration, Requirements, Analysis, SAGRA (2015)

43. Gardelli, L., Viroli, M., Omicini, A.: Design patterns for self-organising systems. In: Burkhard, H.-D., Lindemann, G., Verbrugge, R., Varga, L.Z. (eds.) CEEMAS 2007. LNCS (LNAI), vol. 4696, pp. 123–132. Springer, Heidelberg (2007)

44. Juziuk, J., Weyns, D., Holvoet, T.: Design patterns for multi-agent systems: a systematic literature Review. In: Shehory, O., Sturm, A. (eds.) Research Directions in Agent-Oriented Software Engineering. Springer, Heidelberg (2015)

45. de Jonge, D., Rosell, B., Sierra, C.: Human interactions in electronic institutions. In: Chesñevar, C.I., Onaindia, E., Ossowski, S., Vouros, G. (eds.) AT 2013. LNCS, vol. 8068, pp. 75–89. Springer, Heidelberg (2013)

46. Omicini, A., Ricci, A., Viroli, M., Castelfranchi, C., Tummolini, L.: Coordination artifacts: environment-based coordination for intelligent agents. In: Third International Joint Conference on Autonomous Agents and Multiagent Systems (2004)

47. Ricci, A., Piunti, M., Viroli, M.: Environment programming in multi-agent systems: an artifact-based perspective. Auton. Agent. Multi-Agent Syst. **23**, 2 (2011)

48. Musil, J., Musil, A., Weyns, D., Biffl, S.: An architecture framework for collective intelligence systems. In: Working International Conference on Software Architecture, WICSA (2014)

49. Sauter, J., Matthews, R., Van Dyke Parunak, H., Brueckner, S.A.: Performance of digital pheromones for swarming vehicle control. In: Fourth international joint conference on Autonomous agents and multiagent systems, AAMAS (2005)

50. Ricci, A., Viroli, M., Omicini, A.: CArtAgO: a framework for prototyping artifact-based environments in MAS. In: Weyns, D., Van Dyke Parunak, H., Michel, F. (eds.) E4MAS 2006. LNCS (LNAI), vol. 4389, pp. 67–86. Springer, Heidelberg (2007)

51. Odell, J., Van Dyke Parunak, H., Fleischer, M.: The role of roles. J. Object Technol. **2**(1), 39–51 (2003)

52. Castelli, G., Mamei, M., Rosi, A., Zambonelli, F.: Developing social applications in SAPERE. In: IEEE 10th International Conference on Ubiquitous Intelligence & Computing and IEEE 10th International Conference on Autonomic & Trusted Computing (2013)

Connecting Agents, Environments, and Humans

Agent Bodies: An Interface Between Agent and Environment

Julien Saunier[1][✉], Carlos Carrascosa[2], Stéphane Galland[3],
and Patrick Simo Kanmeugne[4]

[1] Normandie Université, INSA de Rouen, LITIS EA 4108, Avenue de l'Université,
BP 8, 76801 Saint-Étienne-du-Rouvray, France
julien.saunier@insa-rouen.fr
[2] DSIC, Universitat Politècnica de València, Camino de Vera Sn,
46022 Valencia, Spain
carrasco@dsic.upv.es
[3] Université Bourgogne Franche-Comté, UTBM, IRTES EA7274,
90010 Belfort, France
stephane.galland@utbm.fr
[4] Université Pierre et Marie Curie, Laboratoire d'Informatique de Parie 6,
Paris, France
patrick.simo-kanmeugne@lip6.fr

Abstract. Interfacing the agents with their environment is a classical problem when designing multiagent systems. However, the models pertaining to this interface generally choose to either embed it in the agents, or in the environment. In this position paper, we propose to highlight the role of agent bodies as primary components of the multiagent system design. We propose a tentative definition of an agent body, and discuss its responsibilities in terms of MAS components. The agent body takes from both agent and environment: low-level agent mechanisms such as perception and influences are treated locally in the agent bodies. These mechanism participate in the cognitive process, but are not driven by symbol manipulation. Furthermore, it allows to define several bodies for one mind, either to simulate different capabilities, or to interact in the different environments - physical, social- the agent is immersed in. We also draw the main challenges to apply this concept effectively.

Keywords: Multi-agent systems · Embodied agent · Environment · Interface · Influence · Laws · Rules

1 Introduction

Immersing agents in dynamic physical, virtual or mixed environments is still a challenge for Multiagent systems (MAS) researchers. As has been established in [31], an essential part of such systems is the MAS environment, in order to provide the services allowing agents to interact with it. However, to define what is the interface between the agents and their environment is not obvious. A key

© Springer International Publishing Switzerland 2015
D. Weyns and F. Michel (Eds.): E4MAS 2014 – 10 years later, LNAI 9068, pp. 25–40, 2015.
DOI: 10.1007/978-3-319-23850-0_2

aspect is to both respect their autonomy and ensure that environment rules are enforced. In the following, we call *agent environment* the software layer between the external world and the agents.

As has been shown in several simulation models, adding a component between the agents and the agent environment enables to encapsulate responsibilities such as influence-reaction mechanisms [14, 26] and observability and perception management [10], while keeping the internal integrity of the agents. A suitable concept to manage this interface is the agent *body*, *i.e.* a component that is attached to each agent to manage its interface with the environment.

The distinction between *mind* and *body* when talking about AI systems in general has been proposed mainly for robotics [3], and more recently virtual companions [28]. Its application to multiagent systems, where there is not necessarily a physical body, has not been discussed extensively in the literature. In this paper, we argue that introducing agent bodies enables to propose a flexible agent design separating sensory and control modules from high level reasoning, thus allowing to design the mind once for several action/perception capabilities, while keeping the agent adaptive -to its body and to its dynamic environment(s).

Investigating the concept of body implies to also investigate the different kinds of environment an agent can be in. The physical metaphor is obvious, and that is why it is firstly in the simulation domain that the concept appeared. However, abstracting the concept of environment as being any topological space, such as social spaces, in which the agent may interact with others, also allows to envision different uses of bodies depending on the environment type, while being consistent across all the agents environments.

This article is a position paper in support of the introduction of agent bodies as environment abstractions. In Sect. 2, we review the state of the art related to the use of this concept as interfaces between agents and environment. Then, we propose a tentative definition of the concept in Sect. 3, and draw on this definition to distinguish agent body and mind responsibilities. Section 4 discusses the advantages and limits of this approach. Section 5 proposes a typology of bodies and minds across two dimensions: cardinality and type of environment, and we discuss how these relate to functionalities that have to be implemented in the different components of the MAS. Finally, we identify in Sect. 6 the main issues and challenges for the introduction of this concept in mainstream MAS, and link them to previously established challenges in environment design.

2   State of the Art

Although the situatedness of the agents has been part of the multiagent systems community practice for a long time, it has long been tackled in an *ad hoc* way [32]. Situated agents interacting with their environment have shown the advantages of using the environment for problem solving via indirect interactions such as stigmergy [19] and limited cognitive capabilities of the agents [30]. Works of E4MAS workgroup have then put forward the view of the environment as a first-order abstraction for the design of MASs [31]. However, the body/mind differentiation has not received the same attention as the environment role.

As we have seen in introduction, the distinction between mind and body in the context of artificial intelligence was mainly proposed in robotics [3]. Nevertheless, there has been a few works on the concept of body in the MAS community. Two works addressing explicitly bodies in the MAS literature are the ELMS model [15] and Soft-Bodies [16]. In these works, the body is considered as controlled by the environment, and encapsulates several responsibilities including observability and accessibility of the public state of the agents.

Other works introduce the use of a mediator between agents and environment, such as Interaction Objects [10] and Smart Objects [27], which can be viewed as functionally similar to bodies. Artifacts [20, 21] are dynamic objects, independent from the agents, that enable the agent to interact with its environment.

In the simulation domain, the addition of an interface between mind and agent environment has been done in a number of works, although never using the same naming [1, 2, 7, 14, 23, 25, 28]. These works deal with situated interactions, where the modeling of imperfect coupling between the decision process and its effects on the environment (and the other agents) is necessary. In these works, the body is a component of the environment (Fig. 1). It contains a collection of sensors and effectors related to the associated environment. It is able to filter the percepts and the actions according to its state variables and attributes. The body has its own dynamics that can not be controlled by the agents.

The agent environment controls the dynamic properties of the bodies (position, orientation, etc.) in order to ensure that they follow the rules and laws of the universe [15, 16]. However, the agent can influence its body by using a mechanism such as the Influence/Reaction model [14].

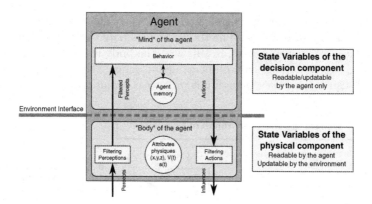

Fig. 1. The body at the interface between the agent mind and the environment, extracted from [7].

In a specific kind of environments, Intelligent Virtual Environments, the meta-model MAM5 [1, 23] has been developed. It allows to model the Virtual Environment by means of artifacts, including the distinction between mind (agent) and body. It defines the body as an artifact belonging to the Virtual

Environment. In Virtual Environments, the body is naturally represented. For instance, in games users and agents avatars may have different bodies, with different capabilities or features. In this case it is not unusual to be able to switch between different bodies so that each body may relate to a particular environment, while it is always controlled by the same mind.

Furthermore, let us note that the representation (observability) role of the body is not its only role. It mediates the whole processes between mind and environment in terms of perception, action and accessibility.

3   Refining the Body Concept

In this section, we define the concept of body and its major responsibilities in a MAS. We also propose a formalization of the perception process to illustrate this approach.

3.1   Definition

Drawing on the related works, we propose the following definition of an agent body:

The agent body is a component of the multiagent system working as an interface between mind (agent) and environment. It is embedded in the environment to enforce body rules and ecological laws, but is influenced by -and allows introspection for- the mind. An agent may have one or more bodies in the environment(s) it participates in.

Figure 2 illustrates this definition in a UML class diagram. The goal of the body is to embed parameters and methods that mediate the interaction between the agent and its environment(s). In this way, the body is not a simple interface between the agent and the environment, defining how they interact with each other. It is also a dynamic - though not proactive - component.

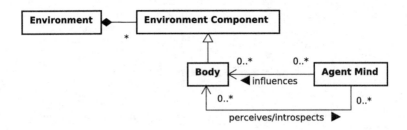

Fig. 2. UML class diagram of the model.

The body embeds tendencies that influence the mind as well as the mind influences the body. In this sense, the body has its own dynamics that is not controlled by the mind. Furthermore, the body is situated in an environment, and follows its rules. Hence, while respecting the agent integrity - the mind is autonomous from the body, the body ensures its situation in the multiagent system by (1) being consistent with the environment rules and (2) enforcing the dynamics.

However, since the body state and processes may evolve without agent action, agreement or even knowledge, it has to propose some kind of introspection primitives, for the mind to be aware of the state of its body.

Finally, in most simulation cases, *mind* and *body* are related 1 to 1, so that there is one mind, that is one agent, associated to one and only one body. But the concept of body fits more complicated relations. For instance, one mind can be related to several different bodies, each one with different interfaces with the environment, or each one with access to different parts of the environment. This can be related to [11], where several environments –one for each specific aspect of the application– are composed through a unified modeling. In this work, actuators and sensors are defined in each environment and reified in the agents.

Moreover, different minds can have access to the same body, at different times or even at the same time, having some mechanism, as for instance a negotiation process or multiple influences fusion, to decide which action to carry out. The different cardinalities are discussed in Sect. 5.1.

3.2   Component Responsibilities

Figure 3 shows the different interactions between body, mind and environment. The introduction of agent bodies (or *soft-bodies*) imply the introduction of feedback loops, since it is a dynamic entity that may change without influences from the mind, and its reactions to the mind's influences are not ensured.

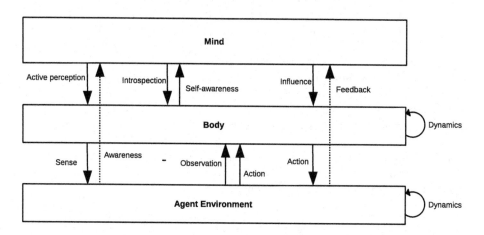

Fig. 3. Mind, body and environment interactions.

From our definition, we can derive the following responsibilities of the agent body in the multiagent system design:

1. Representation of the agent
2. Perception mediation
3. Action mediation
4. Life cycle
5. Activity (rules and dynamics)

In the following, we detail each of these responsibilities.

Agent Representation. Deriving from the works on virtual companions with a physical representation, the body acts as a representative of the agent in the agent environment. Hence, it provides the *public* part of the agent in terms of observability. In virtual reality environments, this public part is a 2D or a 3D model; in software agents (such as in [16] it is a set of attributes or even a set of accessible methods (like in artifacts) to interact with this agents. This can be related to the affordance [9] concept, the object carrying its functionalities itself.

In non-physical agent environments, this representation may be a profile - as in social media; or any set of properties and interfaces.

Perception Mediation. Concerning perception, the body defines the perception capabilities of the agent, the simplest example being a maximal field of view. It may also provide more refined perception methods, such as aggregate or "macroscopic" views of the agent (or real) environment. Hence, it both defines capabilities and limits, in a similar way to perception filters [24] or active perception [33].

This approach enables to define a mixed *bottom up* and *top down* approach of perception [13]: the classical perception methods, which are requests from the agent to the environment, are top-down, since they are driven by the agent, may be mixed with "awareness" filters, defining percepts that are perceived by the agents event if they do not request them [16,25].

Another part of perception, from the point of view of the mind, is that of its own body through *introspection*. Since the agent body state is not decided by the agent, but only influenced by it, the body has to provide self-awareness methods for the agent to adapt to it. Hence, the layer provides observability for its owner agent, for both attributes, inner and outer methods.

Furthermore, it may provides alerts (in a bottom up style) if its state is modified by the environment to internal (dynamics) or external (environment or other agents interaction with it) influences.

Action Mediation. In the same way as perception, the body defines action capabilities of the agents, for example the set of actions it is able to achieve in the agent environment. These action methods are limited by the rules of the environment, and possible rules of this particular body, which may differ from one agent to another, in terms of action set, but also of accuracy, success rate, performance... This combines into an influence, that is then received by the environment for it to compute its reaction.

Since the agents actions are mediated by both its body and the environment, the result of its actions (or perceptions attempts) is not ensured. Hence, *feedback methods* are provided, in order for the agent to learn how its influences are met. These feedback are both those from the environment and those from the body, when the agent tries to modify its state.

These feedback may be processed online, for an agent to adapt to its action and perception results, or offline by the agent designer.

Life Cycle. As has been evoked in the previous sections, an agent may have one or more bodies in the different agent environments it participates in. Furthermore, the agent body may change at run-time, for example in modular robotics [34].

Hence, bodies are considered as a service of the agent environment. An agent may request one or more bodies from an environment in order to interact with it. Let us note that since bodies are embedded in the environment, the agent may not receive a body, or not one with the characteristics it requested.

Dynamics and Rules. The body must respect the laws of the agent environment. Furthermore, it may be embedded with a set of dynamics that correspond to the laws of the environment. For example, in [25], the agents are influenced by their neighbor's emotion contagion, and each agent body has its own emotion dynamics.

This set of laws is enforced at run-time by the body, under the responsibility of the environment.

3.3   Example of Formalism: The Perception Process

In order to illustrate this definition, we propose a formalization of the perception process. This enables to show how the perception, or more generally the interactions between mind, body and environment, becomes a composition of successive processes managed by each component.

Equation 1 illustrates the four steps of perception for the body and agent i on the instant state of the environment σ_t:

$$
\begin{aligned}
Perception_i(\sigma_t) &= Assimilation_i \circ Filter_i \circ Alter_i \circ Extract_i(\sigma_t) \\
&= Assimilation_i(Filter_i(Alter_i(Extract_i(\sigma_t)))) \qquad (1) \\
&= \Gamma_d^i
\end{aligned}
$$

where the characteristics of an agent or more generally an entity, form the set Γ. The first step is the raw extraction from the environment. For an agent ag_i in can be expressed as the function $Extract_i$ detailed on (2).

$$Extract_i : \Sigma \times \Gamma \longrightarrow \sigma$$
$$\sigma_t, \Gamma_e^i \longmapsto E_t, E_t \subseteq \sigma_t \tag{2}$$

The second step is the alteration of the produced subset in the agent body. This alteration, for ag_i can be expressed as the function $Alter_i$ detailed on equation (3) where Ξ_t is the altered subset. As a reminder, the produced subset may not be a subset of σ_t.

$$Alter_i : \Sigma \times \Gamma \longrightarrow \Xi$$
$$E_t, \Gamma_e^i \longmapsto \Xi_t^i \tag{3}$$

The third step consists in filtering the provided subset depending on the request of the agent mind. This filtering can be expressed, for ag_i, as the function $Filter_i$ detailed on (4).

$$Filter_i : \Xi \times \Gamma \longrightarrow \Xi$$
$$\Xi_t^i, \Gamma_d^i \longmapsto \Xi_t^{i'} \tag{4}$$

Finally, the assimilation, for ag_i, can be expressed as the function $Assimilation_i$ detailed on (5).

$$Assimilation_i : \Xi \times \Gamma \longrightarrow \Gamma$$
$$\Xi_t^{i'}, \Gamma_d^i \longmapsto \Gamma_d^{i'} \tag{5}$$

4 Discussion

The definition of agent bodies and their responsibilities enumerated in the previous section present several advantages in terms of software engineering, flexibility, and cyber-physical systems.

From a Software Engineering point of view, since the environment controls the body, it may enforce rules regarding body dynamics in the case of several agent designers, thus acting as an electronic institution [4] in all aspects of agent interactions. Secondly, it enables to manage the design complexity by separating high-level decision from low-level (operational) mechanisms.

Concerning the flexibility in agent design, designing one mind that can be coupled with different bodies enables to manage body heterogeneity without changing the high-level decision process; for example in the case of multiagent simulation where a population of agents with different parameter sets coexist.

Finally, in cyber-physical systems were agents are immersed in both software and physical worlds, it enables to create agents that can be interfaced with physical or simulated worlds seamlessly, as long as the interface is consistent. This multiple interface may be done simultaneously or not, depending on the context.

The main limits of this approach are (i) that another component, the agent body, is added, and (ii) that the choice of where to divide mind/body/environment responsibilities is yet to be fully understood.

Concerning the first point, the functionalities have to be implemented in any case, so that their location is a design choice that does not add complexity.

Concerning the second point, we have proposed a division of functionalities in the previous section. This is a basis for further discussion about the location of each basic module to unify this view of a MAS architecture. However, the responsibilities may in certain cases be divided in other ways. For example, some authors have proposed to not separate body and mind processes, considering only interconnected modules [17] that make up the whole cognition. Although we also consider that both body and mind processes are components of the cognition, not separating nor defining the responsibilities of each fails to simplify the agent design from an architecture point of view.

5   Typology

Having defined the responsibilities of agent bodies, we then study how agents (or minds) and bodies relate, on two scales: cardinality and environment nature. Then, we propose examples for each type of subdivision.

5.1   Based on Cardinality

One possible typology of the relationship between body and mind in agents is the one given by the cardinality of such relationship:

- 1 to 1: one body is related to one mind. So, an agent can be identified as a mind and its corresponding body.
  In this case, the transition between an integrated agent approach and a body/mind differentiation is straightforward, considering it as a decomposition of previous modules in order to improve modularity.
- n to 1: n bodies are related to the same mind. As the body can be seen as interfaces to the environment, this case is related to one agent which is able to access in different ways to the environment (i.e. normal or supervisor modes; different bodies in a video-game kind of application, with different capabilities; an evolving body as in a modular robots) or to different environments.
  In this case, the mind has to be able to manage each body, considering each of those may have different capabilities in terms of action, perception and internal dynamics. A solution is to transparently merge these capabilities across the agent environments, as in [11].
- 1 to n: 1 body controlled by n minds. This seemingly *schizophrenic* relation represents the use of a common vessel for different intentions. In this case, the body may be subject to contradictory influences, and must therefore either have a rights management system and an influence disambiguation mechanism to manage the different influences. It is quite similar to previous works on influence reaction mechanisms, which in this case must be implemented in the body itself.

5.2   Based on the Environment Nature

Another parallel classification of the agent's body - mind relationship is the one according to environment nature, that is, according to the features that the body may have:

- Physical: Either the environment is the true physical world (as could be if the body corresponds to a robot) or it is a simulated world (as in *Second Life* or *World Of Warcraft*). The body has some physical features such as shape, volume, position, ..., that also define the sensing and actuation that can be carried out by means of such body.
- Non-Physical: The agent is not situated in a physical-related environment, but it may be related to a *body* seen as an interface it can be perceived and a that gives it some way of perceiving the environment. In a social network, it will be related to the agent's profile.

It should be underlined here that this classification is parallel to the previous one. So, for instance, an agent's mind could be controlling one or several robots, or to different social network's profiles. We propose in Table 1 examples across both classifications.

Table 1. Examples

Cardinality	Physical - real	Physical - virtual	Social
1 Agent/N bodies	Centralized control robot swarm	Macro or mesoscopic simulation	One representation in each social space e.g. several Social Networks
1 agent/1 body	Robot	Virtual agent	Personal profile e.g. Online Social Networks
N Agents/1 body	Decentralized control robot	Decentralized controlled agent	Organization/Group interface; e.g. profile: macro/aggregate view

6   Modeling and Deployment Challenges

As we have mentioned earlier in this article, the *realization* of the mind/body paradigm is far from being an easy task. Let us acknowledge the risk that the Mind/Body paradigm could be counterproductive if the significance of both concepts is not rigorously established. In this section, we discuss the different challenges that have to be carried out in order to concretely take advantage of the distinction between the mind and body from a modeling and deployment perspective, and how they relate to previous challenges identified by the E4MAS workgroup.

6.1   Mastering the Body Concept

If the body is part of the environment, it means that the way we build an instance of an agent in a multi-agent system needs to be examined closely. This is related to *the definition of the abstractions and concepts that may be used for defining an agent environment* [12,29] that has constituted one of the major challenges on the environment in MAS during the past 10 years. The introduction of the body concept raises the question: what is specific to the body and could be implemented regardless of the mind? To answer this critical question we suggest the following two tracks.

The Body is Part of the Environment. The fact that the body is part of the environment means that the former provides conditions for the body to exist. Furthermore, assuming that the body is an interface between the agent and its environment, we can also conclude that the environment embodies an important part of the capacities of agents, namely, those that allow the agent to act on its environment and to interact with other agents. Therefore the action model and the interaction model could be embedded within the environment regardless of agents' Mind : agents are not driven by the environment, but it is clearly the environment that defines the means for their perception, action and interaction. We believe that this is a critical separation that has to be handled by designers at the very start of a MAS modeling process.

In [11], the authors argue for this responsibility separation. In particular, they note that this enables the agent environment to be independent from the agent design. The environment providing its means to interact with it (and through it with the other agents), the agent design is thus simplified, even in the case of multiple environments. We propose to take this idea one step further, including other aspects of software bodies such as dynamics and observability.

According to [31], *suitable software architectures*, and *suitable architectural patterns and reference architectures for the agent environment* must be defined. The previous separation principle participates to the building of a general software architecture for the agent environment. Figure 1 illustrates that the bodies are at the interface between the agent environment and the agents. The body-mind separation may also be a starting point for determining if general-purpose or special-purpose simulation environments for executing multi-agent simulations involving dynamic agent environments are needed, that was a challenge considered in [12]. In [5,6], the authors consider two dimensions of the agent environment: the physical and communication dimensions. The body concept is used in the two dimensions (the physical body, and the Internet avatar) as the representations of the agents in these dimensions. This concept may be considered as a general abstraction, and may participate to the definition of a general-purpose simulation environment.

The Environment Holds its Own Dynamics. Another important aspect to account for is the notion of body tendencies. Since the environment is dynamic, the body, being part of the environment, inherits the dynamicity of this environment. Tendencies could be seen as a realization of this dynamicity and therefore implemented within agents' bodies regardless of their mind. Tendencies could be considered as permanent : agents can cope with them, eventually influence them, but cannot erase them. An important challenge from a modeling perspective could be therefore to define the different type of bodies' tendencies that are relevant for the agent behaviour and how the agent cope with it. Previous works (e.g. [11,31] propose to use an ontology of the environment, a part of which should concern (and be embedded in) the agent bodies to increase the environment openness to heterogeneous agents [32].

6.2 Mastering the Mind Concept

As with the body concept in the previous section, the following question could be raised concerning the mind concept : what is specific to the mind and could be implemented regardless of the body? We suggest the following tracks to shape the discussion.

Activities Specific to the Mind. With the introduction of the body concept, it is legitimate to consider the activity of the mind specifically. It seems natural to assume that the proper of the mind is concepts (symbol) manipulation and reasoning. Those activities are ruled by constraints, different from that of the body, that could be native or acquired from the experience. Rigorously speaking, the mind life cycle does not depend on that of the body, both entity evolving in parallel. Hence, their respective activities could be implemented separately. Anyway, the mind experience proceed from the evolution of the body in the environment, so *feedbacks* from the evolution of the body to the mind have to be clearly established by the designer.

One of the responsibilities of the environment is *ensuring the locality of the perception and of the actions* [32]. The body participates to the solving of this challenge by providing sensors that are defined or constrained by geometries. For example, the view perception may be supported by a camera in the real world [8], or by a geometrical shape in a simulated environment [7]. In this last case, the shape of the field-of-view is defined by geometrical elements that have a position relative to the position of the agent's body in the physical environment. On the one hand, this definition ensures a local perception for the agents. On the other hand, the actions are local since they are always related to an object in the environment such as moving the object or doing an action on it.

Connexion Between the Mind and the Body. We believe that one of the biggest challenge is to instantiate the link between the Mind and the Body, since both entities are implemented separately. The mind activity is different by nature with that of the body, but they are strongly coupled.

Several works are already proposed in the literature for defining the connexion between the mind and the body. For example, the influence/reaction [14] model models the joint actions of the actions. Another example is the model of smart objects [27] that defines how the agents obtain the possible actions in the environment. These approaches constitute answers for the *handling of the interferences between the agents' actions* that constitute one of the research challenges related to the environment in MAS [12].

To properly apprehend the coupling, at least three types of knowledge have to be considered: (i) knowledge of the agent about the capacities of its body, (ii) knowledge of the agent about the consequences of its actions on the integrity of its body only, (iii) knowledge about the consequences of its actions on the environment in general (beyond the agent's body). The dynamics of these three types of knowledge need to be addressed early in the design.

6.3 Supporting the Body in the Engineering of the Agent Environment

One of the past 10-years research challenges concerned the *difference between the agent environment and the agents that inhabit it* [32]. The distinctions that were highlighted (activity vs proactivity, maintenance-driven behaviour vs goal-driven behaviour, dynamics embodiment vs reaction, observability vs opacity) clearly support the view of the body as an abstraction, or even service, of the environment.

Based on the principle that agents are autonomous entities, and that the environment is not autonomous and does not contain (in a software sense) autonomous entities, the question of defining what is an agent and what is not has arisen. In our view, every entity that exists in the agent environment and is perceivable by agents is a component of this environment: a body represents one or more agent(s) in the agent environment. The agents become therefore the autonomous entities that control the bodies. They are able to perceive and act in the agent environment through their bodies.

Another research challenge is related to the *need of a specific language for describing the agent environment, including its structural and dynamical features* [12]. Artifact [18] and CArtAgO [22] may be considered for proposing a language that is able to describe the bodies and their dynamics, for instance. They provides programming languages for describing the artifacts inside the agent environment that may be used for defining a programming language that has keywords dedicated to the body concept.

The introduction of agent bodies does not solve the architectural issues in effectively engineering environments [31], however it can serve –once properly defined– as an architectural building element and pattern for agent-environment interactions.

7 Conclusions

The interface between agent and environment has given rise to a number of different proposals in the multiagent systems literature. This paper has argued that this interface can be reified through the concept of agent body, and that it answers partially to previous research challenges for agent environments, such as perception and action local management, local dynamics and rules, and multiple environments management. We have discussed the main questions raised by the adoption of this new abstraction: the localization of the interface between agent and body, the definition of body properties and processes, the cardinality of agent/body relationships, and the relations of the bodies with different kinds of environment.

To take advantage of the Mind/Body paradigm, we have stressed that several aspect need to be considered early in the modeling process. They are organized into three main issues: (i) Body-specific, (ii) Mind-specific, (iii) Body/Mind interface. These considerations give an overview of the challenges raised by the Mind/Body paradigm from a modeling and deployment perspective.

In order to mainstream this paradigm, the next step is therefore the integration of the body and environment components in agent-oriented methodologies and in agent-oriented platforms. The heterogeneity of previous related works does not allow to draw methodological guidelines for the design of this component, hence calling for more work in this direction.

Finally, we have also given an informal definition of the agent body. Another challenge is then to propose a formal definition of the concept of body in order to propose an architectural building block for an agent environment unified model.

References

1. Barella, A., Ricci, A., Boissier, O., Carrascosa, C.: MAM5: Multi-agent model for intelligent virtual environments. In: 10th European Workshop on Multi-Agent Systems (EUMAS 2012), pp. 16–30 (2012)
2. Behe, F., Galland, S., Gaud, N., Nicolle, C., Koukam, A.: An ontology-based meta-model for multiagent-based simulations. Int. J. Simul. Model. Pract. Theor. **40**, 64–85 (2014). http://authors.elsevier.com/sd/article/S1569190X13001342
3. Brooks, R.A.: Intelligence without representation. Artif. Intell. **47**(1), 139–159 (1991)
4. Campos, J., López-Sánchez, M., Rodríguez-Aguilar, J.A., Esteva, M.: Formalising situatedness and adaptation in electronic institutions. In: Hübner, J.F., Matson, E., Boissier, O., Dignum, V. (eds.) COIN 2008. LNCS, vol. 5428, pp. 126–139. Springer, Heidelberg (2009)
5. Galland, S., Balbo, F., Gaud, N., Rodriguez, S., Picard, G., Boissier, O.: Contextualize agent interactions by combining social and physical dimensions in the environment. In: Demazeau, Y., Decker, K. (eds.) 13th International Conference on Practical Applications of Agents and Multi-Agent Systems (PAAMS), June 2015
6. Galland, S., Balbo, F., Gaud, N., Rodriguez, S., Picard, G., Boissier, O.: A multidimensional environment implementation for enhancing agent interaction. In: Bordini, R., Elkind, E. (eds.) Autonomous Agents and Multiagent Systems (AAMAS 2015), Istanbul, Turkey, May 2015
7. Galland, S., Gaud, N., Demange, J., Koukam, A.: Environment model for multiagent-based simulation of 3D urban systems. In: the 7th European Workshop on Multiagent Systems (EUMAS 2009), Ayia Napa, Cyprus, December 2009 (paper 36)

8. Gechter, F., Contet, J.M., Lamotte, O., Galland, S., Koukam, A.: Virtual intelligent vehicle urban simulator: application to vehicle platoon evaluation. Simul. Model. Practice Theor. (SIMPAT) **24**, 103–114 (2012)
9. Gibson, J.J.: The Theory of Affordances. Hilldale, USA (1977)
10. Gouaïch, A., Michel, F., Guiraud, Y.: MIC*: a deployment environment for autonomous agents. In: Weyns, D., Van Dyke Parunak, H., Michel, F. (eds.) E4MAS 2004. LNCS (LNAI), vol. 3374, pp. 109–126. Springer, Heidelberg (2005)
11. Gouaïch, A., Michel, F.: Towards a unified view of the environment (s) within multi-agent systems. Informatica (Slovenia) **29**(4), 423–432 (2005)
12. Helleboogh, A., Vizzari, G., Uhrmacher, A., Michel, F.: Modeling dynamic environments in multiagent simulation. Int. J. Auton. Agents Multiagent Syst. **14**(1), 87–116 (2007)
13. Ketenci, U.G., Bremond, R., Auberlet, J.M., Grislin, E.: Drivers with limited perception: models and applications to traffic simulation. Recherche transports sécurité, RTS (2013)
14. Michel, F.: The IRM4S model: the influence/reaction principle for multiagent based simulation. ACM, May 2007
15. Okuyama, F.Y., Bordini, R.H., da Rocha Costa, A.C.: ELMS: an environment description language for multi-agent simulation. In: Weyns, D., Van Dyke Parunak, H., Michel, F. (eds.) E4MAS 2004. LNCS (LNAI), vol. 3374, pp. 67–83. Springer, Heidelberg (2005)
16. Platon, E., Sabouret, N., Honiden, S.: Environmental support for tag interactions. In: Weyns, D., Van Dyke Parunak, H., Michel, F. (eds.) E4MAS 2006. LNCS (LNAI), vol. 4389, pp. 106–123. Springer, Heidelberg (2007)
17. Ribeiro, T., Vala, M., Paiva, A.: Censys: a model for distributed embodied cognition. In: Aylett, R., Krenn, B., Pelachaud, C., Shimodaira, H. (eds.) IVA 2013. LNCS, vol. 8108, pp. 58–67. Springer, Heidelberg (2013)
18. Ricci, A., Viroli, M., Omicini, A.: Programming MAS with artifacts. In: Bordini, R.H., Dastani, M., Dix, J., El Fallah Seghrouchni, A. (eds.) PROMAS 2005. LNCS (LNAI), vol. 3862, pp. 206–221. Springer, Heidelberg (2006)
19. Ricci, A., Omicini, A., Viroli, M., Gardelli, L., Oliva, E.: Cognitive stigmergy: towards a framework based on agents and artifacts. In: Weyns, D., Van Dyke Parunak, H., Michel, F. (eds.) E4MAS 2006. LNCS (LNAI), vol. 4389, pp. 124–140. Springer, Heidelberg (2007)
20. Ricci, A., Piunti, M., Viroli, M.: Environment programming in multi-agent systems: an artifact-based perspective. Auton. Agent. Multi-Agent Syst. **23**(2), 158–192 (2011)
21. Ricci, A., Viroli, M., Omicini, A.: Environment-based coordination through coordination artifacts. In: Weyns, D., Van Dyke Parunak, H., Michel, F. (eds.) E4MAS 2004. LNCS (LNAI), vol. 3374, pp. 190–214. Springer, Heidelberg (2005)
22. Ricci, A., Viroli, M., Omicini, A.: CArtAgO: a framework for prototyping artifact-based environments in MAS. In: Weyns, D., Van Dyke Parunak, H., Michel, F. (eds.) E4MAS 2006. LNCS (LNAI), vol. 4389, pp. 67–86. Springer, Heidelberg (2007)
23. Rincon, J.A., Garcia, E., Julian, V., Carrascosa, C.: Developing adaptive agents situated in intelligent virtual environments. In: Polycarpou, M., de Carvalho, A.C.P.L.F., Pan, J.-S., Woźniak, M., Quintian, H., Corchado, E. (eds.) HAIS 2014. LNCS, vol. 8480, pp. 98–109. Springer, Heidelberg (2014)
24. Saunier, J., Balbo, F., Pinson, S.: A formal model of communication and context awareness in multiagent systems. J. Logic Lang. Inform. **23**(2), 219–247 (2014). http://dx.doi.org/10.1007/s10849-014-9198-8

25. Saunier, J., Jones, H.: Mixed agent/social dynamics for emotion computation. In: Proceedings of the 2014 international conference on Autonomous agents and multi-agent systems, pp. 645–652. International Foundation for Autonomous Agents and Multiagent Systems (2014)
26. Simonin, O., Ferber, J.: Modeling self satisfaction and altruism to handle action selection and reactive cooperation. In: 6th International Conference on the Simulation of Adaptive Behavior (SAB 2000 volume 2), pp. 314–323 (2000)
27. Thalmann, D., Musse, S.R.: Crowd Simulation. Springer, London (2007)
28. Thiebaux, M., Marsella, S., Marshall, A., Kallmann, M.: Smartbody: Behavior realization for embodied conversational agents. In: Proceedings of the 7th international joint conference on Autonomous agents and multiagent systems, vol. 1, pp. 151–158 (2008)
29. Viroli, M., Holvoet, T., Ricci, A., Schelfthout, K., Zambonelli, F.: Infrastructures for the environment of multiagent system. Int. J. Auton. Agent. Multi-Agent Syst. **14**(1), 49–60 (2007)
30. Weyns, D., Boucké, N., Holvoet, T.: Gradient field-based task assignment in an agv transportation system. In: Proceedings of the fifth international joint conference on Autonomous agents and multiagent systems, pp. 842–849. ACM (2006)
31. Weyns, D., Omicini, A., Odell, J.: Environment as a first-class abstraction in multi-agent systems. Auton. Agent. Multi-Agent Syst **14**(1), 5–30 (2007). special Issue on Environments for Multi-agent Systems
32. Weyns, D., Van Dyke Parunak, H., Michel, F., Holvoet, T., Ferber, J.: Environments for multiagent systems state-of-the-art and research challenges. In: Weyns, D., Van Dyke Parunak, H., Michel, F. (eds.) E4MAS 2004. LNCS (LNAI), vol. 3374, pp. 1–47. Springer, Heidelberg (2005)
33. Weyns, D., Steegmans, E., Holvoet, T.: Towards active perception in situated multi-agent systems. Special Issue J. Appl. Artif. Intell. **18**(9–10), 867–883 (2004)
34. Yim, M., Shen, W.M., Salemi, B., Rus, D., Moll, M., Lipson, H., Klavins, E., Chirikjian, G.S.: Modular self-reconfigurable robot systems [grand challenges of robotics]. IEEE Robot. Autom. Mag. **14**(1), 43–52 (2007)

Where Are All the Semantic Web Agents: Establishing Links Between Agent and Linked Data Web Through Environment Abstraction

Oğuz Dikenelli, Oylum Alatlı[(✉)], and Rıza Cenk Erdur

Computer Engineering Department, Ege University,
35100 Bornova, İzmir, Turkey
{oguz.dikenelli, oylum.alatli, cenk.erdur}@ege.edu.tr

Abstract. Semantic Web Agents have been considered as main type of software to consume the semantic data since the Semantic Web concept was raised first time in the well-known "The Semantic Web" article in 2001. More than a decade passed and there is no collaboration between multi-agent systems and semantic web (or its current realization: linked data web) communities that can be considered important. In this paper, it is argued that initial vision was right and two communities need each other to scale up their current practice. Thus, a conceptual framework is proposed to establish necessary links between agent and linked data web infrastructures. Environment abstraction has a special role in this framework and this role is especially discussed throughout the paper.

1 Introduction

In the beginning of the Semantic Web movement, agents have been considered as first-class abstractions. The first article that put the Semantic Web concept forward is the well-known "The Semantic Web" article written by Berners-Lee et al. [4]. The first two paragraphs of that article describe a semantic web scenario where Lucy tries to schedule a series of physical therapy sessions for her mom together with her brother Pete. The second paragraph of the article is rewritten below to emphasize the importance of Semantic Web Agent concept in the initial vision.

"At the doctor's office, Lucy instructed her **Semantic Web agent** through her handheld Web browser. The **agent** promptly retrieved information about Mom's *prescribed treatment* from the doctor's agent, looked up several lists of *providers*, and checked for the ones *in-plan* for Mom's insurance within a *20-mile radius* of her *home* and with a *rating* of *excellent* or *very good* on trusted rating services. **It** then began trying to find a match between available *appointment times* (supplied by the **agents** of individual providers through their Web sites) and Pete's and Lucy's busy schedules. (The italicized keywords indicate terms whose semantics, or meaning, were defined for the **agent** through the Semantic Web.)"

As the sample scenario given above indicates, (semantic web) agents are playing the leading role in the scenario. Six years later, James Hendler wrote a letter as IEEE Intelligent System editor in May–June 2007 issue and asked an important question "Where are all the Intelligent Agents". He commented in the letter that the key obstacle

D. Weyns and F. Michel (Eds.): E4MAS 2014 – 10 years later, LNAI 9068, pp. 41–51, 2015.
DOI: 10.1007/978-3-319-23850-0_3

to the wider deployment of agents is the need for interoperability and intercommunication. He also argued that well established web services standards (and vendor(s) support) provide necessary interoperability infrastructure and semantic web standards provide the knowledge sharing infrastructure for intelligent agents' intercommunication.

In 2007 when Hendler wrote the letter, RDF, RDF Schema and OWL had become standards. There was huge research effort on many areas of the semantic web such as the development of new standards (e.g. SPARQL), inference optimization, construction of new ontologies for different domains, development of ontology mapping and alignment languages and so on. Also, there were significant efforts on tool development, which resulted with some great open source tools such as Protégé, Pellet, Jena and many others that can be used to create and manipulate ontologies.

Despite the huge research efforts in mid-2000s, it was very doubtful to argue that there was a Semantic Web in that time as envisioned. Because, the Semantic Web was defined as a universal knowledge graph from the beginning where every concept named by a URI and these concepts are progressively linked into a universal web [4]. In 2007, there were lots of necessary standards, tools, and independent information systems that use these standards and tools, but universal linked knowledge web was lacking. Thus, the question would be "Where is the Semantic Web We Envisioned" for that time.

But, today it is certain that we are living in the era of transformation of web into a knowledge web which is also called Linked Data Web. There were 1014 linked data sets in the Linked Data Cloud as of April 2014 including billions of triples and more than 500 million out links [2]. Linked data web, which includes data sets in many domains such as government, media, life sciences, geographic places, social web, is constantly and exponentially growing.

Thus, it is time for agent researchers and practitioners to ask themselves how they can link agents to this new web. Since abstraction of the resources at low level deployment context is one of the many duties of the agent environments, agent-linked data web linkage can be achieved by means of them. Thus, in this paper, a conceptual framework for such an environment is proposed. This framework allows agents to access and monitor the data on the linked data web through an abstraction layer as given in [8].

2 Architectural Patterns of Linked Data Web

In July of 2006, Tim Berners-Lee published a personal note named as Linked Data-Design Issues [4]. The note was beginning with the following sentences; "The Semantic Web isn't just about putting data on the web. It is about making links, so that a person or machine can explore the web of data." We believe that this note is crucial for the Semantic Web evolution. Because, it changed the focus of the whole community to real problem; creating a web of data by making links. At that time, community was considering the ontologies like silver bullet and putting them into almost any information system problem known. There were many projects which use ontologies and related tools and many proposed domain ontologies, but creating a web of data was not a common vision within the community. Tim Berners-Lee reminded the community the original vision and renamed this vision as Linked Data Web to get rid of the confusion within the community.

After the publishment of Linked Data-Design Issues, community has taken the message and began to create linked data web. Actually, there were only 4 principles in Linked Data-Design Issues note:

1. Use URIs as names for things.
2. Use HTTP URIs, so that people can look up those names.
3. When someone looks up a URI, provide useful information, using the standards (RDF, SPARQL).
4. Include links to other URIs, so that they can discover more things.

By applying these principles, community has created a Linked Data Cloud which included billions of triples and more than 500 million out links in April 2014 (last measurement, but constantly expanding). Today, we have a well-established infra-structure to publish and consume the linked data from the cloud.

To publish data, there are various ready-to-use data wrappers and converters for all widely used structural and semi-structural data models. Since most of the structural data on the Web are stored by relational databases, the most mature wrappers are for transforming relational databases structures to RDF model. W3C published a recom-mendation in September 2012 for a standard language called as R2RML to express customized mappings from relational databases to RDF datasets. R2RML has been widely accepted by tool developers, even well-known open source D2R [5] uses R2RML as the mapping language.

There are, of course, many tools to convert application specific format such as CVS, Excel, and XML ext. into RDF. These tools are known as RDFizing tools and a list of them can be found in [6]. The output of these tools can be static RDF files accessed through a web server or converted RDF data can be loaded to a RDF Store.

Once the internal data sources are converted to RDF and/or necessary mappings are defined through wrappers to create RDF view, these created RDF data can be accessed via Web by two ways: querying with SPARQL protocol through SPARQL endpoints (RDBtoRDF wrappers and RDF stores provides endpoint support) or accessing RDF files (by dereferencing URL address) through web server.

Now consider that there hundreds (thousands in very near future) data sources publishing their data, there are many links (billions of them) between published sources and there is very dynamic environment where new sources enters and new links are created constantly in an uncontrolled manner. Although the tools and approaches for publishing RDF data are stable and deployed successfully in hundreds of data sources in LOD cloud, consuming the desired data from such a highly dynamic environment is a very challenging task. So, linked data community's main focus is to find effective ways to consume data from linked data cloud. This focus is also very critical for semantic agent researchers since agents have been considered as the main consumer as it is discussed in the introduction.

There are three well understood architecture patterns for consuming linked data depending of the applications' requirements: the On-The-Fly Dereferencing Pattern, the Crawling Pattern and the Query Federation Pattern. These patterns have been described in detail in [3], and they are briefly introduced in the following paragraphs to identify the alternative ways of consuming linked data cloud.

On-The-Fly Dereferencing Pattern is also known as follow your nose approach. This pattern conceptualizes the web as a graph of documents which contains derefe-rencable URIs. So, an application executes a query by accessing an RDF file by dere-ferencing the URL address then follows the URI links by parsing the received file on-the-fly. The problem with this pattern is the performance of the complex operations especially when it is needed to dereference thousands of URIs.

The Crawling Pattern follows the approach of web search engines like Google, Yahoo. In this approach, collection of data and usage of the collected (cached) data are two separate tasks. So the data collection task constantly crawls the web by dereferencing URLs, following links and integrating the discovered data on the local site. The main advantage of the crawling pattern is its performance. Applications can use high volume of integrated data in much higher performance than other patterns. On the other hand, the main disadvantage of this pattern is that original data may change while you use it from replicated local cache (stale data problem). Also, integration of the discovered data is a very challenging task since different publishers may use different URLs to identify the same concept. In this case, one has to resolve this identity problem and also to consider the quality of the data (using the provenance knowledge) while integrating the all collected data.

Query Federation Pattern is based on dividing a (complex) query into sub-queries and distributing sub-queries to relevant datasets which are selected using metadata about datasets. It rises on the findings of the database literature on distributed query processing. Query federation contains two main steps before performing a query. Firstly, query is divided into sub-queries and datasets relevant with sub-queries are selected using some metadata which reflects dataset content. Then, the query execution plan is constructed using statistics about datasets in the query optimization step. For the purpose of executing sub-queries on distributed data sources, query federation requires accessing datasets via SPARQL endpoints. SPARQL endpoints have become the standard approach to publish high volume of data since all relational database wrappers and RDF stores support data publishing through endpoints. Also, publishing metadata about the data sources was added to the Linked Data-Design Issues note as a new principle in 2009 and an RDF scheme called as VoID (Vocabulary of Interlinked Datasets) which is used to express metadata about the data sources was proposed [11] and has become a defacto standard. So, there is a well-established infrastructure to execute Query Federation Pattern and it is the one of the most researched topic within the linked data community. The main problem is again performance of the complex queries especially when query needs to join data from large number of data sources. But, recent federated query engines like SPLENDID [12], and WODQA [10] show reasonable performances even with complex queries.

When these three patterns are examined, it can be easily noticed that Query Federation an On-the-fly Dereferencing patterns query data from its original data sources, on the other hand Crawler pattern brings and integrates all crawled data in the application's local site. At this point, an important question that needs to be answered is which pattern(s) are more suitable for semantic agent and linked data cloud interaction. Let's remember the semantic web scenario again to answer this question.

Lucy's semantic agent looks up several lists of providers, and checks for the ones in-plan for Mom's insurance within a 20-mile radius of her home and with a rating of excellent or very good on trusted rating services. In the world of linked data web, it can be easily assumed that there are two datasets publishing medical providers' knowledge (types of services, location ext.) and rating knowledge as SPARQL end points. There will be links in these datasets and also links from medical provider data to the insurance dataset published somewhere else. So, the answer of the question is clear, semantic agents first able to discover right dataset(s) and query linked data in their original place by using Query Federation or On-the-fly Dereferencing patterns. Another issue with the scenario is taking an appointment from a suitable therapist. In order to establish this, the schedule datasets of the therapists with the desired rank and address can be crawled from their original locations periodically and collected in a local knowledge base which can be queried for appointment times. Of course, semantic agents can take role in crawling process like handling identity resolution, quality handling and management of high volume of crawled data, but agent researchers first need to find effective ways to incorporate linked data querying patterns with the agent systems.

3 A Conceptual Architecture for Linking Agents with the Linked Data Web

As it is discussed in the preceding section, semantic agents should be able to discover the relevant dataset(s) and crawl them if necessary according to the agent's running task requirement(s) and then able to query these dataset as the part of task execution. But querying is not enough in situations where agent needs to react to the changing conditions in the linked data cloud. For example, ratings of medical providers may change and agent needs to monitor these changes to inform Lucy about the fall of her medical service rating numbers. In addition to the rating numbers, many parameters of surrounding linked data cloud such as new medical provider entrance, insurance conditions or laws, conditions of provider services may change over time and semantic agent may need to monitor all of these parameters depending on its requirements.

Linked data cloud changes constantly in two dimensions. In the first dimension, cloud itself expands by entrance of new data sources and creations of new links between the sources. Keeping track of these changes is a must for a semantic agent to be able to discover right knowledge sources to query depending of its task's require-ments. In the second dimension, actual data may change in the data sources and these changes may be critical for agent's internal tasks (such as Lucy's medical provider information) and need to be monitored by the agent. Consequently, semantic agent has to monitor and interpret the changes in the linked data cloud structure and also changes in specific data sources which its task(s) depend on. It is obvious that handling all of these linked data dynamism within the agents makes agent implementation very complex and it is against the well-known software engineering best practice known as separation of concerns. Agent researches encountered this problem before and defined the environment abstraction [8] to cope with it.

Environment is defined as the first class entity used during the design of multi-agent systems, and it includes all the resources and services that an agent needs. Thus, environment shields the agent developer from the complexity of the outside world. In the similar manner, it is necessary to shield semantic agent developer from the complexity of handling linked data cloud dynamism. So, it is time to think how linked data dynamism can be managed within the environment abstraction and what kind of services (interfaces) of environment should be provided to semantic agents to simplify the usage of linked data cloud.

To define internal structure of the proposed architecture, the well-known A&A (Agents and Artifact) [9] meta-model will be used. Thus, to form a basis for our discussion on the proposed conceptual architecture, an overview of the A&A meta-model is given first. The artifact concept lies at the core of the A&A metamodel. Artifacts are the building blocks of the environment and provide specific functionalities for agents. An artifact has a usage interface which defines the operations that an agent can execute on that artifact. There are two types of actions provided for an agent that can be performed on an artifact. The first one is the use action through which the agent can execute the operations in the usage interface of the artifact. The other one is the focus action through which an agent can start to observe specific properties of the artifact. These two actions can be used by semantic agents to query the linked data cloud and to monitor the chances in specific data source(s).

Additionally, events generated as a result of the operations triggered by other agents can also be observed by a specific agent. Finally, the artifacts can interact with each other through their link interfaces. A workspace is defined as a logical container of agents and artifacts. It organizes agents and artifacts from a topological perspective and defines the scope for interacting with the environment. In terms of semantic agents' perspective, workspace defines the scope of a specific domain that a group of agents aim to interact. For example Lucy's scenario is in the medical domain and workspace knows and manages the linked data view of (national) medical domain. Of course, not just Lucy's agent but many agents may interact with this workspace and other domains are represented by different workspaces.

The proposed conceptual architecture has two layers as shown in Fig. 1: Agent-Linked Data Integration Services (A&LDIS) layer and Linked Data Access Services (LDAS) layer. A&LDIS layer appears in every workspace. On the other hand, LDAS layer can be used by all workspaces in the environment or can be replicated in different workspaces if data volume or performance considerations requires. The scope of the workspace is defined by the VoID documents stored in the VoID store about the dataset(s) in a specific domain. If there is one VoID store in the environment, then each workspace should be able to access the VoID documents in its domain of interest.

Semantic agents interact with the environment through six specially designed artifacts as seen in the figure. Four of these are artifacts that monitor the four types of SPARQL queries. The other artifacts are Query Engine Artifact which is for federated query processing and the Crawler Artifact for forming a local knowledge base when many distinct datasets with no SPARQL end point should be monitored.

For the Query Artifacts the first problem is to define the basic entity(ies) that is passed by agents to artifacts. As it is discussed before, environment provides three basic services to agents: it executes queries, crawls datasets to form a local knowledge base and monitor changes of data that are requested by agent. For query service, it is obvious that the basic entity is SPARQL query. On the other hand, monitoring service seems more complex since changes in one data source effect other sources if there are link(s) between them. But, SPARQL query can also be considered as the best entity for monitoring linked data cloud. Because, a SPARQL query defines a sub-graph (or a node as the minimal graph) of the linked data cloud and any data (even the linked one) within the cloud can be defined with a SPARQL query. Changes in this sub-graph may occur because of any changes in linked datasets that constitute this sub-graph and observing changes in a SPARQL query enables semantic agents to observe any kind of subgraph within the cloud. Therefore, semantic agents use SPARQL queries for both querying and monitoring the linked data cloud. However, when there are many distributed small datasets like the schedule datasets of the therapists within 20-mile radius of her mother's home in Lucy's scenario, it may be necessary to crawl these datasets frequently, daily e.g., and form a local knowledge base which may be monitored using SPARQL queries. It is important to emphasize that semantic agent only knows the ontology(ies) which are also in the environment's scope and construct SPARQL queries either for querying or monitoring based on its local knowledge. Note that accessing the URL address is not defined as one of the environment services, because it is a simple task for semantic agent to retrieve and interpret an RDF file by itself.

Querying service is handled by Query Engine Artifact. This artifact directly uses Linked Data Query Engine module located in LDAS layer to execute queries. Linked Data Query Engine module incorporates the Query Federation Pattern to the proposed architecture. As discussed in Sect. 2, Linked Data Query Engines execute SPARQL queries in two steps. In the first step, query is divided to sub-queries and datasets relevant with each subquery are selected using the metadata about the datasets. In the proposed architecture, VoID vocabulary is selected to manage datasets' metadata since it is widely accepted as standard vocabulary to represent dataset metadata and there are well known Linked Data Query Engines such as SPLENDID [12], WODQA [11] which use VoID as the metadata vocabulary. In the second step, a query plan is constructed and sub-queries executed on SPARQL end points of selected dataset(s) and intermediate results are joint following the plan. So, semantic agent just deploys the query to the Query Engine Artifact, it then distributes it to relevant datasets according to its view of the cloud (based on its VoID store).

Crawling service is handled by the Crawler Artifact. This artifact crawls the datasets at a given URI and forms a local knowledge base at a local RDF store. This artifact implements the crawling pattern and handles issues like identity resolution, data quality management as discussed by Bizer [3]. The local knowledge base then can be monitored by local Query Artifact using the local SPARQL end point.

Proposed architecture includes only a Linked Data Query Engine for querying which means the exclusion of the On-The-Fly Dereferencing pattern from the architecture. This decision depends on the fact that SPARQL end points become a defacto standard to publish high volume of data to the cloud. But, On-The-Fly Dereferencing algorithms found in the literature [13] can be incorporated to the architecture so that when there is no VoID description is found to execute the query, Query Engine Artifact can create an artifact that is responsible from On-The-Fly Dereferencing execution. This extension makes the architecture more complex but more adaptable in terms of query execution.

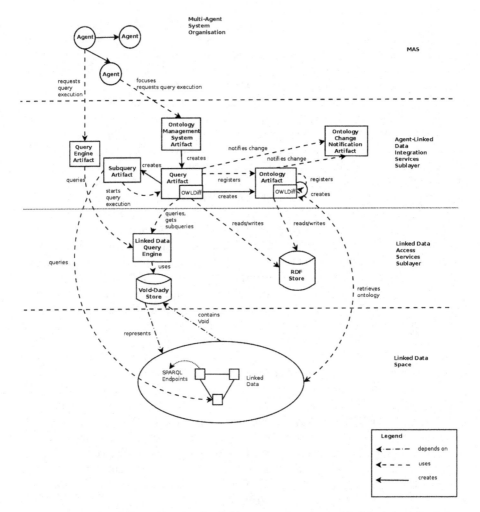

Fig. 1. Environment architecture for linking semantic agents with linked data cloud

Ontology Management System Artifact (OMSA) is responsible of monitoring service. To do so, it creates a separate Query Artifact for each SPARQL monitoring request coming from registered semantic agent(s). Query Artifact first executes query with Linked Data Query Engine and stores the result in the RDF store of the environment. Then it divides the query to sub-queries and selects the relevant dataset(s) using Linked Data Query Engine capabilities and creates a separate Sub-Query artifact for each identified sub-query. Each Sub-Query artifact begins to monitor its query by periodically querying selected dataset(s) and compares the result with the previous one. Once a change is detected by a Sub-Query artifact, it is notified to the related Query Artifact. In this case, Query Artifact re-executes the SPARQL query using Linked Data Query Engine and compares the result with the stored result. If a change is detected, the result is notified to each registered agent(s) and store in the RDF store.

Monitoring the data changes of SPARQL query is not enough. Each SPARQL query depends on one or more ontologies and these ontologies may change dynamically (name of a concept or property may change and/or new concept may added or removed ext.) in the linked data cloud without the control of the semantic agent(s). Therefore, changes of ontologies, that monitored queries are built upon, should be monitored too. Query Artifact creates Ontology Artifact(s) to monitor changes of ontologies used in the query. Each Ontology Artifact creates separate Ontology Artifact (s) for each ontology imported in itself. Then, each Ontology Artifact monitors its assigned ontology by periodically retrieving original ontology and identifies the changes (if any) using an ontology comparison algorithm like OWLDIFF [14]. Ontological changes are notified to registered agents with Ontology Change Notification Artifact using a special ontology which represents the changes within an ontology like the one proposed in [15].

As a result, Lucy's semantic agent can query medical providers' information and ratings from the linked data cloud without any knowledge about the dataset(s) and how they are distributed and linked in the cloud. Moreover, agent may monitor any related information like changes in provider information, rating information, insurance policy or any changes in ontologies it depends on.

4   Evaluation of the Proposed Framework

The reference architecture given in [8] divides the agent environment into three layers:

- basic level which enables agents to access the deployment context,
- abstraction level which fills the conceptual gap between the agents and deployment context by hiding the low level details of the deployment context and the resources in it by providing observation, synchronization, data processing and translation services, and
- interaction-mediation level which regulates resource usage and mediates the interaction among agents by providing perception, communication, interaction and environment dynamics services.

The framework we propose in this paper supports agents at the interaction-mediation, abstraction and basic levels. Perception, interaction and environment dynamics services that should be given at the interaction-mediation level are provided by the A&A metamodel. The services provided by our framework which is built on top of the A&A metamodel are at the abstraction and basic levels.

The artifacts in our framework

- observe the queries given by the agents by running them periodically, which corresponds to a basic level support for accessing the datasets in the deployment context and an abstraction level support for observing the results of those queries,
- comparing the results and processing them for differences, which corresponds to an abstraction level support for data processing,
- updating the cached results when a difference is found, which corresponds to an abstraction level support for data synchronization,

- translating the differences found between two versions of the results of a query into an ontological representation, which corresponds to an abstraction level support for translation.

Although change monitoring and querying are the two basic services a semantic agent needs, there are others like provenance, search, crawling etc. Like monitoring and querying, all these services also belong to the abstraction layer. The agent environment framework we propose can be easily extended with additional functionality due to its artifact based nature. Therefore, our framework can be extended with these additional services as future work.

Another feature of the proposed framework, which is important for agent environment research [17], is its domain independency. Once the VoID documents of the datasets to be used in an application domain are given to the system, data can be monitored regardless of the domain it belongs to. Therefore, it is possible to specialize the framework for the domain at hand.

5   Conclusion

In this paper, an environment architecture is proposed to facilitate the interaction between semantic agents and the linked data cloud. Proposed architecture is based on the experience of the implementation attempt of such a domain independent environment that gives agents support at the abstraction layer [16]. These efforts can be considered as initials steps to attract attention of both agent and linked data researchers to this challenging area of linking agents to linked data web.

Acknowledgements. The development of the environment architecture given in this study has been supported by the Scientific and Technological Research Council of Turkey (TUBITAK) Electric, Electronic and Informatics Research Group (EEEAG) under grant 111E027.

References

1. Berners-Lee, T., Hendler, J., Lassila, O.: The semantic web. Sci. Am. 1–4 (2001)
2. State of the LOD Cloud. http://linkeddatacatalog.dws.informatik.uni-mannheim.de/state/
3. Heath, T., Bizer, C.: Linked data: evolving the web into a global data space. Synthesis Lectures on the Semantic Web: Theory and Technology, 1st edn., vol. 1:1, pp. 1–136. Morgan & Claypool, New York (2011)
4. Linked Data-Design Issues. http://www.w3.org/DesignIssues/LinkedData.html
5. D2R Server. http://d2rq.org/d2r-server
6. RDFizing Tools. http://www.w3.org/wiki/ConverterToRdf
7. Hartig, O., Bizer, C., Freytag, J.-C.: Executing SPARQL queries over the web of linked data. In: Bernstein, A., Karger, D.R., Heath, T., Feigenbaum, L., Maynard, D., Motta, E., Thirunarayan, K. (eds.) ISWC 2009. LNCS, vol. 5823, pp. 293–309. Springer, Heidelberg (2009)
8. Weyns, D., Omicini, A., Odell, J.: Environment as a first class abstraction in multiagent systems. Auton. Agents Multi-Agent Syst. **14**(1), 5–30 (2007)

9. Omicini, A., Ricci, A., Viroli, M.: Artifacts in the A&A meta-model for multi-agent systems. Auton. Agents Multi-Agent Syst. **17**(3), 432–456 (2008)
10. Akar, Z., Halac, T.G., Ekinci, E.E., Dikenelli, O.: Querying the web of interlinked datasets using void descriptions. In: Bizer, C., Heath, T., Berners-Lee, T., Hausenblas, M. (eds.) 5th Linked Data on the Web Workshop (LDOW 2012), CEUR-WS, vol. 937 (2012)
11. Alexander, K., Cyganiak, R., Hausenblas, M., Zhao, J.: Describing linked datasets - on the design and usage of VOID, the 'Vocabulary of Interlinked Datasets'. In: WWW 2009 Workshop: Linked Data on the Web (LDOW 2009), Madrid, Spain (2009)
12. Görlitz, O., Staab, S.: SPLENDID: SPARQL endpoint federation exploiting VOID descriptions. In: Proceedings of the 2nd International Workshop on Consuming Linked Data, Bonn, Germany (2011)
13. Hartig, O.: Zero-knowledge query planning for an iterator implementation of link traversal based query execution. In: Antoniou, G., Grobelnik, M., Simperl, E., Parsia, B., Plexousakis, D., De Leenheer, P., Pan, J. (eds.) ESWC 2011, Part I. LNCS, vol. 6643, pp. 154–169. Springer, Heidelberg (2011)
14. Kremen, P., Smid, M., Kouba, Z.: Owldiff: a practical tool for comparison and merge of owl ontologies. In: Proceedings of the 2011 22nd International Workshop on Database and Expert Systems Applications, DEXA 2011, pp. 229–233. IEEE Computer Society, Washington, DC (2011)
15. Palma, R., Haase, P., Corcho, O., Gomez-Perez, A.: Change representation for OWL-2 ontologies. In: OWLED (2009)
16. Erdur, R.C., Alatli, O., Halac, T.G., Dikenelli, O.: Monitoring the dynamism of linked data space through environment abstraction. In: I-SEMANTIC 2013, pp. 81–88 (2013)
17. Weyns, D., Van Dyke Parunak, H., Michel, F., Holvoet, T., Ferber, J.: Environments for multiagent systems state-of-the-art and research challenges. In: Weyns, D., Van Dyke Parunak, H., Michel, F. (eds.) E4MAS 2004. LNCS (LNAI), vol. 3374, pp. 1–47. Springer, Heidelberg (2005)

Mixed Environments for MAS: Bringing Humans in the Loop

Alessandro Ricci[1]($\boxtimes$), Juan A. Rodriguez-Aguilar[2], Ander Pijoan[3], and Franco Zambonelli[4]

[1] DISI, University of Bologna, Cesena (FC), Italy
a.ricci@unibo.it
[2] Artificial Intelligence Research Institute, IIIA,
Spanish Council for Scientific Research, CSIC,
08193 Cerdanyola, Spain
jar@iiia.csic.es
[3] Deusto Institute of Technology, University of Deusto, Bilbao, Spain
ander.pijoan@deusto.es
[4] Università di Modena e Reggio Emilia, Modena, Italy
franco.zambonelli@unimore.it

Abstract. In many application domains for agents and MAS, the interaction between the systems and human users is a main element. In some cases, the interaction occurs behind a traditional computing device, such as a computer desktop or a smartphone. In other cases, the interaction occurs through the physical world. This is the case, for instance, of smart/intelligent environment applications, and more generally in the wide context of Internet-of-Things based apps. Can the concept of agent environment for MAS play a role in the design of such systems, where humans *are in the loop*? In this position paper we further develop this question, providing some reflections and suggestions for future works.

1 Introduction

Emerging technologies such as wireless sensor networks, Internet of Things (IoT), smart and wearable devices, or even volunteer geographic information, provide a whole new virtual layer where the physical world can be accessed or modified by any computational system. This information gathering capabilities from distributed sources is poised to revolutionize the way MAS environments interact with our real world.

These are main examples of application domains where humans are *in the loop*. By being in the loop we mean to be an essential part of the picture, either as: *(i)* a user of the system, engaging in continuous interactions with it through traditional computational devices (PC, tablet, smartphones, ...) or with the physical environment itself, in the IoT perspective; or *(ii)* part of the system itself, like in the case of socio-technical systems.

Multi-agent systems appear as an effective approach for modelling and designing this kind of systems given their characteristics. In that, the notion

D. Weyns and F. Michel (Eds.): E4MAS 2014 – 10 years later, LNAI 9068, pp. 52–60, 2015.
DOI: 10.1007/978-3-319-23850-0_4

of (application) environment in MAS as elaborated by the community [11] is called to play a relevant role. In fact, in these systems the interaction with a shared distributed physical and social world is a primary aspect, as well as the presence of rich forms of communication, either explicit or implicit, uncoupled, and persistent.

However, research contributions about environments for MAS so far have mainly focused on cases where the first-class citizens acting, perceiving, and interacting have typically been artificial agents—either software or robots. What about first-class agent environments where *both human and artificial agents* are first-class citizens? This is the type of environments we focus on in this paper. Therefore, we are interested in a new type of agent environments that henceforth we shall refer to as *mixed environments* since they are meant to realise mixed multi-agent systems populated by both human and artificial agents.

2   Background: Agent Environment Support Levels

To elaborate the question raised in the introduction above, we start by recalling the three levels describing the environment level of support reported in the literature [11]. These levels include:

- *Basic Level* — At the basic level, the agent environment enables agents to access the deployment context (see Fig. 1). That is, agents know low-level language, details and directly access hardware and software resources.
- *Abstraction Level* — The abstraction level bridges the conceptual gap between the agent abstraction and low-level details of the deployment context (see Fig. 2). Agents access an interface shielding specific details of the resource hidden behind.
- *Interaction-Mediation Level* — The interaction-mediation level offers support to regulate the access to shared resources, ensure restrictions are met and mediate interaction between agents (see Fig. 3).

The three levels of support represent different degrees of functionality provided by the environment that agents can use to achieve their goals. The first question is: *where do we put humans in these layers?*.

3   Modelling Humans in the Loop

On the one side, one could consider humans as part of the deployment context— so the basic level. However, as soon as we consider modern application domains such as pervasive computing/smart environments, we realize that such a modeling is not fully satisfactory, from an abstraction point of view in particular.

An alternative modeling could be considering humans as part of the agents, so that the application environment becomes the glue also among human users and agents at different levels. But in this case we are considering part of the MAS something which is – actually – outside the system, being the *users* of the system.

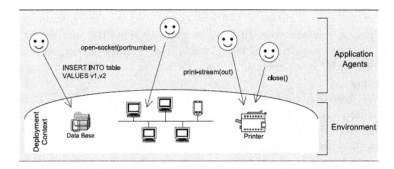

Fig. 1. Basic support level (from [11]).

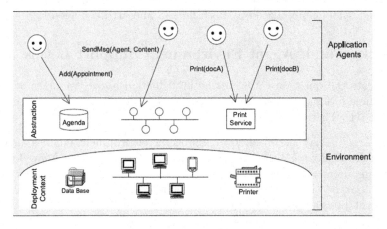

Fig. 2. Abstraction support level (from [11]).

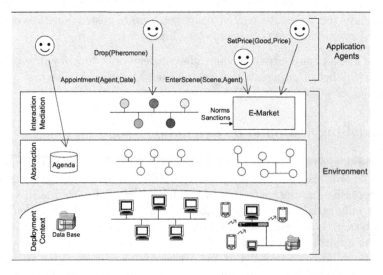

Fig. 3. Interaction-mediation support level (from [11]).

A further solution in the middle could be to introduce "special agents", kind of *user agents*, that have the goal of modeling/representing the human users inside the system, with the goal of reflecting their actions and intentions, and collecting perceptions and information that should be brought back to the human users that they represent. This kind of agents is quite recurrent in agent-based applications. From an agent environment point view, they function as kind of *facilitators*, making it possible to bring inside the system actions that human user aim to perform and bring outside the system the perceptions/information targeted to them. From an abstraction point of view, they could be still considered part of the application environment. In fact, in a conceptual model like A&A [8], these facilitators are better modelled in terms of *artifacts* – not agents – designed in this case to make human actions observable (from an agent point of view) or agents' actions (from a human point of view).

Being represented either as agents or not, the problem is the model adopted to define the interaction between humans and the MAS. This issue is not new for the agent research community: the point here is to understand if the idea of environment as first-class abstraction inside a MAS can be helpful for that purpose.

4   Reifying Human Actions and Perceptions into the Agent Environment

Now we consider some relevant examples in the literature of agent-based systems with humans in the loop.

4.1   Pervasive Ecosystems and Human-Aware Superorganisms

The first is given by pervasive ecosystems and human-aware superorganisms, as introduced and developed by Zambonelli and colleagues in [9,12,13].

Generally speaking, pervasive and ubiquitous computing is a well-known and obvious case where humans are in the loop. These technologies promise to notably change the future ICT landscape, letting us envision the emergence of an integrated and very dense socio-technical infrastructure for the provisioning of innovative general-purpose digital services. The infrastructure will be used to ubiquitously access services for better interacting with the surrounding physical world and with the social activities occurring in it.

Following this line, future urban environments can be depicted as *sociotechnical superorganism* [12], where networks of entities – ICT devices and citizens – will continuously and perhaps invisibly cooperate in highly decentralized and participatory sensing activities. The real-time sharing of the results of such activities at city scale will enable a shared understanding, via computing and thinking, of urban issues and their dynamics. This in turn will make it possible to plan and direct responses or fix problems with specific collective actions.

In order to tackle the design of this kind of systems, the SAPERE project [13] envisioned an approach based on modeling and architecting pervasive service environments as a non-layered spatial *substrate*, laid above the actual pervasive network infrastructure, on top of which human users act as "prosumers" continuously producing and consuming data. The substrate embeds the basic laws of nature (or eco-laws) that rule the activities of the system. There, individuals of different species – agents/services, data, and devices – interact and combine with each other (in respect of the eco-laws and typically based on their spatial relationships), so as to serve their own individual needs as well as the sustainability of the overall ecology.

The approach is clearly data-centric, in that the environment supporting humans/agents interaction and coordination can be implemented as an open distributed set of data spaces, hosting streams of tuples – generated by sensors, actuators, so human actions and reactions – semantically combined, aggregated, manipulated, and diffused according to some nature-inspired laws.

4.2   Human-Agent Collectives

A second example stems from recent works on *human-agent collectives* (HACs) [6]. HACs refer to all those systems where humans and software agents continually and flexibly establish a range of collaborative relationships with one another, to meet their individual and collective goals, operating at a global scale. In HACs, depending on the task at hand, different constellations of people, resources, and information must come together, operate in a coordinated fashion, and then disband. The openness and presence of many distinct stakeholders, each with their own resources and objectives, means participation is motivated by a broad range of incentives – extrinsic (for example, money or tax-benefit), social, or image motivation (for example, public accreditation or leader-board position), or intrinsic (for example, personal interest in a social cause, altruism, or hobby) rather than diktat. Moreover, once presented with such incentives, the stakeholders need to be evaluated and rewarded in ways that ensure they sustain behaviours that are beneficial to the system they partially form.

4.3   Virtual Institutions

A third example comes from research on virtual institutions [2], a concept that combines electronic institutions [1] and 3D virtual worlds.

Virtual worlds technology has recently emerged in computing with enormous strength [7]. A virtual world is an online immersive environment where, using 3D visualisation, humans participate represented as graphically embodied characters (avatars) and interact with others and the environment by using simple and intuitive control facilities. Because humans are social, the concept of virtual worlds is very appealing to mediate their remote interactions. Nowadays, there are millions of people connecting to virtual worlds every day. Such immersive and interactive environment provides many possibilities to represent the system state and the regulations defined by the coordination model. For instance, the other participants are represented also as avatars and their appearance can be used to display the role they are playing. We argue that 3D virtual worlds can be successfully used to incorporate humans into MAS. To illustrate this hypothesis, next we outline the work carried out to open electronic institutions to humans by using virtual worlds.

The aim of virtual institutions is to design regulated environments where both human and software agents can participate. In this context, electronic institutions are used to define the rules that structure participants interactions (for both humans and artificial agents), while 3D virtual worlds facilitate human participation in the system. Notice that virtual institutions provide different interfaces with the interaction-mediation level in Fig. 3 to artificial agents and humans agents. On the one hand, artificial agents are allowed to directly interact with the electronic institutions' coordination infrastructure by means of an agent communication language. On the other hand, humans visualise and interact in a virtual world where they actions are collected and translated to be processed by the electronic institutions' coordination infrastructure. Thus, the environment's façade is different for human and artificial agents.

4.4 Mirror Worlds

A forth example is based on mirror worlds, as introduced in [4]. Originally inspired by Gelernter's book with the same name [5], mirror worlds can be conceived as an agent-based extension of augmented and mixed reality. Both human and artificial agents inhabit an environment which is both physical and augmented of a digital virtual layer (the mirror), coupled to the physical one.

Mirroring is given by the fact that physical things, which can be perceived and acted upon by humans in the physical world, have a digital counterpart (or augmentation, extension) in the mirror, so that they can be observed and acted upon by agents. Viceversa, an entity (artifact) in the MW that can be perceived and acted upon by software agents may have a physical appearance (or extension) in the physical world – e.g. augmenting it, in terms of AR – so that it can be observed and acted upon by humans (by means of e.g. smart-glasses). This implies a form of *coupling*, such that an action on an object in the physical world causes some kind of changes in entities in the mirror, perceivable then by software agents. Viceversa an action by agents on an artifact in the MW can have an effect on things in the physical world, perceivable by people.

In this case, the abstraction support level provided by the agent environment is twofold: from the artificial agents point of view, it provides a way to represent, perceive and interact with physical things, represented and abstracted by artifacts; from the human agents point of view, the virtual environment provides a way to *augment* the physical world with further functionalities, as well as to empower humans with further cognitive/sensing/acting capabilities. The interaction mediation support level in this case allows for designing environment-meditated coordination and cooperative strategies – possibly self-organising, emerging – that exploit both the physical and digital layer, towards new forms of *Behavioural-Implicit Communication* and stigmergy [3,10].

4.5 Commonalities: Stigmergy Among Humans and Agents

In spite of the differences, in all three approaches it is possible to recognise the introduction of different levels of mechanisms that can be framed as *stigmergic*. At a lower level, these mechanisms make it possible to track, reify, and make it persistent and observable information about human/agent actions and their effect, at the semantic level. At a higher level, this information can be continuously aggregated, elaborated and distributed according to high-level rules designed with some social goal in mind, so as to support high-level and emergent forms of coordination and cooperation between human and artificial agents.

5 Humans Inside

There are situations where it is necessary that real-world humans become an integral part of the system and live together within the same virtual environment with intelligent agents. These systems require facing complex decisions for an agent environment as to how model humans, how to design a human-aware communication infrastructure, how to provide decision and co-ordination support, and how to implement laws. More precisely,

- *Real-World Human Modelling:* It is necessary to capture the representative human attributes for the system and translate them into an environment entity that corresponds to reality. These attributes need to be aligned and harmonized with the layers where artificial agents perform their duties.
- *Communication Infrastructure:* Different types of artificial agents in the environment must be able to recognize human entities and have mechanisms to communicate with them. Thus, agents can sense the humans and get information for their decision making processes.
- *Decision and Coordination Support:* Endowing an environment with capabilities to assist humans in their interactions is a must. Decision and coordination support appear as fundamental environment features to help humans reduce the scope of their reasoning with the aim of achieving their goals.
- *Constraints and Laws Implementation:* The agent environment should contain rules that all entities and agents must fulfill so as to define both their existence and behavior with others. The environment and its agents, need to add new restrictions to know how to interact with humans.

Putting real-world humans in the loop entails having elements that can not be controlled, modified or even expected to have a rational behavior. Although the environment enforces its laws on the artificial agents, it is not possible to change a human's state or attributes. Therefore, one of the main questions of this position paper is: *can humans break the environment rules?*

It is now, more than ever, when the need for an explicit environment entity that ensures the integrity and consistency of the entire ecosystem becomes unavoidable. It is necessary to seek consensus on the role the environment must play when unstable situations are given and how to cope with them. The environment needs to be prepared to cope with impossible situations without coming into faulty performance. All events and behaviours that take place inside, need to be decomposed into atomic actions that go from one consistent state to another. Not only that, but considering that the real world is receiving actions from the system too, even with impossible situations the environment must preserve the consistence of the ecosystem and avoid creating damage or harming any human.

6 Towards Environments Where Humans and Agents Are Happy to Live in – Open Challenges

The objective of this position paper was to raise some basic questions about an issue that we believe could be important for future research about environments for MAS.

By considering humans in the loop, we are pushed towards identifying first-class environments that provide effective means for enabling and interaction, coordination, cooperation not only among agents, but among humans and agents too. Open challenges in that path include:

- devising effective environment mechanisms effectively modelling human-agent interaction and coordination, paying particular attention to providing decision and coordination support;
- the introduction of high-level environment abstractions and mechanism to effectively model and design *augmented* realities and worlds where (human/software) agents live in;
- methodologies for designing and developing scalable agent environment technology stacks to deal with open, large-scale human-agent environments, eventually integrating mainstream architectures and technologies related to e.g. Internet-of-Things and the cloud.

Existing explorations and visions about sociotechnical urban superorganisms, mirror worlds or human-agent collectives can be considered just a starting point. We believe that in order to tackle these challenges, a broader inter-disciplinary perspective is needed, bringing together studies and results from both the human and the agent side, with the specific objective of designing environments where both humans and agents are happy to live in.

Acknowledgements. This paper has been partially funded by the following projects: COR (TIN2012-38876-C02-01) and the Generalitat of Catalunya (2009-SGR-1434).

References

1. Arcos, J.L., Esteva, M., Noriega, P., Rodríguez-Aguilar, J.A., Sierra, C.: Engineering open environments with electronic institutions. Eng. Appl. Artif. Intell. **18**(2), 191–204 (2005)
2. Bogdanovych, A.: Virtual institutions. Ph.D. thesis, University of Technology, Sydney, Australia (2007)

3. Castelfranchi, C., Pezzullo, G., Tummolini, L.: Behavioral implicit communication (BIC): communicating with smart environments via our practical behavior and its traces. Int. J. Ambient Comput. Intell. **2**(1), 1–12 (2010)
4. Castelfranchi, C., Piunti, M., Ricci, A.: AmI systems as agent-based mirror worlds: bridging humans and agents through stigmergy. In: Bosse, T. (ed.) Agents and Ambient Intelligence. Ambient Intelligence and Smart Environments, vol. 12, pp. 17–31. IOS Press, Amsterdam (2012)
5. Gelernter, D.: Mirror Worlds - or the Day Software Puts the Universe in a Shoebox: How It Will Happen and What It Will Mean. Oxford University Press, New York (1992)
6. Jennings, N.R., Moreau, L., Nicholson, D., Ramchurn, S., Roberts, S., Rodden, T., Rogers, A.: Human-agent collectives. Commun. ACM **57**(12), 80–88 (2014). doi:10.1145/2629559
7. Messinger, P.R., Stroulia, E., Lyons, K., Bone, M., Niu, R.H., Smirnov, K., Perelgut, S.: Virtual worlds - past, present, and future: new directions in social computing. Decis. Support Syst. **47**(3), 204–228 (2009)
8. Omicini, A., Ricci, A., Viroli, M.: Artifacts in the A&A meta-model for multi-agent systems. Auton. Agents Multi-Agent Syst. **17**(3), 432–456 (2008). doi:10.1007/s10458-008-9053-x
9. Sassi, A., Zambonelli, F.: Coordination infrastructures for future smart social mobility services. IEEE Intell. Syst. **29**(5), 78–82 (2014). doi:10.1109/MIS.2014.81
10. Tummolini, L., Castelfranchi, C.: Trace signals: the meanings of stigmergy. In: Weyns, D., Van Dyke Parunak, H., Michel, F. (eds.) E4MAS 2006. LNCS (LNAI), vol. 4389, pp. 141–156. Springer, Heidelberg (2007)
11. Weyns, D., Omicini, A., Odell, J.: Environment as a first class abstraction in multi-agent systems. Auton. Agents Multi-Agent Syst. **14**(1), 5–30 (2007). doi:10.1007/s10458-006-0012-0
12. Zambonelli, F.: Toward sociotechnical urban superorganisms. IEEE Comput. **45**(8), 76–78 (2012). http://doi.ieeecomputersociety.org/10.1109/MC.2012.280
13. Zambonelli, F., Castelli, G., Ferrari, L., Mamei, M., Rosi, A., Serugendo, G.D.M., Risoldi, M., Tchao, A., Dobson, S., Stevenson, G., Ye, J., Nardini, E., Omicini, A., Montagna, S., Viroli, M., Ferscha, A., Maschek, S., Wally, B.: Self-aware pervasive service ecosystems. Procedia Comput. Sci. **7**, 197–199 (2011). doi:10.1016/j.procs.2011.09.006

Environments for Complex
and Stigmergic Systems

Engineering Environment-Mediated Coordination via Nature-Inspired Laws

Franco Zambonelli[(✉)]

Dipartimento di Scienze e Metodi dell'Ingegneria,
University of Modena and Reggio Emilia, Modena, Italy
`franco.zambonelli@unimore.it`

Abstract. SAPERE is a general multiagent framework to support the development of self-organizing pervasive computing services. One of the key aspects of the SAPERE approach is to have all interactions between agents take place in an indirect way, via a shared spatial environment. In such environment, a set of nature-inspired coordination laws have been defined to rule the coordination activities of the application agents and promote the provisioning of adaptive and self-organizing services.

1 Introduction

Progresses in mobile and ubiquitous computing are making possible to conceive a variety of innovative general-purpose pervasive computing services for interacting with the physical and social worlds around us [2,5,12]. However, the effective design and development of such services requires the capability of promoting flexible and adaptive interactions among a multiple of distributed devices and software components.

To support the vision, a great deal of research activity in pervasive computing has been devoted to meet the requirements of pervasive service systems, i.e.: supporting self-configuration and context-aware composition; enforcing self-adaptability and self-organization; and ensuring that service frameworks can be highly flexible and long-lasting [29]. The SAPERE ("Self-aware Pervasive Service Ecosystems") approach [27,28] tackles the problem at the foundation, conceiving a radically new way of modeling integrated pervasive services and their execution environments, such that the apparently diverse issues of context-awareness, dependability, openness, flexibility, can all be uniformly addressed.

SAPERE models a pervasive service framework as a distributed multiagent system, in which the coordination between the application agents rely on spatially-situated and environment-mediated interactions [21]. In particular, in the SAPERE environment, a set of simple yet very expressive nature-inspired interaction laws dictates how agents will interact with each other, e.g., how they will compose and orchestrate their activities and how they will exchange information.

As it will be backed up in the following of this paper, the SAPERE approach effectively supports the provisioning of adaptive self-organizing services, suitable to meet the requirements of pervasive service systems. In addition, with

© Springer International Publishing Switzerland 2015
D. Weyns and F. Michel (Eds.): E4MAS 2014 – 10 years later, LNAI 9068, pp. 63–75, 2015.
DOI: 10.1007/978-3-319-23850-0_5

SAPERE, we have somewhat answered to some long-standing research questions related to environment engineering in multiagent systems. For instance:

- SAPERE defines a set of general-purpose interaction laws, embedded and enforced in the abstract spatial environment, which shows that valuable application-independent approaches can be defined as far as environmental abstractions are concerned [23].
- The SAPERE approach, with its peculiar environment-mediated coordination model, makes it possible to properly encapsulate any kind of resources and services within the environment, yet preserving the full observability of such resources and of the related coordination events [22]
- In general, SAPERE properly frames the needed abstractions and architectural building elements to engineer environment-mediated (and nature-inspired) multiagent systems [20].

To elaborate on the above, we introduce the SAPERE environment-centered coordination architecture (Sect. 2) and the key characteristics of the SAPERE middleware and its programming model (Sect. 3). Following, we present the set of nature-inspired coordination laws (Sect. 4) and discuss how they can be used to enforce a variety of self-organization scheme (Sect. 5), also with the help of a simple application example. Finally, we discuss related work (Sect. 6) and conclude (Sect. 7).

2   The SAPERE Approach and Its Reference Architecture

SAPERE takes its primary inspiration from nature, and starts from the consideration that the dynamics and decentralization of future pervasive networks will make it suitable to model the overall world of pervasive services, data, and devices as a sort of distributed computational *ecosystem*.

As from Fig. 1, SAPERE conceptually architects such pervasive service ecosystem as a non-layered *spatial environment*, laid above the actual pervasive network infrastructure [8]. The environment embeds the basic *interaction laws* (which we also call *eco-laws*) that rule the activities of the system. The environment mediates all interactions and represents the ground on which components of different species indirectly interact and combine with each other. Such interactions take place in respect of the eco-laws and typically based on the spatial relationships between components, so as to serve their own individual needs as well as the sustainability of the overall ecology. Users can access the ecology in a decentralized way to use and consume data and services, and they can also act as "prosumers" by injecting new data or service components, possibly also for the sake of controlling the ecology behavior.

For the *components* living in the ecosystem, all of which can be abstracted as autonomous software agents (and whether being sensors, actuators, services, users, data, or resources in general), SAPERE adopts a common modeling and a common treatment. Each of them has an associated semantic representation which we call "LSA" (*Live Semantic Annotations*), to be injected in the spatial environment as it it were a sort of shared spatial memory (or tuple space [11]). This is a basic ingredient for enabling dynamic environment-mediated interactions between components. To account for the high dynamics of the scenario and for its need of continuous adaptation, SAPERE defines LSAs as living, active entities, tightly associated to the agent they describe, and capable of reflecting its current situation and context. This supports semantic and context-aware interactions both for service aggregation/composition and for data/knowledge management. In the case of pure data items, the entity and its LSA coincide.

The approach based on LSA makes it possible to encapsulate within the

The *eco-laws* define the basic interaction policies among the LSAs of the various agents of the ecology. In particular the idea is to enforce on a spatial basis, and possibly relying on diffusive mechanisms, dynamic networking and composition of data and services by composing their LSAs and exchanging data via them. Data and services (as represented by their associated LSAs) will be sort of chemical reagents, and interactions and compositions will occur via chemical reactions, relying on semantic pattern-matching between LSAs.

As detailed later on, the set of eco-laws includes: *Bond*, which is the basic mechanism for local interactions between components, and acts as a sort of virtual chemical bond between two LSAs (i.e., their associated agents); *Spread*, which diffuses LSAs on a spatial basis, and is necessary to support propagation of information and interactions among remote agents; *Aggregate*, which enforces a sort of catalysis among LSAs, to support distributed data aggregation; *Decay*, which mimics chemical evaporation and is necessary to garbage collect data. As discussed in Sect. 5, set of eco-laws are general enough to be applicable to a wide range of application domains.

Adaptivity in SAPERE is not in the capability of individual components, but in the overall self-organizing dynamics of the ecosystem. In particular, adaptivity will be ensured by the fact that any change in the system (as well as any change in its components or in the context of the components, as reflected by dynamic changes in their LSAs) will reflect in the firing of new eco-laws, thus possibly leading to the establishment of new bonds or aggregations, and/or in the breaking of some existing bonds between components.

3   The SAPERE Middleware and Its Programming Interface

In this section we shortly overview how SAPERE applications can be programmed, by introducing the API of the SAPERE middleware and exemplifying its usage.

3.1   The Middleware

The execution of SAPERE applications is supported by a middleware infrastructure [26] which reifies the SAPERE architecture in terms of a lightweight software support, enabling a SAPERE node to be installed in tablets and smartphones.

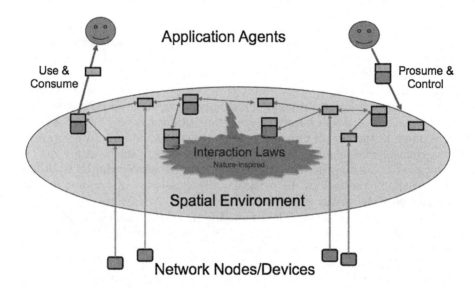

Fig. 1. The SAPERE Architecture based on environment-mediated interactions

Operationally, all SAPERE nodes (whether fixed at the infrastructure level or mobile) are considered at the same level since the middleware code they run could support the same services and provides the same set of functions.

Each SAPERE node hosts a local tuple space [11], that acts as a local repository of LSAs for local agents, and a local eco-laws engine. The LSA-space of each node is connected with a limited set of neighbor nodes based on spatial proximity relations. Such relations consequently determine the spatial shape of the SAPERE substrate. From the viewpoint of individual agents (that will constitute the basic execution unit) the middleware provides an API to access the local LSA space, to advertise themselves (via the injection of an LSA), and to support the agents' need of continuously updating their LSAs. In addition, such API enables agents to detect local events (as the modifications of some LSAs) or the enactment of some eco-laws on available LSAs.

Eco-laws are realized as a set of rules embedded in SAPERE nodes. For each node, the same set of eco-laws applies to rule the dynamics between local LSAs (in the form of bonding, aggregation, and decay) and those between non-locally-situated LSAs (via the spreading eco-law that can propagate LSAs from a node to another to support distributed interactions).

From the viewpoint of the underlying network infrastructure, the middleware transparently absorbs dynamic changes at the arrival/dismissing of the supporting devices, without affecting the perception of the spatial environment by individuals.

3.2 The SAPERE API

In the SAPERE model, each agent executing on a node takes care of initializing at least one LSA (representing the agent itself), of injecting it on the local LSA space, and of keeping the values of such LSA (and of any additional LSA it decides to inject) updated to reflect its current situation. Each agent can modify only its own LSAs, and eventually read the LSAs to which it has been linked by a proper eco-law. Moreover LSAs can be manipulated by eco-laws, as explained in the following sections.

At the middleware level, a simple API is provided to let agents inject LSA – `injectLSA(LSA myLSA)` – and to let agents atomically update some fields of an LSA to keep it "alive" – `updateLSA(field = new-value)`. In addition, it is possible for an agent to sense and handle whatever events occur on the LSAs of an agent, e.g., some match that triggers some eco-laws. E.g., it is possible to handle the event represented by the LSA being bound with another LSA via the `onBond(LSA mylsa)` method.

The eco-laws assure self-adaptive and self-organizing activities in the ecosystems. Eco-laws operate on a pattern-matching schema: they are triggered by the presence of LSAs matching with each other, and manipulate such LSAs (and the fields within) according to a sort of artificial chemistry [29].

3.3 LSAs

LSAs are realized as descriptive tuples made by a number of fields in the form of "name-value" properties. By building over tuple-based models and extending upon them [11], the values in a LSA can be: *actual*, yet possibly dynamic and changing over time (which makes LSAs live); *formal* not tied to any actual value unless bound to one and representing a dangling connection (typically represented with a "?").

Pattern matching between LSAs – which is at the basis of the triggering of eco-laws – happens when all the properties of a description match, i.e., when for each property whose names correspond (i.e., are semantically equivalent) then the associated values match. As in classical tuple-based approaches, a formal value matches with any corresponding actual value.

For instance, the following `LSAa:(sensor-type = temperature; accuracy = 0.1; temp = 45)`, that can express the LSA of a temperature sensor, can match the following `LSAb:(sensor-type = temperature; temp = ?)`, which can express a request for acquiring the current temperature value. LSAa and LSAb match with each other. The properties present in LSAa (e.g., accuracy) are not taken into account by the matching function because it considers only inclusive match.

4 The Eco-Laws Set

Let us now detail the SAPERE eco-laws and discuss their role in the SAPERE ecosystem.

4.1 Bond

Bonding is the primary form of interaction among co-located agents in SAPERE (i.e., within the same LSA space). In particular, bonding can be used to locally discover and access information, as well as to get in touch and access local services. All of which with a single and unique adaptive mechanism. Basically, the bond eco-law realizes a sort of a virtual link between LSAs, whenever two LSAs (or some SubDescriptions within) match.

The bond eco-law is triggered by the presence of formal values in at least one of the LSAs involved. Upon a successful pattern matching between the formal values of an LSA and actual values of another LSA, the eco-law creates the bond between the two. The link established by bonding in the presence of the "?" formal fields is bi-directional and symmetric.

Once a bond is established, the agents holding the LSAs are notified of the new bond and can trigger actions accordingly. After bond creation, the two agents holding the LSAs can read each other LSAs. This implies that once a formal value of an LSA matches with an actual value in an LSA it is bound to, the corresponding agent can access the actual values associated with the formal ones. For instance, with reference to the LSAa and LSAb of the previous subsection, the agent having injected LSAb, upon bonding with LSAa (which the agent can detect with the onBond method) it can access the temperature measure by the sensor represented by LSAb.

As bonding is automatically triggered upon match, debonding takes place automatically whenever some changes in the actual "live" values of some LSAs make the matching conditions no longer holding.

We emphasize that bonding can be used to enable two agents to spontaneously get in touch with each other and exchange information, all of which with a single operation and with both having injected an LSA in the space. That is, unlike in traditional discovery of data and services, without distinguishing between the roles of the involved agents and subsuming the traditionally separated phases of discovery and invocation.

4.2 Aggregate

The ability of aggregating information to produce high-level digests of some contextual or situational facts is a fundamental requirement for adaptive and dynamic systems. In fact, in open and dynamic environments, one cannot know *a priori* which actual information will be available (some information source may disappear, other may appear, etc.) and the availability of ways to extract a summary of all available information (without having to explicitly discover and access the individual information sources) is very important.

The aggregate eco-law is intended to aggregate LSAs together so as to compute summaries of the current system's context. An agent can inject an LSA with the *aggregate* and *type* properties. The aggregate property identifies a function to base the aggregation upon. The type property identifies which LSAs to aggregate. In particular it identifies a numerical property of LSAs to be aggregated. In the current implementation, the aggregate eco-law can perform most common order and duplicate insensitive aggregation functions [4].

The aggregate eco-law supports separation of concern and allows to re-use previous aggregations. On the one hand, an agent can request an aggregation process without dealing with the actual code to perform the aggregation. On the other hand, the LSA resulting from an aggregation can be read (via a proper bond) by any other agent that needs to get the pre-computed result.

4.3   Decay

The decay eco-law enables the vanishing of components from the SAPERE environment. It applies to all LSAs that specify a decay property to update the remaining time to live according to the specific decay function, or actually removing LSAs that, based on their decay property, are expired.

The Decay eco-law therefore is a kind of garbage collector capable of removing LSAs that are no longer needed in the ecosystem or no longer maintained by an agent, for instance because they are the result of a propagation.

4.4   Spread

The above eco-laws act on a local basis, i.e., on a single LSA space. Since the SAPERE model is based on a network of interaction spaces, it is fundamental to enable non-local interactions, by providing a mechanism to send information to remote LSA spaces and making it possible to distribute information and results across a network of LSA spaces.

To this end, in SAPERE we defined the spread eco-law to diffuse LSAs to remote spaces. One of the primary usages of the spread eco-law is to enable searches for components that are not available locally, and vice versa to enable the remote advertisement of services. For an LSA to be subjected to the spread eco-law, it has to include a `diffusion` field, whose value (along with additional parameters) defines the specific type of propagation.

Two different types of propagation are implemented in the SAPERE framework: *(i)* a direct propagation used to spread an LSA to a specified neighbor node, so as to make it possible to realize gossiping schemes and multicasts; *(ii)* a general diffusion capable of propagating an LSA to all neighboring SAPERE nodes, possibly recursively applying such propagation up to a maximum distance form the source node.

General diffusion of an LSA via the spread eco-law to distances greater than one is a sort of broadcast that induces a large number of replicas of the same LSA to reach the same nodes multiple times from different paths. To prevent this, general diffusion is typically coupled with the aggregate eco-law, so as to merge together such multiple replicas.

5   From Eco-Laws to Distributed Self-organization and Its Application to Pervasive Services

The above presented eco-laws form a necessary and complete set to support self-organizing environment-mediated interactions, which can be exploited in a variety of application scenarios.

5.1   Realizing Self-organizing Schemes with Eco-Laws

The eco-laws are necessary to support decentralized adaptive behaviors for pervasive service systems. Bonding is necessary to support adaptive local service interactions, subsuming the phases of discovery and invocation of traditional service systems. Spreading is necessary to diffuse information in a distributed environment and to enable distributed interactions. Aggregation and decay are necessary to support decentralized adaptive access to information without being forced to dynamically deploy code on the nodes of the system, which may not be possible in decentralized environments.

Further, and possibly of more software engineering relevance, the eco-law set is sufficient to express a wide variety of interaction schemes (or "patterns"), there included self-organizing ones. Bonding and spreading can be used to realize local and distributed client-server scheme of interactions as well as asynchronous models of interactions and information propagation. Coupling spreading with aggregation and decay, however, makes it possible to realize also those distributed data structures necessary to support all patterns of nature-inspired adaptive and self-organizing behaviors, i.e., virtual physical fields, digital pheromones, and virtual chemical gradients [4].

In particular, aggregation applied to the multiple copies of diffused LSAs can reduce the number of redundant LSAs so as to form a distributed *gradient* structures, also known as *computational force fields*. As detailed in [14], many different classes of self-organized motion coordination schemes, self-assembly, and distributed navigation can be expressed in terms of gradients.

In addition, spreading and aggregation can be used together to produce distributed self-organized aggregations, i.e., dynamically computing some distributed property of the system and have the results of such computation available at each and every node of the system. Distributed aggregation is a basic mechanism via which to realize forms of distributed consensus and distributed task allocation and behavior differentiation.

By bringing also the decay eco-law into play, and combining it with spreading and aggregation, one can realize pheromone-based data structures, which makes possible to realize a variety of bio-inspired schemes for distributed self-organization [4]. In particular, while general diffusion and progressive decay can be used to realize diffusible and evaporating pheromone-like data structures, direct propagation can be used to navigate by following pheromone gradients.

5.2 Application Areas

Over the course of the SAPERE project, we have shown how the SAPERE approach can be effectively exploited in a variety of application scenarios. We overview here three representative examples.

As a first example, we have used SAPERE to realize a distributed tool for helping people move around in complex and crowdy environment, such as big museum and exhibitions [16]. There, SAPERE eco-laws have been exploited to realize a number of distributed computational force fields reflecting the density of people in the different areas of the environment. Then, a mobile app has been implemented capable of directing people along the gradient of decreasing fields, i.e., in less crowded areas.

As a second example, we have implemented a "social feedback" application [1], where public displays receive LSAs by users expressing their personal food preferences, and are able guide users to individually optimized food providers (e.g., restaurants, pub, cafeteria, etc.). This selection is based on *(i)* the food preferences of users and on *(ii)* the estimated waiting time at the various lunch locations, computed by aggregating (via the aggregate eco-law) the overall number of users in that location; Users can then be directed towards the most proper locations by following the gradients of appropriate computational fields.

Finally, we have developed a number of applications for helping people socializing and coordinating in unknown environment [7,12]. The general idea is to exploit public displays to collect information about users and, by using eco-laws to properly aggregate and diffuse information, be able to put in touch people with similar interests.

6 Related Works

6.1 Environment-Mediated Coordination Models

The issue we face in this article can be framed as the problem of finding the proper coordination model for enabling and ruling interactions of pervasive services, starting from the key consideration that environment-mediated coordination is well suited to the scenarios of interest.

On this base, SAPERE takes as ground the archetypal environment-mediated coordination model, namely LINDA, which simply provides for a blackboard with associative matching for mediating component interactions through insertion/retrieval of tuples.Then, we followed the idea of engineering the coordination space of a distributed system by some policy "inside" tuple spaces, following the pioneer works of approaches like Tucson [15] and MARS [6]. However, our proposal tries to extend these models to include bio-inspired ecological mechanisms, by fine-grained and well structured chemical-like reactions.

In particular, the coordination approach we propose in this paper originates from the chemical tuple space model in [19], though with some notable differences: *(i)* here we provide a detail notational framework to flexibly express eco-laws that work on patterns of LSAs and affect their properties; *(ii)* the chemical concentration mechanisms proposed in [19] to exactly mimic chemistry is not mandatory here—though it can be achieved by a suitable design of rate expressions; *(iii)* the way we conceive the overall infrastructure, and relationship between agents and their LSAs goes beyond the mere definition of the tuple-space model.

6.2   Situatedness and Context-Awareness in Pervasive Services

Considering the issues of situatedness and context-awareness, which is central to pervasive services, many of the approaches in the literature have approaches the problem by extending and modifying service-oriented approaches and architectures [13].

In PLASTIC [3], service descriptions are coupled with dynamic annotations related to the current context and state of a service, to be used for enforcing adaptable forms of service discovery. This is somewhat in line with the idea of LSAs that we in SAPERE. However, due to its environment-mediated approach, SAPERE goes further and gets rid of traditional discovery services and enforces dynamic and adaptive service interaction via simple natural reactions and a minimal middleware.

In many proposals for pervasive computing environments and middleware infrastructures, the idea of "situatedness" has been promoted by the adoption of shared virtual spaces for services and components interactions. The pioneering system Gaia [18] introduces the concept of active spaces, that is active blackboard spaces acting as the means for service interactions.

Later on, a number of Gaia extensions where proposed to enforce dynamic semantic pattern-matching for service composition and discovery [10] or access to contextual information [9]. However, the concept of active space is more that of a shared memory, rather than that of an active environment in which to reify the existence of the pervasive service components and via which to enable and rule their interactions.

6.3   Self-organization

Several recent works exploit the lessons of adaptive self-organizing natural and social systems to enforce self-awareness, self-adaptivity and self-management features in pervasive computing systems.

At the level of individual component modeling, these proposals take the form of either situated reactive agents or proactive and goal-oriented ones [17]. At the level of interaction models, these proposals typically take the form of specific nature- and socially-inspired interaction mechanisms [4], enforced either at the level of component modeling or via specific middleware-level mechanisms.

We believe the SAPERE framework integrates and improves these works in three main directions: *(i)* it abstracts from the specific internal characteristics of components (no matter whether they are simple reactive components or complex goal-oriented ones) and rather proposes an approach that seamlessly applies to both cases; *(ii)* it tries to identify an environment-centered interaction model that is able to represent and subsume the diverse nature-inspired mechanisms under a unifying self-adaptive abstraction (i.e. the semantics chemical reactions); *(iii)* the ecological approach we undertake goes beyond most of the current studies that limit to ensembles of homogeneous components, defining a suitable framework for supporting the vision of novel pervasive and Internet scenarios as made up of self-adaptive devices and services, that autonomously cooperate for the creation of global services.

7   Conclusions and Open Challenges

SAPERE can be somewhat considered the result of several years of experience and research in the area of environment-mediated coordination. The innovative nature-inspired approach of SAPERE is effective to enforce, via environment-mediated interactions, a variety of self-organizing schemes for pervasive computing services, and properly answer to a number of open challenges identified by multiagent systems community with regard to the role of the environment in multiagent systems. These challenges include: the definition of an application-independent approach to handle environmental abstractions are concerned [23]; the possibility of encapsulating any kind of resources and services within the environment yet preserving the observability of the environment of such resources and of the related coordination events [22]; and the proper framing of the needed abstractions to engineer environment-mediated (and nature-inspired) multiagent systems [20].

As the activities within the SAPERE European Project have finished, we will now challenge the SAPERE findings and tools against innovative services in the area of urban computing and smart cities [5]. In particular, we are currently analyzing how to exploit SAPERE to realize the ambitious concept of "urban superorganism" [24,25], i.e., to have all the ICT devices in our urban environment, and the citizens within, be enable to act collectively towards the realization of urban-level objectives aimed at improving quality of life and sustainability. With this regard, and to realize such vision, research on multiagent systems environment will still have to face some open research challenges. For instance:

- How can the adopted environmental abstraction account for the socio-technical nature of future urban computing scenarios, where environment-mediated interactions will involve not only agents but also humans, and will also have to account for their social relationships?
- How can one promote human participation in urban activities by means of a suitable environment-mediated coordination model that is able to effectively incentivize collaboration?

In general, beside the two above open challenges, we think there is still plenty of room for 10 more years of interesting research in the area of environments for multiagent systems.

Acknowledgments. Work supported by the EU project SAPERE, No. 256873.

References

1. Anzengruber, B., Castelli, G., Rosi, A., Ferscha, A., Zambonelli, F.: Social feedback in display ecosystems. In: IEEE International Conference on Systems, Man, and Cybernetics, Manchester, SMC 2013, United Kingdom, 13–16 October 2013, pp. 2893–2898 (2013)
2. Atzori, L., Iera, A., Morabito, G.: From "smart objects" to "social objects": the next evolutionary step of the internet of things. IEEE Commun. Mag. **52**(1), 97–105 (2014)
3. Autili, M., Di Benedetto, P., Inverardi, P.: Context-aware adaptive services: the PLASTIC approach. In: Chechik, M., Wirsing, M. (eds.) FASE 2009. LNCS, vol. 5503, pp. 124–139. Springer, Heidelberg (2009)
4. Babaoglu, O., et al.: Design patterns from biology for distributed computing. ACM Trans. Auton. Adapt. Syst. **1**(1), 26–66 (2006)
5. Bicocchi, N., Cecaj, A., Fontana, D., Mamei, M., Sassi, A., Zambonelli, F.: Collective awareness for human-ict collaboration in smart cities. In: 21st IEEE International WETICE Symposium, pp. 3–8 (2013)
6. Cabri, G., Leonardi, L., Zambonelli, F.: MARS: a programmable coordination architecture for mobile agents. IEEE Internet Comput. **4**(4), 26–35 (2000)
7. Castelli, G., Mamei, M., Rosi, A., Zambonelli, F.: Developing social applications in sapere. In: 10th IEEE International Conference on Ubiquitous Intelligence and Computing, Vietri sul Mare, Sorrento Peninsula, Italy, pp. 314–320 (2013)
8. Castelli, G., Mamei, M., Rosi, A., Zambonelli, F.: Engineering pervasive service ecosystems: the SAPERE approach. TAAS **10**(1), 1:1–1:27 (2015)
9. Costa, P.D., Guizzardi, G., Almeida, J.P.A., Pires, L.F., van Sinderen, M.: Situations in conceptual modeling of context. In: Tenth IEEE International Enterprise Distributed Object Computing Conference (EDOC 2006), Workshops, Hong Kong, China, 16–20 October 2006, p. 6. IEEE Computer Society (2006)
10. Fok, C.-L., Roman, G.-C., Lu, C.: Enhanced coordination in sensor networks through flexible service provisioning. In: Field, J., Vasconcelos, V.T. (eds.) COORDINATION 2009. LNCS, vol. 5521, pp. 66–85. Springer, Heidelberg (2009)
11. Gelernter, D.: Generative communication in linda. ACM Trans. Program. Lang. Syst. **7**(1), 80–112 (1985)
12. Hachem, S., Pathak, A., Issarny, V.: Service-oriented middleware for large-scale mobile participatory sensing. Pervasive Mob. Comput. **10**, 66–82 (2014)
13. Huhns, M.N., Singh, M.P.: Service-oriented computing: key concepts and principles. IEEE Internet Comput. **9**(1), 75–81 (2005)
14. Mamei, M., Zambonelli, F.: Programming pervasive and mobile computing applications: the tota approach. ACM Trans. Software Eng. Methodol. **18**(4), 1–56 (2009)
15. Omicini, A., Zambonelli, F.: Coordination for internet application development. Auton. Agent. Multi-Agent Syst. **2**(3), 251–269 (1999)
16. Pianini, D., Ferscha, A., Viroli, M., Zambonelli, F.: Hpc from a self-organisation perspective: the case of crowd steering at urban scale. In: Workshops of the 2014 IEEE Conference on High Performance Computing, Bologna, Italy (2014)

17. Ricci, A., Omicini, A., Viroli, M., Gardelli, L., Oliva, E.: Cognitive stigmergy: towards a framework based on agents and artifacts. In: Weyns, D., Van Dyke Parunak, H., Michel, F. (eds.) E4MAS 2006. LNCS (LNAI), vol. 4389, pp. 124–140. Springer, Heidelberg (2007)

18. Román, M., Hess, C.K., Cerqueira, R., Ranganathan, A., Campbell, R.H., Nahrstedt, K.: Gaia: a middleware platform for active spaces. Mob. Comput. Commun. Rev. 6(4), 65–67 (2002)

19. Viroli, M., Casadei, M.: Biochemical tuple spaces for self-organising coordination. In: Field, J., Vasconcelos, V.T. (eds.) COORDINATION 2009. LNCS, vol. 5521, pp. 143–162. Springer, Heidelberg (2009)

20. Viroli, M., Holvoet, T., Ricci, A., Schelfthout, K., Zambonelli, F.: Infrastructures for the environment of multiagent systems. Auton. Agent. Multi-Agent Syst. 14(1), 49–60 (2007)

21. Weyns, D., Helleboogh, A., Holvoet, T., Schumacher, M.: The agent environment in multi-agent systems: a middleware perspective. Multiagent Grid Syst. 5(1), 93–108 (2009)

22. Weyns, D., Omicini, A., Odell, J.: Environment as a first class abstraction in multiagent systems. Auton. Agents Multi-Agent Syst. 14(1), 5–30 (2007)

23. Weyns, D., Van Dyke Parunak, H., Michel, F., Holvoet, T., Ferber, J.: Environments for multiagent systems state-of-the-art and research challenges. In: Weyns, D., Van Dyke Parunak, H., Michel, F. (eds.) E4MAS 2004. LNCS (LNAI), vol. 3374, pp. 1–47. Springer, Heidelberg (2005)

24. Zambonelli, F.: Toward sociotechnical urban superorganisms. IEEE Comput. 45(8), 76–78 (2012)

25. Zambonelli, F.: Engineering self-organizing urban superorganisms. Eng. Appl. of AI 41, 325–332 (2015)

26. Zambonelli, F., Castelli, G., Mamei, M., Rosi, A.: Integrating pervasive middleware with social networks in sapere. In: International Conference on Selected Topics in Mobile and Wireless Networking, pp. 145–150. PRC, Shanghai (2011)

27. Zambonelli, F., et al.: Self-aware pervasive service ecosystems. Procedia CS 7, 197–199 (2011)

28. Zambonelli, F., Omicini, A., Anzengruber, B., Castelli, G., De Angelis, F.L., Di Marzo Serugendo, G., Dobson, S.A., Fernandez-Marquez, J.L., Ferscha, A., Mamei, M., Mariani, S., Molesini, A., Montagna, S., Nieminen, J., Pianini, D., Risoldi, M., Rosi, A., Stevenson, G., Viroli, M., Ye, J.: Developing pervasive multi-agent systems with nature-inspired coordination. Pervasive Mob. Comput. 17, 236–252 (2015)

29. Zambonelli, F., Viroli, M.: A survey on nature-inspired metaphors for pervasive service ecosystems. J. Pervasive Comput. Commun. 7, 186–204 (2011)

Introduction and Challenges of Environment Architectures for Collective Intelligence Systems

Juergen Musil[(✉)], Angelika Musil, and Stefan Biffl

Institute of Software Technology and Interactive Systems, CDL-Flex,
Vienna University of Technology, Vienna, Austria
{jmusil,angelika}@computer.org, stefan.biffl@tuwien.ac.at

Abstract. Collective Intelligence Systems (CIS), such as wikis, social networks, and content-sharing platforms, are an integral part of today's collective knowledge creation and sharing processes. CIS are complex adaptive systems, which realize environment-mediated coordination, in particular with stigmergic mechanisms. The behavior of CIS is emergent, as high-level, system-wide behavior is influenced by low-level rules. These rules are encapsulated by the CIS infrastructure that comprises in its center an actor-created artifact network that stores the shared content. In this chapter, we provide an introduction to the CIS domain, CIS architectural principles and processes. Further, we reflect on the role of CIS as multi-agent system (MAS) environments and conclude with an outlook on research challenges for CIS architectures.

Keywords: Collective intelligence · Coordination · Self-organization · Software architecture · Stigmergic information system · Stigmergy

1 Introduction

Since the early 2000s, a new generation of web-based, social platforms has reshaped the way of knowledge creation and sharing. Well-known instances of such systems include social networking services (Facebook[1]), microblogging services (Twitter[2]), wikis and the online encyclopedia Wikipedia[3], content-sharing platforms (YouTube[4]), and review and rating platforms (Yelp[5]). These systems can be regarded as Collective Intelligence Systems (CIS), since these socio-technical platforms all have the capability to harness the collective intelligence of connected groups of people by providing a web-based environment for a community of participating users to share, distribute and retrieve topic-specific information in an efficient way. By contributing new content individually to these

---

[1] http://www.facebook.com/ (last visited 06/18/2015).
[2] http://www.twitter.com/ (last visited 06/18/2015).
[3] http://www.wikipedia.org/ (last visited 06/18/2015).
[4] http://www.youtube.com/ (last visited 06/18/2015).
[5] http://www.yelp.com/ (last visited 06/18/2015).

© Springer International Publishing Switzerland 2015
D. Weyns and F. Michel (Eds.): E4MAS 2014 – 10 years later, LNAI 9068, pp. 76–94, 2015.
DOI: 10.1007/978-3-319-23850-0_6

systems, their users build collectively a continuously growing repository of valuable information, knowledge and data and thus generate collective intelligence of a user community.

CIS are multi-agent systems (MAS), which operate on micro and macro levels and provide benefits both for their users and operators. The individual user benefits from (1) the division of labor, since knowledge emerges from additive contributions of multiple users, and (2) efficient dissemination of knowledge among a large user group and leveraged awareness about activities and contributions of other users. For operators, CIS represent an approach to address complex knowledge-intensive problems on organizational, community and society level, which are improved in two ways. Firstly, hard to access knowledge is continuously aggregated from situated individuals on a global level, whereby *situatedness* of an individual means the *"physical, cultural, and social context, that guides, constrains and partially determines intelligent activities"* [28]. Secondly, the consolidated information is disseminated back to the individuals on a local level. The resulting feedback loop and quality of enabling the continuous adding, updating and restructuring of information gives CIS self-organizational capabilities that make them adaptable and resilient.

Therefore, CIS represent an interesting proving ground for the investigation of MAS-related concepts and theories. One concept that is central in this chapter is the environment [38]. In this chapter, we provide an integrated view of previous work by giving an introduction to the CIS domain as well as the architecting of CIS-specific environments, and conclude with an agenda for CIS architecture research. We argue, that self-organizational CIS are a particular family of MAS environments, which posses a characteristic system model [24]. The model consists of three layers which are a proactive actor base, a passive artifact network and a reactive/adaptive AMD (analysis, management and dissemination) system. Between these layers aggregation and dissemination dynamics exist that create a stigmergic feedback loop connecting the computational environment and the actor base [25]. This system model is the basis to derive an ISO/IEC/IEEE:42010 compliant software architecture framework [16], which should assist software architects to model CIS. So far software architects lack guidance in designing CIS that are tailored for specific application contexts, domains and for individual organizations. Thus, the framework provides consolidated systematic knowledge of the architectural principles and mechanisms that underlie each CIS. The CIS architecture framework (CIS-AF) consists of the three viewpoints CI Context, CI Technical Realization and CI Operation [25]. Each architectural viewpoint comes with its own stakeholders, concerns, model kinds and analytics. While working on this research, we discovered certain needs and limitations, which are described in the research agenda at the end of the chapter. The agenda deals with structure and dynamics of CIS, as well as future application domains. The work of this chapter builds upon advanced concepts of MAS, software architecture, and complex systems. For a deeper understanding of these concepts, we encourage the interested reader to explore the references [15,23,25,34,39].

The remainder of this chapter is structured as follows. Section 2 discusses related work on CIS and Sect. 3 describes CIS characteristics and architectural principles which are illustrated with a real-world CIS platform. In Sect. 4 we present an overview of the architecture framework for CIS comprising three viewpoints with their model kinds. An agenda for future research is discussed in Sect. 5 outlining research challenges in the field of CIS architectures. Finally, Sect. 6 concludes.

2   Related Work

This section presents an overview of related work on CIS foundations: coordination models, environment-mediated interaction and stigmergic coordination as well as IT-enabled collective intelligence.

2.1   Environment-Mediated Interaction and Stigmergic Coordination

Coordination is a key aspect of CIS. Central to the realization of coordination are coordination models, which were described by Gelernter et al. [11] as *"the glue that binds separate activities in an ensemble"* and by Omicini [27] as essential to define *"the abstractions and the computational models for ruling the interaction space in computational systems"*. Ciancarini [5] identified coordination entities, coordination media and coordination laws as the constituents of a coordination model for computational systems. *Coordination entities* are the entities that are being coordinated, like processes, threads, agents or humans. The *coordination media* enable communication among the entities, and serve as means for manipulations among the whole entity base. Examples of coordination media can be simple constructs like semaphores, monitors or complex constructs like tuple spaces [10] and blackboards [7]. Finally, *coordination laws* describe rules, constraints and mechanisms how entities are coordinated by means of the coordination media. The duality between coordination medium and laws was also described by Schmidt and Simone [32] in the context of Computer-Supported Cooperative Work (CSCW) using similar concepts of coordinative artifact and coordinative protocol.

In the last decade, particular focus has been drawn to the environment, which is created by the system, and its impact on the design of modern MAS [38]. Environment-mediated coordination approaches allow the decoupling of processes in space and time, and enable producers and consumers to stay anonymous [29]. A special form of environment-mediated coordination mechanisms is *stigmergy*, which was originally introduced by Grassé [12] to describe the spatial coordination among termite societies. Stigmergy enables not only environment-mediated coordination and indirect communication between agents, it possesses also a positive feedback mechanism [2,3], so that an agent activity causes more activities. The mechanism promotes *awareness* among agents about the activities of other agents, which in turn reinforces their own activities [30]. Additionally, the process behavior of stigmergy is *emergent*, so certain system properties exist on a high-level, but not on a low-level and vice versa [1]. For stigmergy, this means that high-level, system-wide behavior is influenced by low-level rules, encapsulated by artifacts, the environment, and *local* activities. There is no explicit coordination control [8] and the agents are independent and choose autonomously which activities they perform [8,9,28]. In computer science, stigmergy has been explored extensively in various domains [40].

To better understand stigmergy in MAS, the concepts of the environment and artifact are of particular relevance [28,30,35]. Weyns et al. [38] defined the environment as *"a first-class abstraction that provides the surrounding conditions for agents to exist and that mediates both the interaction among agents and the access to resources"*. According to the environment reference model [38], an environment's responsibility with respect to stigmergy is to act as a communication structure maintaining aforementioned dynamics. The *artifact* is used as a coordination medium and as an environment abstraction through which the agents communicate. Extensive discussions of coordination artifacts from a MAS perspective can be found in [8,28] and from a CSCW perspective in [32]. Omicini et al. [28] provided a particular perspective on agents and artifacts in their *agents & artifacts (A&A) meta-model* for MAS. In this approach (1) agents are pro-active components, which autonomously execute activities inside an environment, whereby (2) artifacts are *"passive components which are cooperatively or competitively constructed, manipulated and shared by the agents to support their activities"* [28]. In addition, there are workspaces which represent local environments in which agents can interact with artifacts [28].

Susi et al. [35] provided a conclusive description of using stigmergy to support human cognitive processes and the usage of artifacts as mechanism to mediate emergent human collective behavior. Ricci et al. [30] adapted their work towards a theory of *cognitive stigmergy* for MAS, which proposes the dual usage of artifacts as means (1) to enable emergent coordination processes and (2) to share and represent high-level knowledge for cognitive agents, like humans. In their work they identified the recurring stigmergic mechanisms of diffusion, aggregation, selection and ordering [30]. Parunak [37] surveyed stigmergic computational systems, which are used to coordinate human interactions. A comprehensive discussion of the current state of stigmergy and internet-supported collaboration was provided by Heylighen [15].

2.2   IT-Enabled Collective Intelligence

The phenomenon of *collective intelligence* (CI) has been investigated by researchers in a variety of disciplines like computer science, cognitive science, organization theory, biology and network science [20] and thus in literature a variety of CI definitions exists. According to Malone et al. [21], collective intelligence can be defined as *"groups of individuals doing things collectively that seem intelligent"*. The focus of this section is the discussion of computer science-related research of collective intelligence.

One of the first CI-related system concepts was introduced by Vannevar Bush in 1945 in his essay *As We May Think* [4]. In his work, he envisioned with the *Memex* a hypothetical system that had some of the features of modern CIS, in particular the concept of associative trails. Bush's work influenced other researchers like J.C.R. Licklider and Douglas C. Engelbart. Licklider argued in his work [18] for the needs of a tighter coupling of man and computing system, resulting in a hybrid, mutually-complementing overall system. It was then Engelbart's work on intelligence augmentation and in particular his seminal paper *Augmenting Human Intellect* [6], where he described the concept of a H-LAM/T system, which had two interesting aspects from a MAS environment perspective. Firstly, it highlighted the importance of artifacts, human-artifact interfaces and explicit-artifact processes. Secondly, he introduced the concept of an *executive superstructure*, which operates on a global system level so that *"more human time, energy and productive thought could be allocated to direct-contributive processes, which would be coordinated in a more sophisticated, flexible and efficient manner"* [6]. This executive superstructure can be regarded as an environment architecture and its occurrence, even in this early stage of research, supports the hypothesis that the environment concept is essential for the design of CIS. Interestingly, Engelbart already explicitly recognized the importance of computational automation in the system on a micro level (direct-contributive processes) and macro-level (executive processes).

Research efforts in IT-enabled collective intelligence have continued to gain momentum since the beginning of the Web 2.0 area and the rapid adoption of the first generation of CIS (wikis, social networking services, social media sharing) in a variety of domains and cultures. Besides Surowiecki's book *The Wisdom of Crowds* [34], there have been the works of Lévy [17] and Tapscott and Williams [36], which contributed to the wider adoption of the term collective intelligence. A repeatedly reported characteristic of CIS is the complementary interdependence between human and computing systems on a system level. In literature various terms refer to this attribute, which orbit around the same concept like socio-technical systems [27] or social machines [33]. Studies on the systematization of CI-related systems were conducted by Malone et al. [22], Lykourentzou et al. [19] and Smart et al. [33]. Grasso and Convertino [13] investigated tools and studies on CI in organizations, and Salminen [31] conducted a literature review on CI in humans. Gruber [14] examined how CI of the Social Web can be leveraged using knowledge representation and reasoning techniques from Semantic Web. A discussion of urban-level CIS and their challenges is provided by Zambonelli [39]. Two current collections on scientific CI literature are the book edited by Miorandi et al. [23] and the forthcoming book edited by Malone and Bernstein [20].

3 CIS Environments

This section describes major CIS characteristics and provides an overview of architectural principles as well as the underlying stigmergic process model.

Finally, we illustrate the described architectural principles by applying them on the well-known example case of a Wiki.

3.1   CIS Characteristics

In the context of our research work a *collective intelligence system* is a *socio-technical multi-agent system* which mediates human interaction and provides support for distributed cognitive processes. As a socio-technical system, a CIS is driven by its users who contribute content (knowledge or information) to a globally-shared virtual information space located in a computational system, which in return feeds the consolidated information back to its users. This enables each user to benefit from novel and available information of high quality in her local space. Additionally, each user is stimulated to continue the contribution of further content into the globally-shared space. The feedback loop between the user base and the computational system is an essential feature of CIS, since it bridges the local and global space. Figure 1 shows a CIS process model consisting of 4 steps: (1) Actors (users) contribute/modify content of the shared computational platform. (2) The system analyses and processes content data and extracts consolidated information. (3) The system disseminates the information extracts among its actors. (4) Information stimulates either the actors' local activity or triggers a subsequent content contribution (revisit step 1).

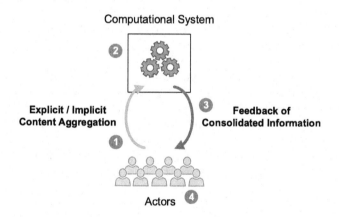

Fig. 1. CIS process with content aggregation and feedback of information

The created bottom-up feedback loop provides CIS with emergent, self-organizational capabilities and differentiates these systems from directed, top-down platforms used for crowdsourcing and human computation, where users are typically provided with task requests that await processing [20].

Another aspect of CIS is the conceptual restriction of the content in the information space to a certain *topic-of-interest*. It can be differentiated between two types of information stored in the space. *Topic-specific information* is data that is closely related to the information space's topic-of-interest, whereby *meta information* provides additional data about the topic-specific information as well as its creation and usage. There are three forms of how topic-specific information can be aggregated by a CIS:

- *Explicit content aggregation (ECA)* depends on the users to actively contribute content to the system. Example instances of such systems are Wikipedia, Facebook and YouTube.
- *Implicit content aggregation (ICA)* captures topic-relevant information as a side-product, while actors are performing a certain activity. A typical example of such a system is a web search engine.
- *Hybrid content aggregation (HCA)* accumulates some of the topic-specific information implicitly, but depends on users to actively contribute a remaining proportion of the data. An example of such a system is the navigation app Waze.

Further, we differentiate CIS by categorizing them according to their organizational structure within which they are typically used. We distinguish between the four levels of group, organization, community and society.

1. *Group level* CIS facilitate the collaboration within groups and teams. System examples comprise wiki systems (MediaWiki) and issue trackers (Redmine). Often systems, which are used on group level, are also applicable on organization level.
2. *Organization level* systems encompass an entire organization and can have an organization-internal or external focus. CIS, which are located on this level, are often associated with the terms Enterprise 2.0 and social collaboration. Representative system types include enterprise-level social networks (Yammer) and wiki farms (Confluence), employee suggestion systems, customer-feedback platforms (UserVoice) as well as a variety of custom-build CIS, which are tailored for a particular application context within the organization.
3. *Community level* CIS are dedicated to a particular aspect of a certain community which may be regional or a community of interest. CIS for regional communities include local review services (Yelp), but also platforms for emerging application domains like smart cities and collective governance. Illustrative examples of systems for communities of interest are TripAdvisor (travel), ResearchGate (social network for scientists), GitHub (code repositories), and MyExperiment (scientific workflows).
4. *Society level* CIS are systems that encompass one or more cultural regions and have developed a sphere of influence in or between these regions. Well-known examples are Wikipedia (encyclopedia), Facebook and VK (social network), Twitter and Sina Weibo (microblogging), as well as YouTube (video sharing).

The concepts that we introduced in the current and previous section provide the theoretical foundation for a systematic architecting approach for self-organizational CIS, which will be presented in the following sections.

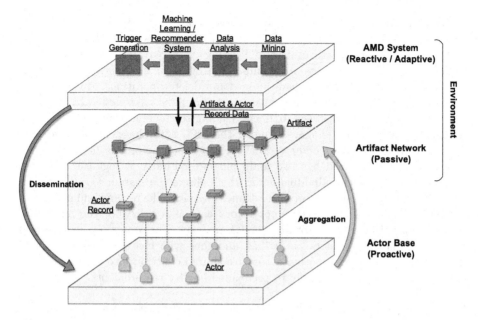

Fig. 2. Multi-layer CIS model with three main components and the stigmergic process

3.2   CIS Architectural Principles

Our CIS approach builds on a multi-layer model (Fig. 2) consisting of three main components: (1) *human actors* as proactive components, (2) a *single, homogeneous CI artifact network* as a passive component, and (3) a *computational analysis, management and dissemination (AMD) system* as a reactive/adaptive component, which fosters information propagation among its actor base. In this configuration, the CIS architecture realizes a composite coordination mechanism facilitating *stigmergic, environment-mediated coordination*, whereby the coordination environment is formed by the artifact network and the AMD system [24]. The architecture enables the *bottom-up building of an artifact network* by allowing its actors to create/modify user-generated content stored in artifacts and thereby effectively accumulate and share information among each other [26]. This continuous flow of actor contributions within the system environment enables the *emergence of collective intelligence* that allows the individual to benefit for own purposes, and concurrently provides groups and organizations with self-organizational knowledge transfer and coordination capabilities. Further, a *perpetual feedback loop* is created between actor base (layer 1) and coordination infrastructure (layer 2 and 3), by instrumenting the actors' contributions to stimulate a subsequent reaction by other actors, causing a *stigmergic process* with aggregation (yellow arrow) and dissemination phase (blue arrow). The following paragraphs provide an overview of the CIS model layers.

1. Actor Base. The actor base layer consists of *human actors*, who independently and actively perform *activities* on the *CI artifacts*.

2. Artifact Network. The CI artifact network layer consists of passive *CI artifacts*, which store the topic-specific content that is generated by the actors. The conceptual content structure of the CI artifact is constrained by the system's topic-of-interest. CI artifacts are manipulated by *actor activities*, which resemble different types of create, read, update and delete operations. An important activity is the linking of artifacts using artifact links. *Artifact links* are links that actors can define between artifacts, leading to the emergent creation of an *artifact network* which is shared among the total actor base. Each performed activity is tracked in an *actor record*, whereby each actor has her own actor record. The actor record has two main purposes: Firstly, it logs the complete actor activities of each individual actor which allows the system to build knowledge about its actors and to provide advanced services like recommendations and shared interests. Secondly, the actor record acts as a proxy for the *ownership relationship* between the actor and the CI artifacts. The ownership relationship defines who is the owner of an artifact and thus who has extensive control to decide (1) to which extent other actors are able to contribute to the CI artifact, and (2) if contributions comply to predefined quality requirements.

3. AMD System. The analysis, management and dissemination (AMD) system is a reactive/adaptive computational system that encompasses subsystems for *data mining*, *data analysis* and *machine learning* that are responsible for executing defined *rule sets*. In this process the subsystems use the aggregated artifact and actor record data and determined *dissemination mechanisms* to create various triggers. In detail, *triggers* are created to propagate changes of CI artifacts and to promote awareness about recent actor activities within the CIS among the total actor base. In addition, these triggers should also act as a stimulus to motivate each individual to react to these activities with a new contribution on an artifact, which in turn should attract other actors to contribute as well. For creating such triggers two different dissemination mechanisms can be applied. Pull-based, or passive, dissemination mechanisms rely on the actor to actively retrieve the updates and changes from the system, e.g. manual looking at the activity feed or dashboard. Push-based, or active, dissemination mechanisms rely on the AMD system and its subsystems to forward updates and changes to the actors in order to make them revisit the platform. A common example is the sending of emails with personalized notifications and reports about artifact updates to actors.

3.3   Example: Wiki System

To illustrate the described architectural design principles of a CIS we map them to the well-known example case of a Wiki. In a Wiki-type CIS groups of people, known as editors, are interested in contributing and sharing knowledge about a certain topic. The actor base is formed by all users who have an active user account. Each actor primarily contributes new content to a Wiki either by creating a new article page or modifying an existing one, which represents the CI artifact. To improve the quality of a particular article, additional contribution activities are supported including adding of comments, starting discussions about an article's content using talk pages, and reviewing changed articles. Activities of each actor are tracked and stored in the actor record (AR)-like log, as is any modification of any article. Each contributed article modification creates a new revision of the article which improves the traceability of modifications by other actors and enables them to undo changes. Typically, all editors have equal ownership rights to all article pages in a Wiki which allows an editor the extensive manipulation of articles created by other editors. Articles can be linked together by actors using Wiki-links (internal links) and categories, creating a network of related articles which improves content discoverability. To improve awareness of artifact changes during an actor's absence the system uses internal and external (e.g. email) notification messages to deliver personalized information.

4   CIS Architecture Framework

To support software architects in the design of new CIS architectures, we developed an architecture framework for realizing CIS solutions (CIS-AF) following the ISO/IEC/IEEE 42010 standard [16]. In this section we present an overview of this CIS-AF which is discussed in detail in [25]. According to the standard, an architecture framework describes *"conventions, principles and practices for the description of architectures established within a specific domain of application and/or community of stakeholders"* [16]. An architecture framework typically addresses a set of concerns that stakeholders have with respect to the system-of-interest. These stakeholder concerns are framed by at least one architecture viewpoint. A viewpoint introduces conventions for constructing, interpreting and analyzing an architecture view which expresses the architecture of a system-of-interest from a specific perspective and addresses particular stakeholder concerns. Therefore, a viewpoint describes model kinds which specify modeling conventions used by architecture models that compose an architecture view.

In the context of the CIS-AF, the architecture framework aims to provide guidance for software architects to systematically describe key CIS elements and model a CIS that is well-suited for the context and goals of an organization. Therefore, the CIS-AF defines foundational principles of CIS, introduces key stakeholders and their concerns that need to be addressed in models and analysis, as well as provides architectural practices how to systematically design such CIS. Thereby, the focus of the framework is on CIS-specific concerns of the system realization from inception to operation and it consolidates architectural knowledge independent of a domain or technology. Hence, software architects may use additional architectural approaches to deal with other traditional stakeholder concerns, such as performance, availability or scalability.

The CIS-AF is based on our proposed meta-model for CIS [24] that defines key CIS elements which we described previously. The CIS-AF comprises three complementary architecture viewpoints together with their model kinds which define conventions for the construction and use of architecture views and models to deal with the identified essential CIS stakeholder concerns. An overview of the CIS-AF is illustrated in Fig. 3. The framework defines the following architecture viewpoints for realizing new CIS solutions: (1) *CI context viewpoint*, (2) *CI technical realization viewpoint*, and (3) *CI operation viewpoint*. Main stakeholder groups whose concerns are considered in the CIS-AF are architect(s) who design and describe the system architecture, owner(s) who define the CIS's purpose and business goals, manager(s) who are responsible for the management and operation of the provided services, builder(s) who develop the CIS, analyst(s) who are responsible for monitoring and assessment of the CIS performance and behavior, and actors who access and contribute to the CIS.

CI Context Viewpoint. The context viewpoint deals with the design of CI-specific system capabilities especially with regards to the usefulness and perpetuality concerns of architects, owners and actors and describes the conventions to derive an architecture view which addresses these main stakeholder concerns. The viewpoint supports capturing relevant architectural design decisions to achieve the essential bottom-up information aggregation, management and distribution capabilities for hard-to-access dispersed knowledge and information. It defines three model kinds. The As-Is Workflow model kind governs models that show the current workflow of interest in the organization or context with the activities performed by users and an existing system environment that may be improved/extended by a CIS. A model created based on the Stigmergic Coordination model kind describes the domain items based on a particular topic-of-interest in the organization or context, the rules to interact with the

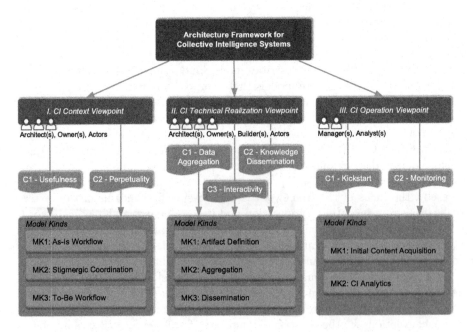

Fig. 3. Overview of architecture framework for Collective Intelligence Systems

domain items and for the dissemination mechanisms that use the network of domain items to generate stimuli in order to motivate the actor base. Finally, models based on the To-Be Workflow model kind express the future workflow of interest in the organization or context with the activities performed by users and the CIS environment, along with feedback from the CIS to the users.

CI Technical Realization Viewpoint. The technical realization viewpoint provides a more detailed perspective on the realization of the CIS and its specific capabilities and supports the concrete implementation of a new system with respective models. The viewpoint describes the conventions to derive an architecture view that frames the data aggregation, knowledge dissemination, and interactivity concerns of architects, owners, builders, and actors. It defines three model kinds. The Artifact Definition model kind governs models that describe the structure of the CI artifacts, how they can be linked, and which operations can be applied upon an artifact's content. A model created based on the Aggregation model kind shows details about how new data is aggregated from the actors, what activities can be performed by the actors to interact with the CI artifacts, what kind of data is aggregated, and to what extent these actor activities are captured. Models governed by the Dissemination model kind provides relevant information about the rules which realize the essential stigmergy-based dissemination of knowledge, the kind of content and ways how to effectively distribute this content in order to stimulate subsequent actor activities.

CI Operation Viewpoint. The operation viewpoint deals with the kickstart and monitoring concerns of system managers and analysts of CIS related to the successful startup of the perpetual feedback loop of a new CIS and its operation. Thus the viewpoint defines two model kinds to derive an architecture view that provides relevant information about initial data acquisition strategy and actor group as well as relevant indicators to measure CIS aggregation and dissemination performance. The Initial Content Acquisition model kind governs models that show potential sources from which initial content for the CI artifacts can be migrated and potential groups of initial actors to build up an actor community. A model created based on the CI Analytics model kind describes relevant metrics to measure the CIS performance and analysis results according to measurement profiles with probes to capture the data necessary for calculating the metrics.

First results of case studies, that we conducted to evaluate the framework's applicability and understandability among software architects, demonstrated that the framework effectively supports stakeholders with providing consolidated architectural knowledge in a documented and established form, a shared vocabulary of CIS concepts, and practical guidance to systematically apply the stigmergic principles of CIS. For a detailed description of the CIS-AF and the case studies results we refer the interested reader to [25].

5   Agenda for Future Research

Since the research of CIS architectures is at the beginning, we present in this section potential directions for future research. We discuss an agenda consisting of 11 research challenges across the areas of software architecture, technologies and system dynamics.

Nevertheless, CIS are complex systems and are dependent on areas that go beyond this research agenda. Figure 4 presents an extended overview of CI relevant areas with the four main areas of System, Influences, Agents and Stakeholders. A CIS is a hybrid system of agents and a computational system which consists of structure and dynamics. Its structure decomposes into the architecture and its conceptual design as well as its actual implementation using technologies. Its dynamics arise from the feedback mechanisms and the interplay of the agents and the system structure. Dynamics and the structure are dependent on each other. Additionally, a set of influences has an impact on the system's behavior and performance by enforcing various sets of constraints and rules. Influences are defined and negotiated between the stakeholders and, to varying extent, by the agent base. Main influences are ethics, culture, governance, and business, whereby each can be refined into more granular subject areas.

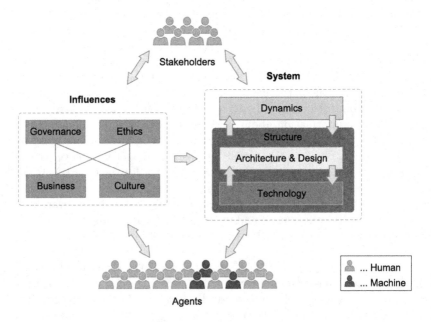

Fig. 4. CIS overview with system, agent base, influences and stakeholders

The following paragraphs focus on selected challenges from the areas architecture, technology and dynamics, that we expect to have high impact on future CIS design, development and research.

5.1   Architecture and Design

Architecture and Design challenges are concerned with conceptual and software architectural aspects of CIS and how they change over time and across application domains.

1. *CIS MAS Architecture Models:* This chapter has illustrated that a coordination model like stigmergy can have a significant impact on the architectural structure of a CIS. Therefore, it would be interesting to explore if there are other nature-inspired coordination models [40] (i.e. chemical, biochemical, physical) that facilitate collective intelligence. How can these models be integrated into generalized architectural models, and what are strengths and limitations of these architectures? Also, how are these models translated into advanced software architectural models like architecture frameworks and reference architectures so that they are more applicable by practitioners?

2. *Platform Evolution Support:* CIS as service platforms tend to constantly advance over time to better address the needs of their actor base. This makes architectural evolution, erosion and architectural technical debt relevant issues that gain importance the longer the system is in service. Therefore, it is necessary to deepen the understanding of a CIS life-cycle, its different phases and their impact on the system architecture, as well as evolutionary transitions between life-cycle phases that support future growth paths. This is of particular relevance the larger a CIS's artifact network and actor base become, because then platform operators are more inclined to evolve the CIS into a more comprehensive form like a multi-sided platform or a software ecosystem. Besides the life-cycle, is there also a differentiation in maturity levels, which depend on the grade of a CIS's set of capabilities?

3. *Exploration of Architecture Variations:* A challenge is the current lack of architecture-relevant knowledge about commonalities and significant variabilities among key elements of CIS. Therefore, it is important to systematically investigate variations of existing CIS and how these variations are affected by underlying architectural elements and design decisions.

4. *Correlating Architectural Models and Dynamics Models:* A particular challenge represents the correlation of software architectural models with CIS dynamic models. A success in this area would allow new inter-disciplinary perspectives on the modeling of complex dynamic software systems. A promising future application scenario represents the *simulation* of CIS and their architectures which would enable to predict the effectiveness of system features before they are actually implemented.

5. *Beyond Human-to-Human Interactions:* CIS are typically understood as socio-technical systems, which mediate interaction between humans. A promising direction for future research would be to investigate the benefits of

CIS environments with different types of actors, in particular human-machine and machine-machine configurations. This opens up new future application domains like *cloud robotics*, where robots can rely on humans as knowledge sources, or where robots can share task execution experiences among each other.

5.2 Technology

Technology challenges focus on how to support the implementation of CIS.

1. *CIS Middleware Frameworks:* The availability of advanced architectural models and frameworks enables the development of a new generation of CIS middleware frameworks that support the implementation of CI-intensive systems for particular application domains. The development of such frameworks will support the diversity of functionality and a wider range of technology stacks.

2. *Measurement and Analysis Components:* In order to support *data-driven development* practices in software development teams, it is important to explore the development of easy to use analysis and measurement components that provide architects and developers with CI-specific measures on system component and feature level. By this, developers are provided with a more accurate basis for making design and implementation decisions.

3. *Model-Driven CIS Engineering:* An efficient way to create new CIS implementations would be to apply methods from model-driven software engineering. In particular, how to adapt CIS architecture meta-models so that they can be the basis for model and code generation approaches? In combination with architecting tool support this would improve the utility and applicability of systematic CIS architecting and engineering among practitioners in industry.

5.3 System Dynamics

System Dynamics challenges are concerned with micro and macro level dynamics, the networks of CIS and effects on the system architecture.

1. *Network Models:* Since the artifact network is the central structure of a CIS, it is critical to also understand its characteristics also from a network science perspective. Findings from such investigations may inform CI-specific models on the dynamics *of* the network itself (changes of nodes and ties) as well as dynamics *on* the network (spreading processes like information cascades). Of particular interest is here the impact of the network on aggregation, dissemination as well as bottom-up and top-down feedback dynamics between the computational system and actor base.

2. *Growth and Perpetuality as First Class Concerns:* CIS are dependent on user-generated content and sustained high user activity levels. Therefore, it is important to understand factors that influence content growth and actor engagement like trust, content curation, and incentive mechanisms, and to document them in a way so they can support architectural decision making with regards to growth and perpetuality.

3. *Controllability:* The emergent, bottom-up nature of CIS is inherently non-deterministic and therefore only allows probabilistic estimates of the system's actual behavior [40]. Subsequently in order to improve CIS controllability, the underlying control principles, control points and their measures as well as observability and robustness aspects of CIS need to be better understood and validated. Advances in this area would not only provide the basis for novel mechanisms for the *dynamic adaptation* of CIS workflows and rules to achieve a certain system behavior, it would also extend the future applicability of CIS towards more critical domains.

We expect that research efforts in collective intelligence systems will continue to grow in the foreseeable future, making it a promising field of investigation. Therefore, finding solutions for the challenges described in this section will not only contribute to a better understanding of CIS and complex systems in general, it will also provide a benefit for the involved disciplines of software architecture, software engineering, multi-agent systems and network science alike.

6   Conclusion

This chapter provided an introduction to collective intelligence systems and how environment-oriented coordination mechanisms and abstractions can be used to describe them. The subsequent adaptation and integration of these concepts in an architecture framework enables software architects to adequately apply them for architecture descriptions of CIS. Additionally, the chapter presented research challenges that need to be addressed in future work for moving the field of CIS environment architectures forward. Advancing the presented models and approaches will not only increase our understanding on how CI-intensive systems work, it will also facilitate the exploration and invention of novel applications and usage scenarios.

Acknowledgments. This work was supported by the Christian Doppler Forschungs-gesellschaft, the Federal Ministry of Economy and Science, and the National Foundation for Research, Technology and Development, Austria.

References

1. Bedau, M.A., Humphreys, P.: Emergence: Contemporary Readings in Philosophy and Science. MIT Press, London (2008)

2. Bonabeau, E., Dorigo, M., Theraulaz, G.: Swarm Intelligence: From Natural to Artificial Systems. Oxford University Press, Oxford (1999)

3. Brun, Y., Di Marzo Serugendo, G., Gacek, C., Giese, H., Kienle, H., Litoiu, M., Müller, H., Pezzè, M., Shaw, M.: Engineering self-adaptive systems through feedback loops. In: Cheng, B.H.C., de Lemos, R., Giese, H., Inverardi, P., Magee, J. (eds.) Software Engineering for Self-Adaptive Systems. LNCS, vol. 5525, pp. 48–70. Springer, Heidelberg (2009)

4. Bush, V.: As we may think. The Atlantic **176**(1), 101–108 (1945)

5. Ciancarini, P.: Coordination models and languages as software integrators. ACM Comput. Surv. **28**(2), 300–302 (1996)

6. Engelbart, D.C.: Augmenting human intellect: a conceptual framework. Technical report, Stanford Research Institute, Menlo Park, CA (1962). http://www.dougengel bart.org/pubs/papers/scanned/Doug_Engelbart-AugmentingHumanIntellect.pdf

7. Erman, L.D., Hayes-Roth, F., Lesser, V.R., Reddy, D.R.: The Hearsay-II speech-understanding system: integrating knowledge to resolve uncertainty. ACM Comput. Surv. **12**(2), 213–253 (1980)

8. Esparcia, S., Argente, E.: A functional taxonomy for artifacts. In: Corchado, E., Graña Romay, M., Manhaes Savio, A. (eds.) HAIS 2010, Part II. LNCS, vol. 6077, pp. 159–167. Springer, Heidelberg (2010)

9. Franklin, S.: Coordination without communication. Technical report, Institute for Intelligent Systems, University of Memphis (1996). http://ccrg.cs.memphis.edu/~franklin/coord.html

10. Gelernter, D.: Generative communication in Linda. ACM Trans. Program. Lang. Syst. **7**(1), 80–112 (1985)

11. Gelernter, D., Carriero, N.: Coordination languages and their significance. Commun. ACM **35**(2), 96–107 (1992)

12. Grassé, P.P.: La reconstruction du nid et les coordinations inter-individuelles chez Bellicositermes natalensis et Cubitermes sp. La théorie de la stigmergie: Essai d'interprétation du comportement des Termites constructeurs. Insectes Soc. **6**(1), 41–80 (1959)

13. Grasso, A., Convertino, G.: Collective intelligence in organizations: tools and studies. Comput. Support. Coop. Work (CSCW) **21**(4–5), 357–369 (2012)

14. Gruber, T.: Collective knowledge systems: where the social web meets the semantic web. Semant. Web Web 2.0 **6**(1), 4–13 (2008)

15. Heylighen, F.: Stigmergy as a Universal Coordination Mechanism: components, varieties and application. In: Lewis, T., Marsh, L. (eds.) Human Stigmergy: Theoretical Developments and New Applications. Springer, Berlin (2015). http://pespmc1.vub.ac.be/papers/stigmergy-varieties.pdf

16. ISO/IEC/IEEE 42010: Systems and Software Engineering - Architecture Description (2011). http://www.iso-architecture.org/ieee-1471/index.html

17. Lévy, P.: Collective Intelligence: Mankind's Emerging World in Cyberspace. Perseus Books, Cambridge (1997)

18. Licklider, J.C.R.: Man-computer symbiosis. IRE Trans. Hum. Factors Electron. HFE **1**(1), 4–11 (1960)

19. Lykourentzou, I., Vergados, D.J., Kapetanios, E., Loumos, V.: Collective intelligence systems: classification and modeling. J. Emerg. Technol. Web Intell. **3**(3), 217–226 (2011)

20. Malone, T.W., Bernstein, M.S. (eds.): Handbook of Collective Intelligence. MIT Press (2015) (in press)

21. Malone, T.W., Laubacher, R., Dellarocas, C.: Harnessing Crowds : Mapping the Genome of Collective Intelligence (2009) (Working Paper No. 2009–001). http://cci.mit.edu/publications/CCIwp2009-01.pdf

22. Malone, T.W., Laubacher, R., Dellarocas, C.: The collective intelligence genome. MIT Sloan Manag. Rev. **51**(3), 21–31 (2010)

23. Miorandi, D., Maltese, V., Rovatsos, M., Nijholt, A., Stewart, J. (eds.): Social Collective Intelligence: Combining the Powers of Humans and Machines to Build a Smarter Society. Springer International Publishing, Switzerland (2014)

24. Musil, J., Musil, A., Biffl, S.: Towards a coordination-centric architecture meta-model for social web applications. In: Avgeriou, P., Zdun, U. (eds.) ECSA 2014. LNCS, vol. 8627, pp. 106–113. Springer, Heidelberg (2014)

25. Musil, J., Musil, A., Weyns, D., Biffl, S.: An Architecture framework for collective intelligence systems. In: Proceedings of the 12th Working IEEE/IFIP Conference on Software Architecture (WICSA 2015), pp. 21–30. IEEE Computer Society (2015)

26. Musil, J., Musil, A., Winkler, D., Biffl, S.: A first account on stigmergic information systems and their impact on platform development. In: Proceedings of the WICSA/ECSA 2012 Companion Volume (WICSA/ECSA 2012), pp. 69–73. ACM (2012)

27. Omicini, A., Contucci, P.: Complexity and interaction: blurring borders between physical, computational, and social systems. In: Bădică, C., Nguyen, N.T., Brezovan, M. (eds.) ICCCI 2013. LNCS, vol. 8083, pp. 1–10. Springer, Heidelberg (2013)

28. Omicini, A., Ricci, A., Viroli, M.: Artifacts in the A&A meta-model for multi-agent systems. Auton. Agents Multi-Agent Syst. **17**(3), 432–456 (2008)

29. Papadopoulos, G.A., Arbab, F.: Coordination models and languages. Adv. Comput. **46**, 329–400 (1998)

30. Ricci, A., Omicini, A., Viroli, M., Gardelli, L., Oliva, E.: Cognitive stigmergy: towards a framework based on agents and artifacts. In: Weyns, D., Van Dyke Parunak, H., Michel, F. (eds.) E4MAS 2006. LNCS (LNAI), vol. 4389, pp. 124–140. Springer, Heidelberg (2007)

31. Salminen, J.: Collective intelligence in humans: a literature review. In: Proceedings of Collective Intelligence Conference 2012 (2012). eprint arXiv:1204.3401, http://arxiv.org/abs/1204.3401

32. Schmidt, K., Simone, C.: Coordination mechanisms: towards a conceptual foundation of CSCW systems design. Comput. Support. Coop. Work (CSCW) **5**(2–3), 155–200 (1996)

33. Smart, P., Simperl, E., Shadbolt, N.: A taxonomic framework for social machines. In: Miorandi, D., Maltese, V., Rovatsos, M., Nijholt, A., Stewart, J. (eds.) Social Collective Intelligece, pp. 51–85. Springer International Publishing, Switzerland (2014)

34. Surowiecki, J.: The Wisdom of Crowds. Abacus , London (2005)

35. Susi, T., Ziemke, T.: Social cognition, artefacts, and stigmergy: a comparative analysis of theoretical frameworks for the understanding of artefact-mediated collaborative activity. Cogn. Syst. Res. **2**(4), 273–290 (2001)

36. Tapscott, D., Williams, A.D.: Wikinomics: How Mass Collaboration Changes Everything. Portfolio, New York (2006)

37. Van Dyke Parunak, H.: A survey of environments and mechanisms for human-human stigmergy. In: Weyns, D., Van Dyke Parunak, H., Michel, F. (eds.) E4MAS 2005. LNCS (LNAI), vol. 3830, pp. 163–186. Springer, Heidelberg (2006)

38. Weyns, D., Omicini, A., Odell, J.: Environment as a first class abstraction in multiagent systems. Auton. Agents Multi-Agent Syst. **14**(1), 5–30 (2007)
39. Zambonelli, F.: Engineering self-organizing urban superorganisms. Eng. Appl. Artif. Intell. **41**, 325–332 (2015)
40. Zambonelli, F., Omicini, A., Anzengruber, B., Castelli, G., De Angelis, F.L., Serugendo, G.D.M., Dobson, S., Fernandez-Marquez, J.L., Ferscha, A., Mamei, M., Mariani, S., Molesini, A., Montagna, S., Nieminen, J., Pianini, D., Risoldi, M., Rosi, A., Stevenson, G., Viroli, M., Ye, J.: Developing pervasive multi-agent systems with nature-inspired coordination. Pervasive Mobile Comput. **17**, 236–252 (2015)

Specification and Analysis of Open-Ended Systems with CARMA

Jane Hillston[1] and Michele Loreti[2,3]([⊠])

[1] Laboratory for Foundations of Computer Science,
University of Edinburgh, Edinburgh, UK
[2] Dipartimento di Statistica, Informatica, Applicazioni "G. Parenti",
Università di Firenze, Florence, Italy
[3] IMT, Lucca, Italy
michele.loreti@unifi.it

Abstract. CARMA is a new language recently defined to support quantified specification and analysis of collective adaptive systems. It is a stochastic process algebra equipped with linguistic constructs specifically developed for modelling and programming systems that can operate in open-ended and unpredictable environments. This class of systems is typically composed of a huge number of interacting agents that dynamically adjust and combine their behaviour to achieve specific goals. A CARMA model, termed a "collective", consists of a set of components, each of which exhibits a set of attributes. To model dynamic aggregations, which are sometimes referred to as "ensembles", CARMA provides communication primitives based on predicates over the exhibited attributes. These predicates are used to select the participants in a communication. Two communication mechanisms are provided in the CARMA language: multicast-based and unicast-based. A key feature of CARMA is the explicit representation of the environment in which processes interact, allowing rapid testing of a system under different open world scenarios. The environment in CARMA models can evolve at runtime, due to the feedback from the system, and it further modulates the interaction between components, by shaping rates and interaction probabilities.

1 Introduction

Collective adaptive systems (CAS), comprised on multiple agents working in collaboration, competition or a combination of both, are predicted to form the underlying infrastructure for the next generation of software systems and services. Their transparent and pervasive nature makes it imperative that the behaviour of such systems should be thoroughly explored and evaluated at design time and prior to deployment. In this paper we present a novel modelling language which has been developed to capture the behaviour of such systems and support their analysis through a variety of techniques.

This work is partially supported by the EU project QUANTICOL, 600708.

© Springer International Publishing Switzerland 2015
D. Weyns and F. Michel (Eds.): E4MAS 2014 – 10 years later, LNAI 9068, pp. 95–116, 2015.
DOI: 10.1007/978-3-319-23850-0_7

CARMA (Collective Adaptive Resource-sharing Markovian Agents) is a stochastic process algebra-based language which means that it represents systems as interacting agents which undertake actions; actions are assumed to have a duration which is represented as a random variable, governed by an exponential distribution. The quantitative information represented by action durations, extends the reasoning power of the language beyond functional analysis to assess the correct behaviour of the system, to non-functional properties such as performance, availability and dependability. Such analysis supports quantitative prediction and checking of system behaviour, including ensuring that resources will be efficiently and equitably shared — an important and strongly desirable feature of infrastructures. Moreover, the underlying interleaving Markovian semantics of CARMAsupports a form of *local synchrony* as discussed in [33]. Independent actions proceed at their own pace, and this autonomy is lost only when agents are constrained to act together through an explicit interaction.

The compositional nature of the language allows components capturing the behaviour of agent types to be defined and then combined to build up the behaviour of the system. The interaction between agents is represented by explicit communication, both multicast-based and unicast-based, and through implicit communication. Moreover a distinguishing feature of CARMA is the inclusion of an *environment*, represented as a distinct element of the model, which captures the operating principles of the world in which the agents exist. This environmental influence includes controlling the rate and effectiveness of communication between agents. Moreover, the environment itself can evolve during the lifetime of the system, reflecting the adaptive operating conditions of the system. The environment also has a state, which can be used to represent implicit asynchronous communication between agents, analogous to pheromone trails in ant systems. This is broadly in-keeping with the architecture proposed by Weyns *et al.* proposed in [34].

In this paper we present an overview of the language constructs of CARMA, including the representation and role of the environment. The style of presentation is intended to be intuitive and the interested reader can find the formal semantics of CARMA in [25]. Specifically, we illustrate the features of the language in a running example, a *Smart Taxi System*. In this system we consider a set of *taxis* operating in a city, providing service to *users*; both taxis and users are agents, or components within our system. In order to manage the system and allocate user requests among the operating taxis, our city is subdivided into a number of patches arranged in a grid over the geography of the city. The users arrive randomly in different patches, at a rate that depends on the specific time of day. After arrival, a user makes a call for a taxi and then waits in that patch until they successfully engage a taxi and move to another randomly chosen patch. Unengaged taxis move about the city, influenced by the calls made by users.

The rest of the paper is organised as follows. In the next section we give a brief overview of related modelling techniques for CAS. Section 3 gives a detailed account of the CARMA language and demonstrates its use to model the Smart Taxi System. Section 4 presents the result of quantitative analysis of the Smart

Taxi System, illustrating the types of measures that can be derived from CARMA models. Previous work on modelling the stochastic dynamic behaviour of a system under the influence of an environment is discussed in Sect. 5, and we conclude in Sect. 6.

2   Related Work

Stochastic process algebras, such as PEPA [23], MTIPP [22], EMPA [5], Stochastic π-Calculus [29], Bio-PEPA [12], MODEST [6] and others [9,21], have been available to support quantitative analysis of systems for approximately two decades. Whilst some offer support for large populations of agents, they have not been designed with CAS in mind, and typically only support synchronous unicast communication. In recent years there have been languages targeted towards systems consisting of populations, collectives or ensembles of agents [15,16,28], which feature attribute-based communication and explicit representation of locations and the development of CARMA has been informed by these.

SCEL [15] (Software Component Ensemble Language), has been designed to support the programming of autonomic computing systems. The language distinguishes between *autonomic components* representing the collective members, and *autonomic-component ensembles* representing collectives. Each component is equipped with an interface, consisting of a collection of attributes, describing different features of components. There is an underlying knowledge base associated with each component and rich forms of reasoning on attributes are supported. Attributes from the knowledge base are used by components to dynamically form ensembles and to select partners for interaction. The stochastic variant of SCEL, called StocS [24], has been used to investigate a number of different stochastic and probabilistic semantics. Moreover, SCEL has inspired the development of the core calculus AbC [3] that focuses on a minimal set of primitives that defines attribute-based communication without the rich underlying knowledge base, and investigates their impact. Communication among components takes place in a broadcast fashion, with the characteristic that only components satisfying predicates over specific attributes receive the sent messages, provided that they are willing to do so.

PALOMA [16] is a process algebra that takes as starting point a model based on located Markovian agents each of which is parameterised by a location, which can be regarded as an attribute of the agent. The ability of agents to communicate depends on their location, through a *perception function*, which can be used to define the range of a communication. Examples include *local* – agents must be co-located, *all* – communication is global, or use of predicates. This can be regarded as an example of a more general class of attribute-based communication mechanisms. Both multicast and unicast communication are supported [17], but in both cases only agents who enable the appropriate reception action have the ability to receive the message. The scope of communication is thus adjusted according to the perception function. PALOMA is supported by an individual-based Markovian semantics, a population-based Markovian semantics and a continuous semantics in the style of [32].

The attributed pi calculus [28] is an extension of the pi calculus [27] that supports attribute-based communication, and was designed primarily with biological applications in mind. As in the languages discussed above, processes may have attributes and these are used to select partners for interaction, but note that communication is strictly synchronisation-based and binary. The language is equipped with both a deterministic and a Markovian semantics, and in the Markovian case the rates may depend on the attribute values of the processes involved. The possible attribute values are defined by a language $\mathcal{L}$, and the definition of the attributed pi calculus is parameterised by $\mathcal{L}$. The language $\mathcal{L}$ also defines the possible rates and constraints that can be applied to attributes, giving the possibility to capture diverse behaviours within the framework when rates and probabilities of interaction are all dependent only on local behaviour and knowledge.

CARMA supports both unicast and broadcast communication, providing locally synchronous, but globally asynchronous communication. This richness is important to enable the spatially distributed nature of CAS, where agents may have only local awareness of the system, yet the design objectives and adaptation goals are often expressed in terms of global behaviour. Representing these rich patterns of communication in classical process algebras or traditional stochastic process algebras would be difficult, and would require the introduction of additional model components to represent buffers, queues and other communication structures. Moreover the inclusion of a distinct environment, allows many possibilities including rates of behaviour based on the global state, or observed data from a system.

Modelling frameworks and languages have also been developed within the multi-agent community, but generally with a focus on specification, qualitative or functional analysis, rather than quantitative assessment of the modelled system e.g. [7,11,20,26]. For example, Helleboogh et al. consider the requirements for modelling multi-agent systems, with a particular emphasis on the modelling of physical applications via simulation [20]. As with CARMA, the authors make a distinction between the *simulated environment* and the *simulating environment*, which is transparent to the modeller. However, in the work presented in [20], the distinction between the simulated environments and the agents within it is not strong (cf. the framework of Weyns et al. [34]). In CARMA we prefer to have a clear separation of concern which allows the same collective of agents to be easily considered in the context of different environments. Moreover, whereas in CARMA agents explicitly interact, in Helleboogh et al.'s approach the behaviour of agents is specified in a declarative way with the environment playing a coordinating role in the evolution of agents.

3   CARMA in a Nutshell

In this section we present the CARMA language and its specific features. To simplify the presentation, and to help the reader to appreciate CARMA features, we will consider a simple running scenario. The latter is a *Smart Taxi System* used to coordinate the activities of a group of taxis in a city. In our scenario we assume that the city is subdivided in patches forming a grid. Two kinds of agents populate the system: *taxis* and *users*. Each taxi stay can either stay in a patch, waiting for user requests, or move to another patch. Users randomly arrive at different patches with a rate that depends on the specific time of day. After arrival, a user waits for a taxi and then moves to another patch.

The *smart taxi scenario* represents well the typical scenarios modelled with CARMA. Indeed, a CARMA system consists of a *collective* (N) operating in an *environment* ($\mathcal{E}$). The collective consists of a set of components. It models the behavioural part of a system and is used to describe a set of interacting *agents* that cooperate to achieve a given set of tasks. The environment models all those aspects which are intrinsic to the context where the agents under consideration are operating. The environment also mediates agent interactions.

Example 1. In our running example the collective N will be used to model the behaviour of *taxis* and *users*, while the environment will be used to model the city context where these agents operate.

In CARMA collectives are defined in a style that is borrowed from process algebras. We let COL be the set of collectives N which are generated by the following grammar:

$$N ::= C \mid N \parallel N \qquad C ::= \mathbf{0} \mid (P, \gamma)$$

where C denotes a *component* while $N \parallel N$ represents the parallel composition of two collectives.

A component C can be either the *inactive component*, which is denoted by $\mathbf{0}$, or a term of the form (P, γ), where P is a *process* and γ is a *store*. A term (P, γ) models an *agent* operating in the system under consideration: the process P represents the agent's behaviour whereas the store γ models its *knowledge*. The latter is a function which maps *attribute names* to *basic values*. In the rest of this paper we let:

- ATTR be the set of *attribute names* $a, a', a_1, \ldots, b, b', b_1, \ldots$;
- VAL be the set of *basic values* $v, v', v_1, \ldots$;
- Γ be the set of *stores* $\gamma, \gamma_1, \gamma', \ldots$, i.e. functions from ATTR to VAL, of the following form:

$$\{a_0 = v_0, \ldots, a_n = v_n\}$$

Example 2. To model our *smart taxi system* in CARMA we need two kinds of components. One for each of the two groups of agents involved in the system, i.e. *taxis* and *users*. Both the kind of components use the local store to publish the relevant data that will be used to represent the state of the agent.

The local store of components associated to taxis contains the following attributes:

- *loc*: identifies current taxi location;

- *occupancy*: ranging in $\{0, 1\}$ describes if a taxi is free (*occupied* $= 0$) or engaged (*occupied* $= 1$);
- *destination*: if occupied, this attribute indicates the destination of taxi journey.

Similarly, the local store of components associated with users contains the following attributes:

- *loc*: identifies user location;
- *destination*: indicates user destination.

The behaviour of a component is specified via a process P. We let PROC be the set of processes P, Q,... defined by the following grammar:

$$P, Q ::= \mathbf{nil} \mid A[X] \mid P \mid Q$$

where **nil** denotes the inactive process, $A[X]$ denotes *process automaton* A in state X, while $P \mid Q$ denotes the behaviour obtained from the concurrent execution of P and Q. Each process automaton, and its states, are defined as follow:

process $A =$
$$X_0 : [\pi_i^0] act_0^0.R_0^0 + \cdots + [\pi_i^{k_0}] act_0^{k_0}.R_0^{k_0}$$
$$\vdots \qquad \vdots \qquad\qquad\qquad \vdots$$
$$X_n : [\pi_i^n] act_n^n.R_n^n + \cdots + [\pi_n^{k_n}] act_n^{k_n}.R_n^{k_n}$$
endprocess

Above, π_i^j is a *guard*, act_i^j are CARMA actions, while R_i^j can be a state in $\{X_0, \ldots, X_n\}$, the inactive process **nil** or the term **kill**. A process $A[X_i]$, that is active in a component with store γ, can execute any of the actions $act_i^{k_i}$ such that π_i^j is satisfied by γ. When one enabled action act_i^j is executed, process $A[X_i]$ terminates, when $R_i^j = \mathbf{nil}$, evolves to $A[X_l]$, when $R_i^j = X_l$ and *destroys* the enclosing component when $R_i^j = \mathbf{kill}$.

In CARMA processes can perform four types of actions: *broadcast output* $(\alpha^\star[\pi]\langle\overrightarrow{e}\rangle\sigma)$, *broadcast input* $(\alpha^\star[\pi](\overrightarrow{x})\sigma)$, *output* $(\alpha[\pi]\langle\overrightarrow{e}\rangle\sigma)$, and *input* $(\alpha[\pi](\overrightarrow{x})\sigma)$, where:

- α is an *action type* in the set of action types ACTTYPE;
- π is an *predicate*;
- x is a *variable* in the set of variables VAR;
- $\overrightarrow{\cdot}$ indicates a sequence of elements;
- σ is an *update* of the form:

$$\{a_0 \leftarrow re_0, \cdots, a_k \leftarrow re_k\}$$

where all the attributes a_i are distinct and re is a *random expression* defined by the following syntax:

$$re ::= \mathsf{now} \mid v \mid x \mid \mathsf{this}.a \mid \delta_{\mathrm{VAL}} \mid re \; b_{op} \; re \mid u_{op} \; re \mid f(re_0, \ldots, re_n)$$

where now is used to refer to current system time, δ_{VAL} is a probability distribution over VAL^1, b_{op} and u_{op} are *binary* and *unary* operators, while f denotes an *n*-ary function over expressions.

In the rest of this paper we will say that an expression *er* is *ground* if it does not contain any variable, while it is *deterministic* if no probability expression δ_{VAL} occurs in *re*. Moreover, we will use *e* to denote a *deterministic expression*.

The admissible communication partners in each of these actions are identified by the predicate π. This is a predicate on *attribute names*. Note that, in a component (P, γ) the store γ regulates the behaviour of P. Primarily, γ is used to evaluate the predicate associated with an action in order to filter the possible synchronisations involving process P. In addition, γ is also used as one of the parameters for computing the actual rate of actions performed by P. The process P can change γ immediately after the execution of an action. This change is brought about by the *update* σ. The update is a function that when given a store γ returns a probability distribution over Γ which expresses the possible evolutions of the store after the action execution.

The *broadcast output* $\alpha^\star[\pi]\langle\overrightarrow{e}\rangle\sigma$ models the execution of an action α that spreads the values resulting from the evaluation of expressions $\overrightarrow{e}$ in the local store γ. This message can be potentially received by any process located at components whose store satisfies predicate π. This predicate may contain references to attribute names that have to be evaluated under the local store. These references are prefixed by the special name this. For instance, if loc is the attribute used to store the position of a component, action

$$\alpha^\star[\text{distance}(\text{this.loc}, \text{loc}) \leq L]\langle\overrightarrow{v}\rangle\sigma$$

potentially involves all the components located at a distance that is less than or equal to a given threshold L. The *broadcast output* is non-blocking. The action is executed even if no process is able to receive the values which are sent. Immediately after the execution of an action, the update σ is used to compute the (possible) *effects* of the performed action on the store of the hosting component where the output is performed.

To receive a broadcast message, a process executes a *broadcast input* of the form $\alpha^\star[\pi](\overrightarrow{x})\sigma$. This action is used to receive a tuple of values $\overrightarrow{v}$ sent with an action α from a component whose store satisfies the predicate $\pi[\overrightarrow{v}/\overrightarrow{x}]$. The transmitted values can be part of the predicate π. For instance, $\alpha^\star[x > 5](x)\sigma$ can be used to receive a value that is greater than 5.

The other two kinds of action, namely *output* and *input*, are similar. However, differently from broadcasts described above, these actions realise a *point-to-point* interaction. The *output* operation is blocking; in contrast to the non-blocking broadcast output.

---

[1] For any denumerable set X, we let $Dist(X)$ denote the set of probability distributions over X while δ_X is a generic element in $Dist(X)$.

Example 3. We are now ready to describe the behaviour of *taxis* and *users*. Behaviour of a user is modelled via process *User* defined below:

$$
\begin{aligned}
\mathsf{process}\ User\ =\ & \\
W : \mathsf{call}^\star[\top]\langle\mathsf{this.loc}\rangle.W & \\
+ & \\
\mathsf{take}[\mathsf{loc} == \mathsf{this.loc}]\langle\mathsf{this.dest}\rangle.\mathbf{kill} & \\
\mathsf{endprocess} &
\end{aligned}
$$

Process *User* has only one state, W, that can either *call* or *take* a taxi. To call a taxi, a *User*$[W]$ executes a *broadcast output* over call to all taxis. A *unicast output* over take is executed to take a taxi. This action is used to send user destination (this.dest) to a taxi that shares the same location as the user. To identify the target of this action, prediate (loc == this.loc) is used. The latter is satisfied only by those components that have attribute loc equal to this.loc. Here prefix this is used to refer to actual values of local attributes. After this action, user disappears (he/she enters the taxi).

The behaviour of a taxi is described via process automaton *Taxi*:

$$
\begin{aligned}
\mathsf{process}\ Taxi\ =\ & \\
F : \mathsf{take}[\top](d)\{\mathsf{dest} \leftarrow d, \mathsf{occupied} \leftarrow 1\}.G & \\
+ & \\
\mathsf{call}^\star[\mathsf{this.loc} \neq \mathsf{loc}](d)\{\mathsf{dest} \leftarrow d\}.G & \\
G : \mathsf{move}^\star[\bot]\langle\circ\rangle\{\mathsf{loc} \leftarrow \mathsf{dest}, \mathsf{dest} \leftarrow \bot, \mathsf{occupied} \leftarrow 0\}.F & \\
\mathsf{endprocess} &
\end{aligned}
$$

Process *Taxi* has two state: F and G. When in state F the taxi is *available* and can either take a user in the current location or receive a *call* from another patch. In the first case an input via take is performed and the user destination is received. In the second case, the location where a user is waiting for a taxi is received. In both the cases, the received location is used, after action execution, to update taxi destination (dest $\leftarrow d$). However, after take input, the taxi also records that it is occupied (occupied $\leftarrow 1$).

When in state G, process *Taxi* just executes a *spontaneous* broadcast over action move. Indeed, no process can receive this message since predicate $\bot$ is used. This models taxi movements. After the movement the taxi position is updated and the taxi is ready to take users in the new location.

To model the arrival of new users, the following process automaton is used:

$$
\begin{aligned}
\mathsf{process}\ Arrivals\ =\ & \\
A : \mathsf{arrival}^\star[\bot]\langle\circ\rangle.A & \\
\mathsf{endprocess} &
\end{aligned}
$$

Process *Arrivals* has a single state A where spontaneous action arrival is executed. This process is executed in a separated component where attribute loc indicates the location where users arrive. The precise role of this process will be clear in a few paragraphs when the environment will be described.

CARMA collectives operate in an environment $\mathcal{E}$. This environment is used to model the intrinsic rules that govern, for instance, the physical context where our system is situated. An environment consists of two elements: a *global store* γ_g, that models the overall state of the system, and an *evolution rule* ρ. The latter consists of three functions that are used to express the probability to receive a message by a component, compute the execution rate of an action, determine the updates to the environment on both the global store and the collective. Syntax of an environment $\mathcal{E}$ is the following:

$$\text{environment } \gamma \; [$$
$$\mu_p$$
$$\mu_r$$
$$\mu_u$$
$$]$$

Element μ_p is used to compute the probability to receive a message. Syntax of μ_p is the following:

$$\text{prob}\{$$
$$\pi_0, \alpha_0 \rightarrow e_0$$
$$\vdots$$
$$\pi_{k_p}, \alpha_{k_p} \rightarrow e_{k_p}$$
$$\text{default } e$$
$$\}$$

In the above, each π_i is a boolean expression over the stores of the two interacting components, i.e. the sender and the receiver, and while α_i denotes the action used to interact. In π_i attributes of sender and receiver attributes are referred to using sender.a and receiver.a, while the values published in the global store are referenced by using global.a. A receiver with store γ_1 receives a message sent by a component with store γ_2 under global store γ with probability p if there exists an index i such that:

$$\gamma_1, \gamma_2, \gamma \models \pi_i \qquad \text{and} \qquad [\![e_i]\!]_{\gamma_1, \gamma_2, \gamma} = p$$

or, if none of the π_is are satisfied, $p = [\![e]\!]_{\gamma_1, \gamma_2, \gamma}$. This probability value may depend on the number of components in a given state. For this reason in the environment the syntax of expressions is extended by considering terms of the form:

$$re ::= \cdots \mid \#(\Pi, \pi)$$

where $\#(\Pi, \pi)$ denotes the number of components in the system satisfying predicate π where a process of the form Π is executed. In turn, Π is a pattern of the following form:

$$\Pi ::= \star \mid A[\star] \mid A[X] \mid \Pi | \Pi$$

Example 4. One can use $\#(\mathit{Taxi}[F], \text{loc} == \ell)$ to count the number of available taxis at patch ℓ. This expression can be used as follows:

$$\mathsf{prob}\{$$
$$\top, \mathsf{take} \;\rightarrow\; \frac{1}{\#(\mathit{Taxi}[F],\mathsf{loc}==\mathsf{sender.loc})}$$
$$\top, \mathsf{call}^\star \;\rightarrow\; p_{lost}$$
$$\mathsf{default}\ \ 1$$
$$\}$$

Above, we say that each taxi receives a user request with a probability that depends on the number of taxis in the patch. Moreover, call* can be missed with a probability p_{lost}. All the other interactions occur with probability 1.

Function μ_r is similar and it is used to compute the rate of an unicast/broadcast output. This represents a function taking as parameter the local store of the component performing the action and the action type used. Note that the environment can disable the execution of a given action. This happens when the function μ_r (resp. μ_p) returns the value 0. Syntax of μ_r is the following:

$$\mathsf{rate}\{$$
$$\pi_0, \alpha_0 \;\rightarrow\; e_0$$
$$\vdots$$
$$\pi_{k_r}, \alpha_{k_r} \;\rightarrow\; e_{k_r}$$
$$\mathsf{default}\ \ e$$
$$\}$$

Differently from μ_p, in μ_r guards π_i are evaluated by considering only the attributes defined in the store of the component performing the action, referenced as sender.a, or in the global store, whose elements are accessed via global.a.

Example 5. In our example rate can be defined as follow:

$$\mathsf{rate}\{$$
$$\top, \mathsf{take} \;\rightarrow\; \lambda_t$$
$$\top, \mathsf{call}^\star \;\rightarrow\; \lambda_c$$
$$\top, \mathsf{move}^\star \;\rightarrow\; mtime(\mathsf{now}, \mathsf{sender.loc}, \mathsf{sender.dest})$$
$$\top, \mathsf{arrival}^\star \;\rightarrow\; atime(\mathsf{now}, \mathsf{sender.loc})$$
$$\mathsf{default}\ \ 0$$
$$\}$$

We say that actions take and call* are executed at a constant rate; the rate of a taxi movement is a function of actual time (now) and of starting location and final destination. Rate of user arrivals depends on current time now and on location loc.

Finally, the function μ_u is used to update the global store and to install a new collective in the system. Syntax of μ_u is:

$$\mathsf{update}\{$$
$$\pi_0, \alpha_0 \;\rightarrow\; \sigma_0, N_0$$
$$\vdots$$
$$\pi_{k_u}, \alpha_{k_u} \;\rightarrow\; \sigma_{k_u}, N_{k_u}$$
$$\}$$

Like for μ_r, guards in function μ_u are evaluated on the store of the component performing the action and on global store. However, the result is a pair (σ_i, N_i). Within this pair, σ_i identifies the update on the global store whereas N_i is a new collective installed in the system. If none of the guards are satisfied, or the performed action is not listed, the global store is not changed and no new collective is instantiated. In both cases, the collective generating the transition remains in operation. This function is particularly useful for modelling the arrival of new agents into a system.

Example 6. In our scenario function update is used to model the arrival of new users and it is defined as follows:

update{
      $\top$, arrival* $\rightarrow$ { }, $(User[W], \{$loc $=$ sender.loc, dest $= destLoc($now, sender.loc$))$
}

When action arrival* is performed a component associated with a new user is created in the same location as the sender (see Example 3). The destination of the new user will be determined by function $destLoc$ that takes current system time and starting location and returns a probability distribution on locations.

To extract data from a system, a CARMA specifications also contains a set of *measures*. Each measure is defined as:

$$\text{measure } m \ = e;$$

Example 7. In our scenario, we could be interested in measuring the number of waiting users at a given location. These measures can be declared as:

$$\text{measure waitingAt}_\ell \ = \#(User[\star], \text{loc} == \ell)$$

When the system is simulated a time-ordered sequence of values is generated for each measure specified.

4   The Smart Taxi System: Simulation and Analysis

In this section we present the Smart Taxi System in its entirety and demonstrate the quantitative analysis which can be undertaken on a CARMA model.

In the previous section we have shown how in CARMA a system specification in fact consists of two parts: a collective and an environment. One of the main advantages of this approach is that one can evaluate the same behaviour (collective) under different models for the enclosing environment.

In this section we consider a scenario with a grid of 3×3 patches, a set of locations (i, j) where $0 \leq i, j \leq 2$, and we instantiate the environment of the *smart taxi system* with respect to two different specifications for the environment:

```
//Component definitions
process User =
     W : call*[⊤]⟨this.loc⟩.W
          +
          take[loc == this.loc]⟨this.dest⟩.kill
endprocess

process Taxi =
     F : take[⊤](d){dest ← d, occupied ← 1}.G
          +
          call*[this.loc ≠ loc](d){dest ← d}.G
     G : move*[⊥]⟨o⟩{loc ← dest, dest ← ⊥, occupied ← 0}.F
endprocess

process Arrivals =
     A : arrival*[⊥]⟨o⟩.A
endprocess
```

//Environment definitions

$\#(Taxi[F], \mathsf{loc} == \ell)$

```
prob{
     ⊤, take → ────────1────────
                 #(Taxi[F],loc==sender.loc)
     ⊤, call* → p_lost
     default 1
}
```

```
rate{
     ⊤, take → λ_t
     ⊤, call* → λ_c
     ⊤, move* → mtime(now, sender.loc, sender.dest)
     ⊤, arrival* → atime(now, loc)
     default 0
}
```

```
update{
     ⊤, arrival* → { }, (User[W], {loc = sender.loc, dest = destLoc(now, sender.loc))
}
```

measure waitingAt$_\ell$ = $\#(User[\star], \mathsf{loc} == \ell)$

function $mtime(t, l_1, l_2) = \lambda_{step} \cdot \max\{|\pi_1(l_1) - \pi_1(l_2)| + |\pi_2(l_1) - \pi_2(l_2)|, 1\}$;
function $atime(time, l) = \lambda_a \cdot \frac{1}{|L|}$;
function $destLoc(time, l) = $ if $(l == (1,1))$ then $rand(L - l)$ else $(1,1)$;

```
collective{
     (Taxi[F], loc = (0,0) , dest = ⊥ , occupied = 0) ∥
 ··· ∥ (Taxi[F], loc = (i,j) , dest = ⊥ , occupied = 0) ∥
 ··· ∥ (Taxi[F], loc = (2,2) , dest = ⊥ , occupied = 0) ∥
     (Arrval[A], loc = (0,0)) ∥ ··· ∥ (Arrval[A], loc = (2,2))}
```

Fig. 1. The CARMA model of the Smart Taxi System

Scenario 1: Users arrive in all the patches at the same rate;

Scenario 2: At the beginning users arrive with a higher probability to the patches at the border of the grid; subsequently, users arrive with higher probability in the centre of the grid.

In both the scenarios users in the border will use the taxi to go to the *centre*, while users collected in the centre will use the taxi to go to any other location (the destination is probabilistically selected). In both the scenarios we assume that the movement rate is constant and is proportional to the number of patches to be traversed to reach the destination. In both the considered scenarios the collective has the structure reported below:

$$(Taxi[F], \text{loc} = (0,0) \ , \ \text{dest} = \perp \ , \ \text{occupied} = 0) \ \|$$
$$\cdots \ \| \ (Taxi[F], \text{loc} = (i,j) \ , \ \text{dest} = \perp \ , \ \text{occupied} = 0) \ \|$$
$$\cdots \ \| \ (Taxi[F], \text{loc} = (2,2) \ , \ \text{dest} = \perp \ , \ \text{occupied} = 0) \ \|$$
$$(Arrivals[A], \text{loc} = (0,0)) \ \| \ \cdots \ \| \ (Arrivals[A], \text{loc} = (2,2))$$

Above we consider $k = 5$ taxis in each location.

To instantiate the environment for **Scenario 1** considered above, we have just to instantiate functions *mtime* and *atime* of Example 5 and function *destLoc* of Example 6:

function $mtime(t, l_1, l_2) = \lambda_{step} \cdot \max\{|\pi_1(l_1) - \pi_1(l_2)| + |\pi_2(l_1) - \pi_2(l_2)|, 1\};$
function $atime(t, l) = \lambda_a \cdot \frac{1}{|L|};$
function $destLoc(t, l) = $ if $(l == (1,1))$ then $rand(L - l)$ else $(1,1);$

Above λ_{step} is the rate needed to move from one location to an adjacent one, π_1 (resp. π_2) is a function that returns the first (resp. the second) element of a pair, λ_a is the arrival rate of a user in the system, L is the set of the considered localities while *rand* is used to select randomly an element in the set received as parameter. The complete CARMA specification of our system is presented in Fig. 1. The results of the simulation of the resulting CARMA model is reported in Fig. 2. In the left side of the figure we can observe the average number of users that are waiting for a taxi in the location $(1,1)$ and in one location in the border of the grid, namely $(0,0)$[2]. In the right hand side of the same figure we can present the proportion of free taxis that are waiting for a user at location $(1,1)$ and $(0,0)$, respectively, and the fraction of taxis that are moving from one patch to another without a user (these are the taxis that are relocating after a *call* has been received). The remaining taxis (not shown) are engaged by users.

We can notice that, on average and after an initial startup period, around 2.5 users are waiting for a taxi in the location in the periphery of the grid while only 1.5 users are waiting for a taxi in location $(1,1)$. This is due to the fact that in **Scenario 1** a larger fraction of users are delivered to location $(1,1)$, that is the central patch. For this reason, a larger fraction of taxis will soon be available

---

[2] Due to the symmetry of the considered model, any other location in the border presents similar results.

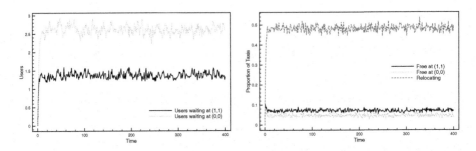

Fig. 2. Smart Taxi System: Scenario 1

to collect users at the centre whereas to collect a user from the border, a taxi has to change its location. This aspect is also witnessed by the fact that, in this scenario, a large fraction of taxis (around 50%) are continually moving between the different patches.

The simulation of **Scenario 2** is reported in Fig. 3. The environment for this scenario is exactly the same as considered for the previous one except for function *atime*. Now this function takes into account the current time (parameter now) to model the fact that the arrival of new users depends on current time, just as we might expect traffic patterns within a city to vary according to the time of day. We assume that from time 0 to time 200, 3/4 of users *arrive* on the border while only 1/4 request a taxi in the city centre. After time 200 these values are switched. New definition of function *atime* is the following:

$$\text{function } atime(t, l) = \text{if } l == (1, 1) \text{ then}$$
$$\text{if } t < 200 \text{ then } \tfrac{1}{4} \cdot \lambda_a \text{ else } \tfrac{3}{4} \cdot \lambda_a$$
$$\text{else}$$
$$\text{if } t < 200 \text{ then } \tfrac{3}{4} \cdot \lambda_a \text{ else } \tfrac{1}{4} \cdot \lambda_a;$$

We can notice that the results obtained from time 0 to time 200 are similar to the ones already presented for the first scenario. However, after time 200, as expected, the number of users waiting for a taxi in the border decreases below 1 whilst the average waiting for a taxi in the centre increases to just over 1. Since after time 200 a large proportion of users request a taxi in the centre, the fraction of taxis that change their location without a user decreases from 40% to 20%.

In both the scenarios one can observe that even if only a small number of users are waiting for a taxi, a significant fraction of taxis are continually moving from one patch to another without users (i.e. in a free state). This is mainly due to the fact that the action used to *call* a taxi is a broadcast output. As a consequence we have that even if only a single user needs a taxi at a given location, all the *free* taxis can change their position to satisfy this request. To study this aspect in more detail, we consider now a variant of processes *Taxi* and *User* where action call is no longer a broadcast output, but is instead a unicast output. The CARMA representation of the variants of these two processes is reported below:

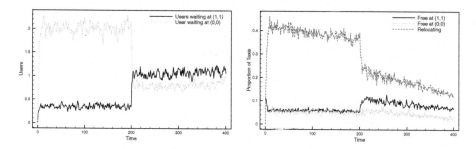

Fig. 3. Smart Taxi System: Scenario 2

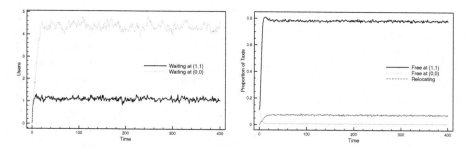

Fig. 4. Smart Taxi System: Scenario 1 (modified specification)

```
process User =
        W : call[⊤]⟨this.loc⟩.W
            + take[loc == this.loc]⟨this.dest⟩.kill
endprocess
process Taxi =
        F : take[⊤](d){dest ← d, occupied ← 1}.G
            + call*[this.loc ≠ loc](d){dest ← d}.G
        G : move*[⊥]⟨○⟩{loc ← dest, dest ← ⊥, occupied ← 0}.F
endprocess
```

The results of simulating the two scenarios with the modified specifications are reported in Figs. 4 and 5. In both cases we can observe that the number of users waiting for a taxi in patches located in the border of the grid doubles, whilst almost all taxis will wait for users' calls in the centre location (around 80 %). This means that after an initial startup period all the taxis will be always staying in the central location and the patch arrangement of the city is, in fact, no longer used in the model.

5   Modelling the Environment

A key feature of CARMA is its distinct treatment of an *environment*. It should be stressed that although this is an entity within our model, it is intended to

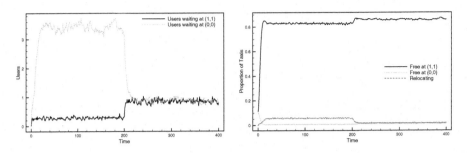

Fig. 5. Smart Taxi System: Scenario 2 (modified specification)

represent something more pervasive and diffuse in the real system, which is abstracted within the modelling to be an entity which exercises influence and imposes constraints on the more physical entities in the system, be they software, human or other forms of agents. For example, in the Smart Taxi System modelled in CARMA the environment determines the rate at which taxis may move through the city, an abstraction of the presence of other vehicles causing congestion which may impede the progress of the taxi to a greater to lesser extent at different times of the day. Thus it should not be considered that the presence of an environment in the model implies the existence of centralised control in the system.

This view of the environment coincides with the view taken by many within the situated multi-agent community e.g. [33]. Specifically, in [34] Weyns *et al.* argue the importance of having a distinct environment within every multi-agent system. Whilst they are viewing such systems from the perspective of software engineers, many of their arguments are as valid when it comes to modelling a multi-agent or collective adaptive system as they are when it comes to building one. Thus our work can be viewed as broadly fitting within the same framework, albeit with a higher level of abstraction. Just as in the construction of a system, in the construction of a model distinguishing clearly between the responsibilities of the agents and of the environment provides separation of concerns and assists in the management of inevitably complex systems. In [34] the authors provide the following definition:

> "The environment is a first-class abstraction that proves the surrounding conditions for agents to exist and that mediates both the interaction among agents and the access to resources."

This is the role that the environment plays within CARMA models through the evolution rules. However, in contrast to the framework of Weyns *et al.* the environment in a CARMA model is not an active entity in the same sense as the agents are active entities; in our case the environment is constrained to work *through* the agents, by influencing their dynamic behaviour or by changes to the number and types of agents making up the system. Despite this difference we consider the CARMA conceptual model to be in line with the Weyns *et al.* framework, the difference primarily arising due to the more abstract approach needed for modelling rather than implementing a CAS. Moreover, note that in CARMA the environment is formally specified and integrated into the operational semantics of the language.

In [31], Saunier *et al.* advocate the use of an *active environment* to mediate the interactions between agents, an active environment that is aware of the current context for each agent. The environment in CARMA also supports this view, as the evolution rules in the environment take into account the state of all the potentially participating components to determine both the rate and the probability of communications being successful, thus achieving a multicast not based on the address of the receiving agents as suggested by Saunier *et al.* This is what we term attribute-based communication in CARMA. Moreover, when the application calls for a centralised information portal, the global store in CARMA can represent it. The higher level of abstraction used in CARMA means that many implementation issues are elided but the CARMA environment could be viewed as capturing the EASI (Environment for Active Support of Interaction) environment of Saunier *et al.* [31], although in CARMA the *filter* is more closely associated with the actions. However, just as in EASI, filters (predicates) may specified separately by the sender, the receiver and the environment. However, our predicates are more strict and "overhearing" type interactions must be anticipated by the modeller, since the effect is taken to be the conjunction of the sender, receiver and environment predicates, thus removing the need for policies to arbitrate between conflicting filters.

The role of the environment is related to the spatially distributed nature of CAS — we expect that *where* an agent is will have an effect on *what* an agent can do. Thus we do find similar features in modelling languages targeted at other domains where location is considered to have influence on the possible behaviours of agents. For example several formalisms developed in the context of biological processes, especially intracellular processes, capture the spatial arrangement of elements in the system because this can have a profound effect on the behaviours that can be observed. In this context, the most important aspect of the spatial arrangement is often hierarchical and logical, rather than the actual physical placement of elements, this is sometimes termed *multi-level* modelling. Moreover the concept of level may also refer to organisational levels, as well as physical levels so that the relationship between levels might be characterised as *consists of* or *contains* [8]. Here we are particularly concerned with modelling techniques that seek to faithfully represent the stochastic dynamic behaviour of systems, allowing properties such as performance, availability and dependability to be assessed.

One example of such a language is the ML-RULES formalism developed by Maus *et al.* [13]. Here the focus is on hierarchical nesting of biological entities and the underlying semantics is given in terms of a population CTMC, intended for analysis by simulation. Entities can be created "on demand" but this must be programmed within the underlying simulation engine by the modeller, and is not supported at the level of the modelling language itself. Rules are used to define the possible reactions in the system and the state updates which result from them; rules are applied by pattern-matching. As in CARMA agents are equipped with attributes and these may be used to filter the rules which may be applied, although there is no explicit naming of attributes making it difficult for other agents to access current values. Moreover it is the modeller's responsibility to ensure that attributes are used consistently across different rules. Explicit function calls are made within agents to determine execution parameters such as Markovian rates or probabilities, thus assuming agents have direct access to a global knowledge. In contrast, in CARMA it is assumed that access to global knowledge is restricted to the environment. Allowing agents to directly access global knowledge makes it more difficult to consider the same set of agents in a different context, because there is less clear separation between the agents and their environment. The multi-level aspect of ML-RULES is used to capture a form of vertical causation, where the application of a rule at one level triggers an update within another level of the model.

The upward and downward causation are also key features of the ML-DEVS formalism, presented in [4], although in a slightly more restricted form since here agents can only trigger changes in the levels immediately above or below them, whereas in ML-Rules an impact can be across arbitrary levels in the hierarchy. ML-DEVS is a modular, hierarchical formalism which is intended to represent a reactive system which interacts asynchronously with its "environment". However the formalism does not support the notion of a distinguished environment, as in CARMA, but rather considers the environment of an agent to be the agents are the same level, with which it may form horizontal couplings, and those in the adjacent levels, with which it may form vertical couplings.

BioSpace [1] is a novel process calculus designed for modelling the physical arrangement of biological molecules in applications such as the formation of polymers and the interactions between microbes and biomaterials [2]. Individual agents in the calculus represent the biological entities, but operate in a type environment against which the legitimacy of their actions can be checked: each action and the entities it involves have types and type consistency is checked before the model evolves. BioSpace^L extends BioSpace by allowing the explicit placement of entities, and giving the modeller the power to program location updates. This reflects the key role that location plays in the considered biological applications, but the physical environment is represented rather implicitly.

In the formalism presented in [8], the formalism supports a multi-level approach which is based on organisational rather than spatial structures. Each level consists of a number of agents whose behaviour may depend on agents at a lower level. In this *system of systems*, agents are represented by automata and automata are organised in tree-structures representing how agents are one level are constituted from their child automata. For example, in a biological setting, the top level might be *tissue* which may alternate between healthy and diseased states; this may be made up by *cells* and the state of the cells within the tissue will influence its health or otherwise; the behaviour and state of cells will depend on the biochemical networks within them, themselves made up of proteins in various states of abundance. Again there are notions of horizontal and vertical couplings, and agents which are above provide the environment to those that are below, in a hierarchical manner.

Similarly the ambient calculus [10], and its biological dialect, bio-ambients [30], capture the behaviour of elements within a system, with respect to a hierarchical arrangement of physical or logical space. As elements move into or out of domains, their behaviour may change because they change their context of operation and communication is limited to be local.

In contrast to these multi-level models, in CARMA we restrict to two levels. The behaviour of the entities within the system are captured by the collective, and this is placed in the context of an environment, which is distinct from any entity and which has the power to constrain the behaviour of the entities through the evolution rule. This reflects our treatment of location in terms of physical space, rather than the hierarchical arrangement of space commonly used in biological modelling where the emphasis is on the containment relationship. It is noteworthy that BioSpace^L, which has similar focus of the physical rather than logical representation on space, also takes a two level approach with the entities and the environment. Within the collective there is no hierarchy, although a single component may have behaviour comprised of multiple process automata. This is intended to represent different aspects of the behaviour of a single entity, such as the taxi having two processes F and G capturing the orthogonal aspects of its behaviour, relating to passengers and movement in search of a passenger respectively.

A two level approach is also found in quantitative formalisms such as PEPA nets [19], Spatial PEPA [18] and STOKLAIM [14]. These languages were motivated by mobile computing and therefore share the aim from modelling CAS to capture systems with behaviour distributed over physical space, in which the current location or position of an entity, and in particular the entities that are co-located, may alter the actions that can be undertaken. In PEPA nets and Spatial PEPA a graphical representation of the physical locations is used either as a Petri net, or as a hyper-graph, and the physical structure is taken to be static. In STOKLAIM, in contrast, the processes within the system may explicitly control the physical structure of the global network. Despite some success in modelling the mobile computing scenarios of the time, these languages are not equipped to represent large populations of entities with similar behaviour, thus they are not well-suited to capture the collective nature of CAS. This large scale nature of CAS systems makes it essential to support scalable analysis techniques, thus CARMA has been designed anticipating both a discrete and a continuous semantics in the style of [32].

6   Conclusions

As we begin to see the deployment of collective adaptive systems in modern infrastructures, it is essential that we have tools and techniques to analyse the behaviour of systems comprised of multiple populations of agents both in terms of their functional and non-functional requirements. In this paper we have introduced CARMA, a novel modelling language which aims to represent collectives of agents working in a specified environment and support the analysis of quantitative aspects of their behaviour such as performance, availability and dependability. CARMA is a stochastic process algebra-based language combining several innovative features such as a separation of behaviour and knowledge, locally synchronous and globally asynchronous communication, attribute-defined interaction and a distinct environment which can be changed independently of the agents. We have demonstrated the use of CARMA on a smart taxi system example, showing the ease with which the same system can be studied under different contexts or environments.

The quantified nature of CARMA, based on Markovian agents whose actions have probability and duration governed by an exponentially distributed random variable, means that CARMA models are amenable to analysis by a variety of techniques. In this paper, based on the semantics presented in [25], we have studied the behaviour of the smart taxi system via stochastic simulation. Future work involves extending the tool support for CARMA and further developing the semantics to also encompass scalable analysis via mean field approximation in the style of [32]. Future work will also include more investigation of the use of the environment to study the adaptivity of systems.

References

1. Compagnoni, A., Giannini, P., Kim, C., Milideo, M., Sharma, V.: A calculus of located entities. In: Proceedings of DCM 2013 (2014)
2. Compagnoni, A., Sharma, V., Bao, Y., Libera, M., Suhkishvili, S., Bidinger, P., Bioglio, L., Bonelli, E.: Biospace: a modeling and simulation language for bacteria-materials interactions. ENTCS **293**, 35–49 (2013)
3. Alrahman, Y., De Nicola, R., Loreti, M., Tiezzi, F., Vigo, R.: A calculus for attribute-based communication. In: Proceedings of SAC 2015 (2015, to appear)
4. Steiniger, A., Krüger, F., Uhrmacher, A.M.: Modeling agents and their environment in multi-level-DEVS. In: Proceedings of the 2012 Winter Simulation Conference, Berlin, Germany. IEEE (2012)
5. Bernardo, M., Gorrieri, R.: A tutorial on EMPA: a theory of concurrent processes with nondeterminism, priorities, probabilities and time. Theor. Comput. Sci. **202**(1–2), 1–54 (1998)
6. Bohnenkamp, H.C., D'Argenio, P.R., Hermanns, H., Katoen, J.: MODEST: a compositional modeling formalism for hard and softly timed systems. IEEE Trans. Softw. Eng. **32**(10), 812–830 (2006)
7. Bordini, R.H., Okuyama, F.Y., de Oliveira, D., Drehmer, G., Krafta, R.C.: The MAS-SOC approach to multi-agent based simulation. In: Lindemann, G., Moldt, D., Paolucci, M. (eds.) RASTA 2002. LNCS (LNAI), vol. 2934, pp. 70–91. Springer, Heidelberg (2004)
8. Bortolussi, L., Hillston, J., Tribastone, M.: Fluid performability analysis of nested automata models. Electr. Notes Theor. Comput. Sci. **310**, 27–47 (2015)
9. Bortolussi, L., Policriti, A.: Hybrid dynamics of stochastic programs. Theor. Comput. Sci. **411**(20), 2052–2077 (2010)
10. Cardelli, L., Gordon, A.D.: Mobile ambients. Theor. Comput. Sci. **240**(1), 177–213 (2000)

11. Celaya, J.R., Desrochers, A.A., Graves, R.J.: Modeling and analysis of multi-agent systems using petri nets. JCP **4**(10), 981–996 (2009)
12. Ciocchetta, F., Hillston, J.: Bio-PEPA: a framework for the modelling and analysis of biological systems. Theor. Comput. Sci. **410**(33), 3065–3084 (2009)
13. Maus, C., Rybacki, S., Uhrmacher, A.M.: Rule-based multi-level modelling of cell biological systems. BMC Syst. Biol. **5**, 166 (2011)
14. De Nicola, R., Latella, D., Massink, M.: Formal modeling and quantitative analysis of klaim-based mobile systems. In: Proceedings of the 2005 ACM Symposium on Applied Computing (SAC), Santa Fe, New Mexico, USA, 13–17 March 2005, pp. 428–435. ACM (2005)
15. De Nicola, R., Loreti, M., Pugliese, R., Tiezzi, F.: A formal approach to autonomic systems programming: the SCEL language. TAAS **9**(2), 7 (2014)
16. Feng, C., Hillston, J.: PALOMA: a process algebra for located Markovian agents. In: Norman, G., Sanders, W. (eds.) QEST 2014. LNCS, vol. 8657, pp. 265–280. Springer, Heidelberg (2014)
17. Feng, C., Hillston, J.: Speed-up of stochastic simulation of PCTMC models by statistical model reduction (2015, Submitted)
18. Galpin, V.: Modelling network performance with a spatial stochastic process algebra. In: Proceedings of International Conference on Advanced Information Networking and Applications, pp. 41–49. IEEE (2009)
19. Gilmore, S., Hillston, J., Kloul, L., Ribaudo, M.: PEPA nets: a structured performance modelling formalism. Perform. Eval. **54**, 79–104 (2003)
20. Helleboogh, A., Vizzari, G., Uhrmacher, A.M., Michel, F.: Modeling dynamic environments in multi-agent simulation. Auton. Agents Multi-Agent Syst. **14**(1), 87–116 (2007)
21. Hermanns, H., Herzog, U., Katoen, J.: Process algebra for performance evaluation. Theor. Comput. Sci. **274**(1–2), 43–87 (2002)
22. Hermanns, H., Rettelbach, M.: Syntax, semantics, equivalences and axioms for MTIPP. In: Herzog, U., Rettelbach, M. (eds.) Proceedings of 2nd Process Algebra and Performance Modelling Workshop (1994)
23. Hillston, J.: A Compositional Approach to Performance Modelling. CUP (1995)
24. Latella, D., Loreti, M., Massink, M., Senni, V.: Stochastically timed predicate-based communication primitives for autonomic computing. In: Bertrand, N., Bortolussi, L. (eds.) Proceedings Twelfth International Workshop on Quantitative Aspects of Programming Languages and Systems, QAPL 2014, Grenoble, France, 12–13 April 2014. EPTCS, vol. 154, pp. 1–16 (2014)
25. Bortolussi, L., Nicola, R.D., Galpin, V., Gilmore, S., Hillston, J., Latella, D., Loreti, M., Massink, M.: Carma: collective adaptive resource-sharing markovian agents. In: Proceedings of the Workshop on Quantitative Analysis of Programming Languages 2015 (2015, to appear)
26. Mili, R.Z., Steiner, R.: Modeling agent-environment interactions in adaptive MAS. In: Weyns, D., Brueckner, S.A., Demazeau, Y. (eds.) EEMMAS 2007. LNCS (LNAI), vol. 5049, pp. 135–147. Springer, Heidelberg (2008)
27. Milner, R., Parrow, J., Walker, D.: A calculus of mobile processes. I. Inf. Comput. **100**(1), 1–40 (1992)
28. John, M., Lhoussaine, C., Niehren, J., Uhrmacher, A.M.: The attributed pi calculus. In: Heiner, M., Uhrmacher, A.M. (eds.) CMSB 2008. LNCS (LNBI), vol. 5307, pp. 83–102. Springer, Heidelberg (2008)
29. Priami, C.: Stochastic π-calculus. Comput. J. **38**(7), 578–589 (1995)

30. Regev, A., Panina, E.M., Silverman, W., Cardelli, L., Shapiro, E.Y.: Bioambients: an abstraction for biological compartments. Theor. Comput. Sci. **325**(1), 141–167 (2004)
31. Saunier, J., Balbo, F., Pinson, S.: A formal model of communication and context awareness in multiagent systems. J. Logic Lang. Inf. **23**(2), 219–247 (2014)
32. Tribastone, M., Gilmore, S., Hillston, J.: Scalable differential analysis of process algebra models. IEEE Trans. Softw. Eng. **38**(1), 205–219 (2012)
33. Weyns, D., Holvoet, T.: A formal model for situated multi-agent systems. Fundam. Inform. **63**(2–3), 125–158 (2004)
34. Weyns, D., Omicini, A., Odell, J.: Environment as a first class abstraction in multiagent systems. Auton. Agents Multi-Agent Syst. **14**(1), 5–30 (2007)

Reconciling Event- and Agent-Based Paradigms in the Engineering of Complex Systems: The Role of Environment Abstractions

Andrea Omicini$^{(\boxtimes)}$ and Stefano Mariani

Alma Mater Studiorum–Università di Bologna, Cesena, Italy
{andrea.omicini,s.mariani}@unibo.it

Abstract. In spite of the growing influence of agent-based models and technologies, the event-based architectural style is still prevalent in the design of large-scale distributed applications. In this paper we discuss the role of environment in both EBS and MAS, and show how it could be used as a starting point for reconciling agent-based and event-based abstractions and techniques within a conceptually-coherent framework that could work as the foundation of a principled discipline for the engineering of complex software systems.

Keywords: Multi-agent systems · Event-based systems · Environment · Situatedness · Coordination models · TuCSoN

1 Introduction

In the last years, the *event-based* architectural style has become prevalent for large-scale distributed applications [16], in order to address some of the most common sources of *accidental complexity*—such as distributed interaction and large-scale concurrency [7]. Meanwhile, *multi-agent systems* (MAS) are expected to provide the most viable abstractions to deal with the modelling and engineering of complex software systems [19,20]. Thus, MAS and event-based systems (EBS) stand nowadays as the two most likely candidate paradigms for modelling and engineering complex systems.

On the one side, events in EBS are the abstractions causing system dynamics; on the other side, environment change [45] is what requires MAS to work as situated systems [44]. Altogether, this suggests that a seamless integration between EBS and MAS – which could preserve conceptual integrity of systems – could be achieved by properly relating the notions of event and change, while suitably re-interpreting event- and agent-based abstractions.

From a MAS perspective, this is also witnessed by the many diverse occurrences of the notion of *event* at different levels of MAS models and technologies. For instance, most of agent architectures adopt some effective notion of event, providing for agent reactiveness—e.g., BDI architectures [37], as implemented, e.g., by AgentSpeak and *Jason* [6]. Also, most of agent middleware provide some

© Springer International Publishing Switzerland 2015
D. Weyns and F. Michel (Eds.): E4MAS 2014 – 10 years later, LNAI 9068, pp. 117–130, 2015.
DOI: 10.1007/978-3-319-23850-0_8

event-based abstractions and mechanisms dealing with asynchronous message passing and environment change—as in the case of JADE [4] and TuCSoN [33]. On the other hand, the literature on EBS clearly exhibits a lack of suitably-expressive abstractions making it possible to harness the complexity of event-based systems.

Environment plays a key-role in both EBS and MAS as a source of unpredictable events and activity, respectively. Therefore, starting from the essential of both paradigms, in this paper we point out the role of the environment in a unifying conceptual framework for MAS and EBS, which could work as the foundation of a coherent discipline for the modelling and engineering of complex software systems.

Accordingly, the remainder of the paper is organised as follows. In Sects. 2 and 3 we recapitulate the role of environment in MAS and EBS, respectively. After Sect. 4 bridges between MAS and EBS, focussing on the environment-related issues, Sect. 5 discusses a case study where the TuCSoN coordination model and architecture [33] is used to illustrate the role of environment abstractions in blending MAS and EBS.

2   The Role of the Environment in MAS

2.1   Environment as a First-Class Abstraction

A common way to look at MAS is to interpret them according to the main first-class abstractions: *agents*, *societies*, and *environment* [44].

Agents are computational entities whose defining feature is autonomy [32]. Agents model activities for the MAS, expressed through their actions along with their motivations—namely, the goals and intentions that determine and explain the agent's course of actions. *Societies* represent the ensembles where the collective behaviours of the MAS are coordinated towards the achievement of the overall system goals. *Coordination models* and *languages* are then the most suitable tools to tackle complexity in MAS [12], as they are explicitly meant to supply the abstractions that "glue" agents together [11,17] by governing agent interaction [42].

Besides agents and societies, *environment* is an essential abstraction for MAS modelling and engineering [44], to be suitably represented, and related to agents. On the one side, the notion of environment captures the unpredictability of the MAS context, by modelling the external resources and features that are relevant for the MAS, along with their evolution over time. On the other side, it makes it possible to model the resources, tools, services that agents and MAS need to carry on their own activities. Along with the notion of *situated action* – as the realisation that coordinated, social, intelligent action arises from strict interaction with the environment, rather than from rational practical reasoning [40] – this leads to the requirement of *situatedness* for agents and MAS, often translated into the need of being sensitive to *environment change* [15].

Along this way, one could state that *(i)* things happen in a MAS because of either agent activity or environment change, and *(ii)* complexity arises from both social and situated interaction. Also, this suggests that *environment-mediated coordination* (as a form of *objective coordination* [30]) – in charge of *managing dependencies* [22], by using, e.g., coordination *artefacts* [31] – could be used to deal in a uniform way with both social and situated interaction [24].

2.2 Environment as an Architectural Component

Situated agency originates from reactive robotics, emerged in the mid-1980s as an approach to build autonomous robots capable of acting efficiently in dynamic environments. The initial reactive agent systems focussed on the importance of *environmental dynamics*. There, environment is considered as external to the system, that is, not as an explicit part of the models or of the architectures [44].

Since early 1990s, researchers have been investigating systems in which multiple agents work together to realise the system functionality. In these systems, the agents exploit the environment to share information and coordinate their behaviour [44]. In its basic form, agents are driven by what they perceive in the environment. Here, the environment may also be an *active* entity that maintains processes independent of the activity of the agents [34]. A classic example is *stigmergic coordination* [18], inspired by social insects, and brought to agents in several forms—as in the case of *digital pheromones* [5,8,35], used by software agents to coordinate their behaviour.

Since the mid-1990s, *situated multi-agent systems* has been the subject of active research [44]. Situated MAS emphasise the importance of *architecture* for agents and the environment, see e.g., [3,15,43]. The environment architecture in situated MAS includes: functionality for perception management, message delivering, action handling, and maintenance processes that manage state in the environment independently of agents. In situated MAS, the environment is an explicit, active *architectural abstraction* with specific responsibilities that differ from agent responsibilities [44].

Stemming from such historical evolution, at least two essential duties can be devised in modern complex MAS for the environment abstraction [44]:

Maintaining Dynamics — Besides the activity of the agents, the environment can have processes of its own, independent of agents. A typical example of dynamics in the environment is the evaporation, aggregation, and diffusion of digital pheromones.

Enforcing Rules — The environment can define and enforce rules to be observed in the whole MAS. Rules may impose domain-driven constraints (e.g., mobility in a network), or reify laws defined by the designer (e.g., limitation of access to neighbouring nodes in a network for reasons of performance). Rules may restrict the access of specific resources or services to particular types of agents, or determine the outcome of agent interactions. By enforcing rules on an agent's activity, the environment acts as an arbitrator constantly striving to preserve the agent system in a consistent state according to the goals and requirements of the application domain.

For instance, such duties are accounted for in the A&A meta-model [32], where *working environment* for agents is conceived as a dynamic set of *artefacts*, organised in terms of *workspaces* [38]. The notion of artefact is the core abstraction of A&A: artefacts can be used to (computationally) represent any kind of *environmental resource* within a MAS, in particular situated ones [24], in a uniform way—from sensors to actuators, from databases to legacy OO applications, from real-world objects to virtual blackboards. Thus, artefacts are the tools for MAS designers to properly model and implement the portion of the environment agents can control/should deal with, working then as the basic building blocks to compose complex working environments [32, 38].

As a side note, the abstraction that encapsulate environment change in CArtAgO – an implementation of the A&A meta-model for environment programming in situated MAS [39] – is precisely that of *event*: seemingly, this further strengthens the intuition that environment abstractions could play a central role in EBS-MAS integration.

3   The Role of the Environment in EBS

According to [16], an EBS is "a system in which the integrated components communicate by generating and receiving *event notifications*", where an *event* is an occurrence of a happening relevant for the system – e.g., a state change in the computational environment –, and a *notification* is the reification of an event within the system, providing for the event description and data. Components in EBS basically act as either *producers* or *consumers* of notifications: producers *publish* notifications, and provide an *output interface* for subscription; consumers *subscribe* to notifications as specified by producers. According to the *event-based architectural style*, producers and consumers do not interact directly, since their interaction is mediated by the *event bus*, which abstracts away all the complexity of the *event notification service*.

Articulated application scenarios like Business Activity Monitoring, Sensor Networks, and Market data [14] raise event management issues that lead to the so-called Complex Event Processing (CEP) [21]. Issues such as *event aggregation* and *transformation* have to be addressed by making individual event notifications meaningful at the level of interpretation required for making consumer activities effective. Relationships (such as causality, timing, or membership) between events should be detected, and event *hierarchies* could be required to provide for different level of abstractions.

Essentially, EBS implicitly exploit *environment-mediated coordination* likewise situated MAS, where coordination is event-based [25]. Process activities are mostly driven by event notifications generated by producers; transformed, aggregated, filtered, distributed by the event bus; and finally interpreted and used by consumers. Producer/consumer coordination is then *mediated* by the event bus, the *environmental resource* working as the system *coordinator*, which encapsulates and possibly automates most of the coordination activities in an EBS. According to the interpretation above, environment in EBS is not much more than an infrastructural service, provided by the event-based middleware to application components for communication purpose, and shielding the application layer from low-level details about event generation, consumption and routing. As such, environment is simply part of the deployment context in which the event-driven application runs, rather than an architectural component that EBS designers can exploit to design the application environment at the most suitable level of abstraction.

3.1   MAS Perspective on EBS Environment

By adopting a MAS perspective, we can recognise that environment in EBS is basically assigned the same duties as environment in MAS:

- producers activities are the source of dynamics, generating events according to an event publication API in response to their course of actions
- consumers subscriptions are the rules governing communication and coordination among components, enforced by the event bus through event notification services.

Also, we can interpret the event bus as the environmental artefact – according to A&A – in charge of such duties: on the one hand, it supports EBS dynamics by capturing events from producers, bringing them to consumers, and by carrying out its own event aggregation, transformation, correlation processes; on the other hand, it mediates – enables and constraints – producer-consumer interactions according to the subscription rules.

Accordingly, our statement (Sect. 3) about implicit environment-mediated coordination in EBS can be rephrased as follows: agents (components) activities are mostly driven by events generated either by other agents or by the environment; transformed, aggregated, filtered, distributed by the event bus artefact; and finally interpreted and used by agents and the environment itself—e.g. by other artefacts. Agent-agent as well as agent-environment coordination (social and situated interaction) is then *mediated* by the event bus, working as the system *coordination artefact*, which encapsulates and possibly automates most of the coordination activities in an EBS.

In the following section, we further elaborate on such an interpretation to provide a unifying conceptual framework for Event-Based Multi-Agent Systems (EBMAS).

4   The Role of the Environment in EBMAS

According to [24], three core concepts motivate MAS abstractions:

- activities are the goal-directed/oriented proceedings resulting into *actions* making things happen within a MAS—motivating agents; through actions, activities in a MAS are *social* [10] and *situated* [40];

- environment change represents the (possibly unpredictable) variations in the properties or structure of the world surrounding a MAS that affect it in any way;
- dependencies arise since activities depend on other activities (social dependencies), and on environment change (situated dependencies); they motivate and cause *interaction* – both *social* and *situated* interaction – thus societies.

Then, [24] advocates the role of *events* as the means through which dependency resolution (that is, coordination) may uniformly happen in MAS: despite their intrinsic diversity, in fact, actions and environment change constitute altogether the only sources of dynamics in a MAS. Thus, in order to provide a uniform modelling of social and situated dependencies, both actions and environment changes can be represented as *events*.

Building on the connection between the notions of change (in MAS) and event (in EBS), in the following we devise out a mapping between EBS and MAS abstractions—that is, both an interpretation of EBS as MAS and vice versa.

4.1   Event Sources

First of all, *(i)* being activities and change the only source of dynamics in MAS, *(ii)* being both dynamics represented as events, and *(iii)* being activities and change the outcome of agent and environment processes, we can state that:

- interpreting MAS as EBS, agents as well as the environment are the *prosumers* of events (simultaneously producers and consumers): the former, account for *internal events*, that is, the designed events happening according to some application criterion; the latter, account for *external events*, that is, those (unpredictable) happenings capturing the uncontrollable dynamics of MAS environment (resources)

Dually, since *(i)* producers are EBS components generating events and *(ii)* consumers are EBS components subscribing to event notifications, we can say that:

- interpreting EBS as MAS, components may be agents or (environmental) artefacts depending on *(i)* which kind of event they deal with: if they are producers/consumers of events originated from application-driven activities (internal events), they are likely to be agents; if they are producers/consumers of events originated from environment change (external events), they are likely to be artefacts

Summing up, the following mapping EBS-MAS can be devised:

EBS $\Longleftrightarrow$ MAS
Producer component $\Longleftrightarrow$ Agent/artefact
Consumer component $\Longleftrightarrow$ Agent/artefact
Internal event (notification) $\Longleftrightarrow$ Agent activity
External event (notification) $\Longleftrightarrow$ Environment change

This involves a higher-level of expressiveness in EBS: since agents encapsulate control along with the criteria for its management – expressed in terms of high-level, mentalistic abstractions –, articulated *events histories* can be modelled along with their *motivations*. In addition, since MAS environment is modelled as a first-class event-based abstraction, all *causes of change* and disruption in a MAS are modelled in a uniform way as *event prosumers* (producers and consumers)—thus improving conceptual integrity.

4.2   Boundary Artefacts

Once EBS and MAS share a common understanding about what generates system dynamics, we can focus on how such dynamics should be supported and coordinated. Being agents activity and environment change heterogeneous sources of dynamics, first of all there is need for a *uniform event model*, then for architectural abstractions suitably supporting event handling by mediating between event producers and the whole system.

In [24], *boundary artefacts* are introduced in MAS as the architectural components working as an interface between the agent (or, the environmental resource) and the MAS *interaction space*, mapping agent activities and environment changes into events. This is, for instance, how Agent Communication Contexts [13] and Agent Coordination Contexts (ACC) [26] work for agents, how the `environment` class works for environment resources in *Jason*, and how transducers work for ReSpecT probes [23]. In the field of event middleware, *event mediators* (or, *correlators*) play the role of boundary artefacts in the Cambridge Event Architecture [2], as implemented for instance by the Hermes distributed event-based middleware architecture [36], or by the OASIS open architecture for open, secure, widely distributed services [1].

Thus, boundary artefacts could be conceived as:

- interpreting EBS as MAS, all those coordination-related services mediating between agents activities and environment change, and the rest of the system—such as coordination operation mapping into coordination events, dependency resolution, etc.
- interpreting MAS as EBS, all those event-related services dealing with the event data model – such as event building, translation between different event models, mapping consumed events into consumer actions and producer actions into generated events, etc. – and with event notification—such as handling subscriptions, event routing, etc.

Accordingly, the following mapping EBS-MAS can be devised:

EBS ⟺ MAS
Event mediators ⟺ ACC/transducers (Artefacts)
Subscription/publication API ⟺ ACC/transducers API

It should be noted that, under such a MAS-oriented interpretation of EBS, the event notification service becomes a sort of environmental resource (an artefact), able to generate and consume events as any other prosumer—according to the mapping in Subsect. 4.1. Thus, event-related services become first-class abstractions in EBS engineering, not merely low-level, infrastructural details; also, EBS engineers may benefit from the A&A literature regarding environment engineering for, e.g., equipping the event bus with malleability, inspectability, and all the other relevant features of A&A artefacts. In fact, once that the event bus is recognised as an artefact, the publication/subscription interaction pattern may be re-interpreted as a much more general event-based coordination model, as detailed in next section.

4.3   Event-Based Situated Coordination

The last step in our quest toward EBMAS aims at completing previous section on system dynamics coordination—in particular, showing how event-based, environment-mediated (that is, situated) coordination can be adopted as a uniform conceptual framework.

First of all, if agents and environment (MAS) work as event prosumers (EBS), coordination abstractions can effectively deal with their interactions of any sort – agent-agent, agent-environment, environment-environment interaction – taking care of their mutual dependencies, by coordinating the many resulting flows of events [22]. Coordination models, in fact, work by *constraining* the space of interaction [42]. In particular, the *coordination primitives* provided by a coordination model constrain the possible agent *actions*, whereas the *coordination media* constrain the possible *targets* of agent actions. Similarly, event notification services (e.g., the event bus) rule the way in which events are produced, consumed, and routed between EBS components, actually constraining the space of interaction too by disciplining event publication and subscription. Accordingly, the publication and subscription API can be interpreted as playing the role of coordination primitives, whereas the event-bus may be regarded as EBS coordination media.

This means that coordination media (artefacts) could work as the core of an event-based architecture for environment-mediated (situated) coordination, and that EBS could be grounded in principle upon a suitably-expressive coordination middleware, designing the event bus around the coordination services [41]. Then, environmental artefacts provide a specific computational model for dealing with event observation, manipulation, and coordination—which should make life easier for programmers and engineers. In the context of EBS, the specific coordination artefact represented by the coordination medium provides a suitable way to automatise event handling, and to encapsulate the logic for the coordination of multiple related flows of events—e.g., counterfeiting the negative effects of inversion of control on the large scale for EBS.

Summing up, the following EBS-MAS mapping can be devised:

EBS $\Longleftrightarrow$ MAS
Publish/subscribe API $\Longleftrightarrow$ Coordination primitives
Event bus $\Longleftrightarrow$ Coordination media (artefacts)

It should be noticed that the last step of our MAS-oriented acceptation of EBS coherently completes the interpretation of the event notification service as an environmental resource and a coordination artefact. In fact, the event bus and the publish/subscribe services altogether constitute the artefacts through which EBS engineers can model and program the environment where EBS components live. In this way, components interaction is mediated by the environment, thus coordination, too, happens through proper event handling carried out by the environment—as in situated MAS. Being events generated by agents activities or environment change, the event notification services actually carries out (event-based) coordination among system components.

5   Case Study: Event-Based Situated Coordination in TuCSoN

The TuCSoN coordination model and infrastructure [33] can be used to illustrate in short the role of environment abstractions in EBMAS, in particular by pointing out the notions of boundary and coordination artefacts.

In detail, the basic TuCSoN architecture can be represented as in Fig. 1, and explained in terms of the following EBMAS components:

ACC — *Agent coordination contexts* [26] represent TuCSoN boundary artefacts devoted to agents. ACC both *enable* and *constraint* agents interactions, mapping every agent operation into events asynchronously dispatched to tuple centres. ACC thus *decouple* agents from MAS in control, reference, space, and time.

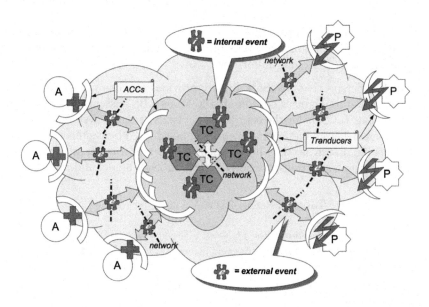

Fig. 1. TuCSoN event-based situated architecture

Probes — TuCSoN environmental resources. They are handled as sources of perceptions (*sensors*) or makers of actions (*actuators*) in a uniform way. Probes do not directly interact with the MAS, but through *mediation* of their transducer.

Transducers — The boundary artefacts devoted to probes [9]. Each probe is assigned to a transducer, specialised to handle events from that sort of probe, and to act on probes through situation operations. Transducers thus decouple probes from tuple centres in terms of control, reference, space and time.

Events — TuCSoN adopts and generalises the ReSpecT *event model* [28]— depicted in Tables 1 and 2. ReSpecT is the logic-based language used to program the behaviour of TuCSoN tuple centres [28]. ACC and transducers translate external events (activities and change) into internal events that tuple centres can handle to implement the policies required for MAS coordination. Thus, internal events essentially correspond to event notifications in standard EBS.

Tuple centres — Tuple centres [28] constitute TuCSoN architectural component implementing coordination artefacts, thus in charge of managing dependencies. As such, they are meant to govern both social and situated interactions [24]. By adopting ReSpecT tuple centres, TuCSoN relies on (*i*) the ReSpecT language to program coordination laws, and (*ii*) the ReSpecT situated event model to implement events [9].

By looking at a TuCSoN-coordinated MAS with a EBS perspective,

– ACC and transducers are the boundary artefacts representing components and environment, respectively, in the MAS, by translating activities and changes in a common event (notification) model;
– tuple centres are the coordination artefacts dealing with both social and situated dependencies by making it possible to program the coordination of events of any sorts in a clean and uniform way.

Under such a perspective, TuCSoN already provides in some way both a model and a technology to engineer coordinated MAS as EBS. Essentially, this means that when using TuCSoN for the coordination of a distributed system, either perspectives – event-based and agent-based – can be adopted by engineers according to their specific design needs, and blended together in a coherent way around the coordination abstractions provided by the TuCSoN model and middleware.[1]

Table 1. ReSpecT situated *event model*.

⟨*Event*⟩ ::= ⟨*StartCause*⟩ , ⟨*Cause*⟩ , ⟨*Evaluation*⟩	
⟨*StartCause*⟩ , ⟨*Cause*⟩ ::= ⟨*Activity*⟩	⟨*Change*⟩ , ⟨*Source*⟩ , ⟨*Target*⟩ , ⟨*Time*⟩ , ⟨*Space:Place*⟩	
⟨*Source*⟩ , ⟨*Target*⟩ ::= ⟨*AgentId*⟩	⟨*CoordArtefactId*⟩	⟨*EnvResId*⟩	⊥	
⟨*Evaluation*⟩ ::= ⊥	{ ⟨*Result*⟩ }	

---

[1] http://tucson.unibo.it.

Table 2. ReSpecT *triggering events.*

$\langle Activity \rangle$ ::=	$\langle Operation \rangle$ | $\langle Situation \rangle$
$\langle Operation \rangle$ ::=	out($\langle Tuple \rangle$) | (in | rd | no | inp | rdp | nop) ($\langle Template \rangle$ [, $\langle Term \rangle$])
$\langle Situation \rangle$ ::=	getEnv($\langle Key \rangle$, $\langle Value \rangle$) | setEnv($\langle Key \rangle$, $\langle Value \rangle$)
$\langle Change \rangle$ ::=	env($\langle Key \rangle$, $\langle Value \rangle$) | time($\langle Time \rangle$) |
	from($\langle Space \rangle$, $\langle Place \rangle$) | to($\langle Space \rangle$, $\langle Place \rangle$)

6   Conclusion

Many large-scale distributed systems are nowadays designed and developed around event-based methods and technologies. At the same time, agent-based abstractions (and, in spite of their limited maturity, agent technologies, too) are more and more adopted to face the intricacies of complex systems engineering, in particular when requirements such pervasiveness, intelligence, mobility, and the like, have to be addressed. Altogether, this suggests that a conceptual framework blending together abstractions and technologies from both EBS and MAS could represent a fundamental goal for the research on complex system engineering.

Our research on the subject started by devising the first formulation of the conceptual framework for EBMAS in [27], then developed by elaborating on the key role of coordination models and technologies [29]. In this position paper we focus instead on the environment, and suggest that a fundamental role in such a conceptual framework could be played by environment-mediated coordination, with the focus on coordination artefacts working as both event-based and agent-based abstractions.

References

1. Bacon, J., Moody, K.: Toward open, secure, widely distributed services. Commun. ACM **45**(6), 59–64 (2002)
2. Bacon, J., Moody, K., Bates, J., Heyton, R., Ma, C., McNeil, A., Seidel, O., Spiteri, M.: Generic support for distributed applications. Computer **33**(3), 68–76 (2000)
3. Bandini, S., Manzoni, S., Simone, C.: Dealing with space in multi-agent systems: a model for situated MAS. In: Castelfranchi, C., Johnson, W.L. (eds.) 1st International Joint Conference on Autonomous Agents and Multiagent Systems (AAMAS 2002). vol. 3, pp. 1183–1190. ACM Press, New York, 15–19 July 2002
4. Bellifemine, F.L., Caire, G., Greenwood, D.: Developing Multi-agent Systems with JADE. Wiley, Chichester (2007)
5. Bonabeau, E., Henaux, F., Guérin, S., Snyers, D., Kuntz, P., Theraulaz, G.: Routing in telecommunications networks with ant-like agents. In: Albayrak, Ş., Garijo, F.J. (eds.) IATA 1998. LNCS (LNAI), vol. 1437, pp. 60–71. Springer, Heidelberg (1998)
6. Bordini, R.H., Hübner, J.F., Wooldridge, M.J.: Programming Multi-agent Systems in AgentSpeak using Jason. John Wiley & Sons, Chichester (2007)
7. Brooks, F.P.: No silver bullet essence and accidents of software engineering. Computer **20**(4), 10–19 (1987)

8. Brückner, S.: Return from the ant. Synthetic ecosystems for manufacturing control. Dissertation, Matematisch-Naturwissenschaftlichen Fakultät II, Humboldt-Universität zu Berlin, Berlin, Germany, June 2000
9. Casadei, M., Omicini, A.: Situated tuple centres in ReSpecT. In: Shin, S.Y., Ossowski, S., Menezes, R., Viroli, M. (eds.) 24th Annual ACM Symposium on Applied Computing (SAC 2009). vol. III, pp. 1361–1368. ACM, Honolulu, 8–12 March 2009
10. Castelfranchi, C.: Modelling social action for AI agents. Artif. Intell. **103**(1–2), 157–182 (1998)
11. Ciancarini, P.: Coordination models and languages as software integrators. ACM Comput. Surv. **28**(2), 300–302 (1996)
12. Ciancarini, P., Omicini, A., Zambonelli, F.: Multiagent system engineering: the coordination viewpoint. In: Jennings, N.R., Lespérance, Y. (eds.) ATAL 1999. LNCS (LNAI), vol. 1757, pp. 250–259. Springer, Heidelberg (2000)
13. Di Stefano, A., Pappalardo, G., Santoro, C., Tramontana, E.: The transparent implementation of agent communication contexts. Concurr. Comput. Pract. Exp. **18**(4), 387–407 (2006)
14. Eckert, M., Bry, F.: Complex event processing (CEP). Informatik-Spektrum **32**(2), 163–167 (2009)
15. Ferber, J., Müller, J.P.: Influences and reaction: a model of situated multiagent systems. In: Tokoro, M. (ed.) 2nd International Conference on Multi-agent Systems (ICMAS 1996), pp. 72–79. AAAI Press, Tokyo, December 1996
16. Fiege, L., Mühl, G., Gärtner, F.C.: Modular event-based systems. Knowl. Eng. Rev. **17**(4), 359–388 (2002)
17. Gelernter, D., Carriero, N.: Coordination languages and their significance. Commun. ACM **35**(2), 97–107 (1992)
18. Grassé, P.P.: La reconstruction du nid et les coordinations interindividuelles chez Bellicositermes natalensis et Cubitermes sp. la théorie de la stigmergie: Essai d'interprétation du comportement des termites constructeurs. Insectes Soc. **6**(1), 41–80 (1959)
19. Jennings, N.R.: On agent-based software engineering. Artif. Intell. **117**(2), 277–296 (2000)
20. Jennings, N.R.: An agent-based approach for building complex software systems. Commun. ACM **44**(4), 35–41 (2001)
21. Sundaram, S., Sundararajan, N., Savitha, R.: Introduction. In: Sundaram, S., Sundararajan, N., Savitha, R. (eds.) Supervised Learning with Complex-valued Neural Networks. SCI, vol. 421, pp. 1–30. Springer, Heidelberg (2013)
22. Malone, T.W., Crowston, K.: The interdisciplinary study of coordination. ACM Comput. Surv. **26**(1), 87–119 (1994)
23. Mariani, S., Omicini, A.: Coordination in situated systems: engineering MAS environment in TuCSoN. In: Fortino, G., Di Fatta, G., Li, W., Ochoa, S., Cuzzocrea, A., Pathan, M. (eds.) IDCS 2014. LNCS, vol. 8729, pp. 99–110. Springer, Heidelberg (2014)
24. Iordache, O.: Methods. In: Iordache, O. (ed.) Polystochastic Models for Complexity. UCS, vol. 4, pp. 17–61. Springer, Heidelberg (2010)
25. Milicevic, A., Jackson, D., Gligoric, M., Marinov, D.: Model-based, event-driven programming paradigm for interactive Web applications. In: 2013 ACM International Symposium on New Ideas. New Paradigms, and Reflections on Programming & Software (Onward! 2013), pp. 17–36. ACM Press, New York, October 2013

26. Omicini, A.: Towards a notion of agent coordination context. In: Marinescu, D.C., Lee, C. (eds.) Process Coordination and Ubiquitous Computing, pp. 187–200. CRC Press, Boca Raton (2002)
27. Omicini, A.: Event-based vs. multi-agent systems: towards a unified conceptual framework. In: 2015 19th IEEE International Conference on Computer Supported Cooperative Work in Design (CSCWD 2015), pp. 1–6. IEEE Computer Society, May 2015
28. Omicini, A., Denti, E.: From tuple spaces to tuple centres. Sci. Comput. Program. **41**(3), 277–294 (2001)
29. Omicini, A., Fortino, G., Mariani, S.: Blending event-based and multi-agent systems around coordination abstractions. In: Holvoet, T., Viroli, M. (eds.) Coordination Models and Languages. LNCS, vol. 9037, pp. 186–193. Springer, Heidelberg (2015)
30. Omicini, A., Ossowski, S.: Objective versus Subjective coordination in the engineering of agent systems. In: Klusch, M., Bergamaschi, S., Edwards, P., Petta, P. (eds.) Intelligent Information Agents. LNCS (LNAI), vol. 2586, pp. 179–202. Springer, Heidelberg (2003)
31. Omicini, A., Ricci, A., Viroli, M.: Coordination artifacts as first-class abstractions for MAS engineering: state of the research. In: Garcia, A., Choren, R., Lucena, C., Giorgini, P., Holvoet, T., Romanovsky, A. (eds.) SELMAS 2005. LNCS, vol. 3914, pp. 71–90. Springer, Heidelberg (2006)
32. Omicini, A., Ricci, A., Viroli, M.: Artifacts in the A&A meta-model for multi-agent systems. Auton. Agent. Multi-Agent Syst. **17**(3), 432–456 (2008)
33. Omicini, A., Zambonelli, F.: Coordination for Internet application development. Auton. Agent. Multi-Agent Syst. **2**(3), 251–269 (1999)
34. Parunak, H.V.D.: "Go to the ant": engineering principles from natural multi-agent systems. Ann. Oper. Res. **75**, 69–101 (1997)
35. Parunak, H.V.D., Brueckner, S., Sauter, J.: Digital pheromone mechanisms for coordination of unmanned vehicles. In: Castelfranchi, C., Johnson, W.L. (eds.) 1st International Joint Conference on Autonomous Agents and Multiagent Systems (AAMAS 2002). vol. 1, pp. 449–450. ACM Press, New York, 15–19 July 2002
36. Pietzuch, P.R., Bacon, J.M.: Hermes: a distributed event-based middleware architecture. In: 22nd International Conference on Distributed Computing Systems Workshops (ICDCS 2002), pp. 611–618. IEEE Computer Society, Vienna, 2–5 July 2002
37. Rao, A.S., Georgeff, M.P.: Modeling rational agents within a BDI architecture. In: Allen, J.F., Fikes, R., Sandewall, E. (eds.) 2nd International Conference on Principles of Knowledge Representation and Reasoning (KR'91), pp. 473–484. Morgan Kaufmann Publishers, San Mateo (1991)
38. Ricci, A., Viroli, M., Omicini, A.: "Give agents their artifacts": the A&A approach for engineering working environments in MAS. In: Durfee, E., Yokoo, M., Huhns, M., Shehory, O. (eds.) 6th International Joint Conference "Autonomous Agents & Multi-Agent Systems" (AAMAS 2007), pp. 601–603. IFAAMAS, Honolulu, 14–18 May 2007
39. Ricci, A., Viroli, M., Omicini, A.: CArtAgO: a framework for prototyping artifact-based environments in MAS. In: Weyns, D., Van Dyke Parunak, H., Michel, F. (eds.) E4MAS 2006. LNCS (LNAI), vol. 4389, pp. 67–86. Springer, Heidelberg (2007)
40. Suchman, L.A.: Situated actions. In: Plans and Situated Actions: The Problem of Human-Machine Communication, pp. 49–67. Cambridge University Press, New York (1987)

41. Viroli, M., Omicini, A.: Coordination as a service. Fundamenta Informaticae **73**(4), 507–534 (2006). Special Issue: Best papers of FOCLASA 2002

42. Wegner, P.: Coordination as constrained interaction. In: Hankin, C., Ciancarini, P. (eds.) COORDINATION 1996. LNCS, vol. 1061, pp. 28–33. Springer, Heidelberg (1996)

43. Weyns, D., Holvoet, T.: A formal model for situated multi-agent systems. Fundam. Inform. **63**(2), 125–158 (2004)

44. Weyns, D., Omicini, A., Odell, J.J.: Environment as a first-class abstraction in multi-agent systems. Auton. Agent. Multi-agent Syst. **14**(1), 5–30 (2007)

45. Wooldridge, M.J., Jennings, N.R.: Intelligent agents: theory and practice. Knowl. Eng. Rev. **10**(2), 115–152 (1995)

Virtual and Simulated Environments

From Physical to Virtual: Widening the Perspective on Multi-Agent Environments

Carlos Carrascosa[1]([⊠]), Franziska Klügl[2], Alessandro Ricci[3],
and Olivier Boissier[4]

[1] DSIC, Universitat Politècnica de València,
Camino de Vera sn, 46022 Valencia, Spain
`carrasco@dsic.upv.es`
[2] School of Natural Science and Technology,
Örebro University, 70182 Örebro, Sweden
`franziska.klugl@oru.se`
[3] DISI, Alma Mater Studiorum - Università di Bologna,
Via Sacchi 3, Cesena, Italy
`a.ricci@unibo.it`
[4] FAYOL - ENS Mines and Laboratoire Hubert Curien CNRS:UMR 5516,
Saint-Etienne, France
`boissier@emse.fr`

Abstract. Since more than a decade, the environment is seen as a key element when analyzing, developing or deploying Multi-Agent Systems (MAS) applications. Especially, for the development of multi-agent platforms it has become a key concept, similarly to many application in the area of location-based, distributed systems. An emerging, prominent application area for MAS is related to Virtual Environments. The underlying technology has evolved in a way, that these applications have grown out of science fiction novels till research papers and even real applications. Even more, current technologies enable MAS to be key components of such virtual environments.

In this paper, we widen the concept of the environment of a MAS to encompass new and mixed physical, virtual, simulated, etc. forms of environments. We analyze currently most interesting application domains based on three dimensions: the way different "realities" are mixed via the environment, the underlying natures of agents, the possible forms and sophistication of interactions. In addition to this characterization, we discuss how this widened concept of possible environments influences the support it can give for developing applications in the respective domains.

1 Introduction

The last decade has seen the increase of the different kinds of environment that Multiagent Systems (MAS) have been applied to/in, due to the increase in numbers and complexity of the application domains as well as their diversification. One category of these environments with a huge development is related to Virtual Environments (VE), proposing more and more sophisticated and credible

© Springer International Publishing Switzerland 2015
D. Weyns and F. Michel (Eds.): E4MAS 2014 – 10 years later, LNAI 9068, pp. 133–146, 2015.
DOI: 10.1007/978-3-319-23850-0_9

simulations of some "reality" for one or more user to be immersed into. Agent technologies have been also proposed for supporting interaction for humans in such environments [13]. VEs are not restricted to traditional virtual reality application domains such as art, entertainment or education, but there is a variety of other sophisticated opportunities for mixing physical, virtual, simulated, etc. With the tremendous development of related technologies, intelligent agents may interact with other agents or with humans in environments in a way far beyond the MAS-environments discussed in the E4MAS community before.

In fact, it is easy to see that current developments are very close to what was only science fiction few years ago. So, nowadays, we are as close as possible to be able to reach what Gelernter defined as "Mirror Worlds" [9]. These are software models of some chunk of reality that can mimic every change in real-time and host a massive number of users each with a different view of the mirror world. In 1991, this definition was as close to science fiction as was the definition of "Metaverse" by Neal Stephenson in 1992 [18], as a computer generated virtual space where people, represented by their avatars may interact in a distributed fashion. Or as was the definition of "Cyberspace" by William Gibson in 1984 [10](though he had introduced the term in 1982) "A consensual hallucination experienced daily by billions of legitimate operators, in every nation, by children being taught mathematical concepts... A graphic representation of data abstracted from banks of every computer in the human system. Unthinkable complexity. Lines of light ranged in the nonspace of the mind, clusters and constellations of data. Like city lights, receding into the distance".

Mirror World, Metaverse, Cyberspace are not unrelated. Their analysis shows three main common dimensions related to (i) the way they are syncing between physical and virtual worlds, (ii) the agents (artificial or human) populating the worlds and cooperating/competing with each other to fulfill their goals, and (iii) the social relations and interactions taking place among the huge number of agents playing different roles in those interactions.

Ten years ago, Weyns et al. formulated in [22] three categories of research challenges as a consequence of following the idea of thinking the environment of a Multiagent System as a first-class citizen: the first category relates to a proper formalization of "environment" making fully clear what is an agent and which element of an overall system is part of the environment. Based on this formal understanding, [22] expected the development of a classification of different kinds of environments also in relation to a corresponding taxonomy of application domains. The second category of challenges drives this further and deals with challenges in exploring the relation between agents and their environment. This can be done with respect to three dimensions: the (software) architectures of agents in relation to the environment, the protocols and laws that govern interaction between agents and their environment as well as between agents mediated by their shared environment and last but not least the constraints that the environmental topology imposes on the agents. The third category of challenges deals with advancing the findings of research addressing the first two categories of challenges into engineering environments – both design and implementation of environments. Over the years, many works have addressed those challenges, from a specialized formalization of the environment as active support of interaction [17] to agent platforms that combine support for complex environmental structures, complex agent reasoning and organization concepts [4] among other frameworks, platforms, and advanced applications as for example in the agreement technologies area [2]. In this collection, one can find many more examples about how research and application related to environments for MAS has been advanced during the last decade.

Ten years ago, despite of its initially wide approach from multiple perspectives, the focus was on a very restricted type of environments, mostly on the required components and infrastructures for MAS. Such environments were identified mostly as the "real" world or a set of non-agent applications. In this contribution, we widen the perspective on the environment for systematically considering also mixed forms. We identify, analyze, and characterize the interesting application domains for MAS paying special attention to the different kind of environments they are situated in and related to. Consequently, we take into account the three different (usual) dimensions allowing to characterize these kind of domains: the environment, the agent and the interaction perspective. The environment cannot be seen as either physical or software-based, but also mixtures of "worlds" must be considered. As a consequence, the characterization of agents must be more fundamental based on its nature (artificial or human). Interaction as the third dimension, may happen on different levels of complexity – richness and intensity – ranging from interaction from simply being situated in the same environment to addressing the question how the mixed environment impacts on agent behavior that is based/resulting in sophisticated sociability. In this contribution, we will not formally define those dimensions, but by discussing different application domains in terms of those three dimensions and analyzing how the environment can support them, we address the first category of challenges adapting the treatment of the environment to modern (and future) developments.

The rest of the paper is structured as follows: in next section, the three different dimensions that we have introduced to classify the application domains, are detailed, Sect. 3 presents the different domains commented in the paper, positioning them in the three commented dimensions. After that, the following section, deals with the different levels of support that the environment, as a first class entity, gives to the different parts of the space given by the three presented dimensions. Lastly, some conclusions and some glimpse at the future are commented.

2   Analysis Dimensions

To drive these considerations beyond visionary literature, we analyze existing proposals taking a multi-agent system perspective. We then consider three dimensions that are worth to compare and position each virtual environment domain with respect to the other: types of *environment*, types of *agents* interacting in these environments and types of *interaction*, taking place in the system. One can easily imagine that the possible types in each dimension are more than the ones presented in these not-so-far-away futuristic scenarios. Hereby the interaction among the entities is actually the decisive factor in what concerns the intensity, mode and richness of the resulting worlds: how the environment mediates the interaction, who may interact with whom along which relation or role. In the following, we characterize the types in each of these three dimensions. We then analyze existing approaches and domains along them in Sect. 3.

2.1 Environment Dimension

The dimension related to the environment is directly accessed by systems . It distinguishes *physical* from *virtual* environments. The *physical* environment refers to the environment which is part of our actual reality, in which we, as humans, interact. There is no clear definition of *virtual environment* in the literature. As we can see in the existing approaches, "virtual environment" may refer to "a high-end user-computer interface that involves real-time simulation and interaction through multiple sensorial channels" [5].

In this paper, virtual environment subsumes two definitions according to the *reference* that the virtual environment may have to another environment. While the *simulated environment* has a reference environment, the *synthetic environment* may not refer to any other environment [12].

- The simulated environment makes only sense as a mapping from a physical environment that it sufficiently precisely represents. Interaction in such environment between simulated agents refers to the way agents of the physical environment interact with the reference environment [11].
- On the contrary, the usefulness of a synthetic environment is not determined by how well it matches another reference environment. It is judged by how much fun it is to interact with such an environment or how well it supports interaction between humans, agents and other entities.

Thus, virtual environments not necessarily refer to a physical environment example, but focus on user interaction, immersion and imagination (the so called *Virtual Reality Triangle* or i^3).

Considering social networks, the need for characterizing "social" environments emerges. They form an abstraction from environments with explicit spatial dimensions by focussing on relations between agents. Space and spatial distance - real or virtual - plays no role. We do not explicitly handle this type of environment, but subsume it under synthetic environments as it may not just reproduce relationships between humans, but enable the establishment of new ones. Additionally it needs a matter for manifestation such as an environment created by facebook or similar.

From the analysis conducted in this section, as we can see in Table 1, the range of types for the environment dimension could be: *physical*, *synthetic* or *simulated*. Let's note that *virtual* subsumes both *synthetic* and *simulated* types.

2.2   Agent Dimension

The second dimension to characterize the considered approaches is the nature of the agents interacting in the system. Traditionally, one may find descriptive values along "passive - active", "reactive, deliberative, cognitive", etc. According to the existing approaches, the types that we will use in this dimension fits to the range of the environment dimension. Hereby, we characterize only agents and let aside objects, resources that are part of the environment. Thus, possible types for an agent along this second dimension are: *human, robot* or *digital*. As humans, robots possess a (physical) body that allows physical interaction, i.e. interaction in the physical environment. Robots exist and interact primarily physically. There is a tendency for equipping them with displays for interaction with humans - e.g. the Giraff robot, which is basically "skype on wheel" (http://www.giraff.org). As in the environment dimension, *digital* subsumes *simulated* agent and *synthetic* agent.

Both types of agents point to an entity that exists in the digital world. Both may refer or not to an entity in the physical world (human or robot). Simulated agents can be Virtual Characters which are often humanoid. Believability of their behavior is an important measure for their quality. Synthetic agents are created for a particular aim - for example a fully digital playing partner for children such as a Tamagotchi. In an extreme form, a synthetic agent may not be explicitly embodied, but may e.g. deliberately display information at a particular location in the virtual world. The overall system may contain different forms of agents at the same time.

Thus, we may identify the range of types for the agent dimension: *human, robot* or *digital*. Let's note that here also *digital* subsumes both *synthetic* and *simulated* types.

2.3   Interaction Dimension

As for agents, characterizing "interaction" is also not done for the first time. See for instance a quite comprehensive example in [8] of kinds of interaction in terms of relations, protocols or organizations that are proposed in the MAS domain. Knowing that background, we are aware of the simplification when we just consider how intensive and on what level of abstraction agents interact with each other and with their shared environment. We identify in the existing approaches a type that we denote as *indirect* (or stigmergy) in which each agent just interacts with its environment. For reasons of limited space, we use this term *"indirect"* to refer to any kind of interaction based on the use of the environment. The next value is what we call *direct* or *message passing* interaction that concern the exchange of messages between agents. In principle, we call *social* the other extreme type in this dimension: one agent knows and intensively interacts with a large set of other agents, if not all others, being aware (and maybe participating) to the social dimension (e.g. organisation) sustaining the agents participating to its environment.

The set of types for the interaction dimension comprises thus: *indirect, direct, social.* As can be noticed, this dimension is of a different nature than the two other dimensions. This dimension doesn't take value in terms of reality or virtuality. It characterizes the existence or non existence of interaction between the entities to interact in the shared environment. However, we still can identify references to the real world in the sense that the kind of interaction that could be installed among the agents can refer or not to some kind of interaction that may exist among the humans or robots that they are simulating. In environments in which humans are immersed, at least the humans may not be able to interact ignoring the social context in which they are embedded. There is clear relation between complexity of an agent and complexity of the interaction that this agent may come up. The first two – interaction based on environment manipulation (indirect) and based on message exchange (direct) – form lower level characterizations based on the mean of interaction. The category of social may be technically reduced to those two forms, nevertheless we assume that this categorization is admissible focusing on the intensity and richness of interaction.

3   Domain Classification

In this section, we structure our analysis of the domains according to the environment dimension presented in the previous section. This organisation is just here to stress the fact that domains follow a smooth path from physical to virtual types. The following table (cf. Table 1) shows a representation of the three dimensions presented above, locating in the 3D corresponding space several application domains where multi-agent systems can be/are used. In this section, we use the coordinate system (a,e,i) to locate each of the corresponding domains. When a coordinate is equal to 'all', we mean that all the values of the coordinate can be considered. After a tabular overview, we shortly justify our characterizations.

3.1   Domains Situated in Physical Environment

Pure Physical Reality domains (e=physical - a=human - i=all) refers to the "ordinary" real world in which humans are living, that means a domain where humans intensively interact with each other (i.e. interaction type of sociability embraces all values of this dimension) and the physical environment.

Robotic domains (e=physical - a=robot - i=all) refers to domains where only robots populate the relevant sectors of the physical environment. Interactions may take all three forms. This might be surprising on the first sight, as with applications consisting of multiple robots often swarm robots are associated. These swarm multi-robot systems form examples based on intensive, yet simple stigmergic interaction. An impressing example is the Swarmanoid project [14], in which a robot swarm's task is to locate and fetch a particular book from a high shelf. Each robot can just perform simple tasks, but based on intensive, carefully designed stigmergic interaction the overall swarm could achieve the task. One may also find complex, social interactions in robotic domains: for

Table 1. Domains classifications according to environment, agent and interaction dimensions. Let's note that even if the right column appears to be redundant as it has the same value for all rows, we intentionally kept it here as it is not intuitively clear that all domains contain all forms of interactions.

Domain	Environment	Agent	Interaction
Pure physical reality	Physical	Human	All
Robotic	Physical	Robot	All
Humans-robots system	Physical	Human, robot	All
Ambient intelligence	Physical, synthetic	Human, robot	All
Data-driven simulations	Physical, simulated	Human, robot, digital agent	All
Situated Multi-agent systems	Physical, virtual	Digital agent, robot	All
Augmented reality	Physical, virtual	Human	All
Mirror world	Physical, virtual	Human, digital agent, robot	All
Multi-agent based simulations	Simulated	Digital agent	All
Interactive simulations	Virtual	Human, digital agent	All
Virtual reality	Virtual	Human, digital agent	All
Social networks	Synthetic	Human	All

example in RoboCup applications multiple robots form complex organizations with corresponding interactions for achieving a shared goal. This can be clearly characterized as social interaction.

Humans-Robots System are domains (e=physical - a=human, robot - i=all) where humans may participate in shared activities or otherwise interact with robots. This raises challenges for overall system design as the autonomous robots may need to be aware of what humans are doing (for a general overview of human activity recognition see [1]). Interaction with one human for shared activity works quite well, interacting with multiple humans is still a challenge.

3.2 Domains Situated in Physical-Virtual Environment

Ambient Intelligence is a domain (e=physical, synthetic - a=human, robot - i=all) where the environment is real and the agents are human and robots. An important form of robots for this kind of domain are sensors. No matter whether they are mobile or stationary, sensors are physical hardware placed in the physical world. Thus, we subsume them under robotic agents. Sensors may be embedded into a control loop for regulating environmental features, or may be organized in sensor networks for producing complex information necessary to support human activity or well-being. In this domain, the task of the robots is to support the human by adapting the environment and providing access to different functionalities in it, by eventually interacting through a synthetic environment. Examples are agents in charge of adjusting temperature and light intensity for individual humans. Depending on the task and the number of agents, there might be intensive interaction between the agents, but the main focus is on supporting the human.

Data-Driven Simulations refers to domains (e=physical, simulated - a=human, robot, digital agent - i=all) that connect simulation to reality based on sensor data integrated during simulation runtime. Thus, environment is basically real, but simulations are done for extrapolating the current environmental state, for example for supporting decision making about the current state. An example could be found in the OLSIM[1] system: the highway network of North-Rhine Westfalia – a densely populated area in Germany – is connected to a simulation of relevant highway segment via sensors that count vehicles entering those highways. Every time a vehicle enters a ramp an agent is generated in a simulation and vice-versa for agents leaving the segment. A traveler can access the simulated (predicted) congestion via Internet for making decisions about routing. As for all kinds of simulations, the reproduced interaction may eventually range from simple to complex.

Situated Multi-Agent Systems as a domain that is established (e=physical, virtual - a=digital agent - i=all) and concerns all those multi-agent systems operating in some physical environment, where a virtual environment is introduced in order to provide some functionality concerning either the agent access to the physical layer, or agent coordination. A main example is the decentralized control of AGV case proposed by D. Weyns et al. [21].

Augmented Reality (e=physical, virtual - a=human - i=all) is characterized by an environment, but populated with human agents and artificial ones [15]. Introduced the term "Mixed Reality" to describe a continuum of environments from fully physical via augmented reality and augmented virtuality to fully virtual environments. In Augmented Reality the main part of the environment is real. This mix of virtual and physical environment enables new forms of interaction in the overall system mixing for example haptic experiences or smells with virtual information displays. This is interesting not only for entertainment (see for example the INVIZIMALS[2] game), but also information services depending on physical location.

Mirror Worlds (e=physical, virtual - a=human, digital, robot - i=all) – as defined in [7] – can be conceived as an agent-based extension of augmented and mixed reality. Both human and artificial agents inhabit an environment which is both physical and augmented of a digital virtual layer (the mirror), coupled to the physical one. Mirroring is given by the fact that physical things, which can be perceived and acted upon by humans in the physical world, have a digital counterpart (or augmentation, extension) in the mirror, so that they can be observed and acted upon by agents. Vice versa, an entity (artifact) in the Mirror World that can be perceived and acted upon by software agents may have a

---

[1] http://www.autobahn.nrw.de/index_e.html.

[2] http://invizimals.eu.playstation.com/.

physical appearance (or extension) in the physical world – e.g. augmenting it, in terms of Augmented Reality – so that it can be observed and acted upon by humans (by means of e.g. smart-glasses). This implies a form of *coupling*, such that an action on an object in the physical world causes some kind of changes in entities in the mirror, perceivable then by software agents. Vice versa an action by agents on an artifact in the Mirror World can have an effect on things in the physical world, perceivable by people.

3.3 Domains Situated into Virtual Environment

Multi-Agent Based Simulations is a well established domain (e=simulated - a=digital agent - i=all) in the research community. It clearly forms an extreme domain since environment is virtual (i.e. simulated), agents are artificial (i.e. simulated), interactions are defined following observable or hypothesed interactions in the given reference system possibly embracing all three values of this dimension.

Interactive Simulations refers to a domain (e=virtual - a=human, digital agent - i=all) that generalizes from the pure multi-agent simulation approaches and raises multiple sub-domains: the environment is virtual, one or more agents may be human, others may be artificial. The environment may refer to the real world or may be completely synthetic. Interaction between humans and simulated entities may happen on different levels of immersion. A human may perform a simulated biological experiment or may be immersed in a flight simulator. Usually some (more or less realistic) physics are simulated, capturing how the environment (including other agents) reacts to user actions. In multiagent simulation, participatory approaches (such as [3]) play a more and more important role mainly in cases in which reliable empirical data is missing for model development. Another motivation for immersing humans into multi-agent simulations can be found if stakeholders should be supported in learning about possible system responses. Hereby, human stakeholders are involved or even immersed in role-playing game-like simulations, yet those approaches mainly .

Virtual Reality defines a domain (e=virtual - a=human, digital agent - i=all) that is nearby interactive simulations and multi-agent based simulations: the environment is virtual, it may include humans and artificial agents - more humans than in multiagent-based simulations and interactive simulations. The environment may refer more to a real environment than in interactive simulations, yet without the need of reproducing a particular original system. Again, we include also here entertainment simulations (e.g. games, "Second Life" where humans interact with other humans and artificial agents in a shared immersive virtual environment). This domain includes not only the Metaverse of Neal Stephenson, but also the Cyberspace of William Gibson. The original idea was to differentiate between Virtual Reality and Cyberspace, by having the former as an individual experience, and the last as a social one. We selected "virtual" as the value for the environment capturing both synthetic and simulated - so the environment in the Virtual Reality domain may have a reference to a real environment or not, however the stringency of connecting the environment to an original one may not be as strong as in the simulation applications. Here, whether the environment is interesting or believable is more important than its validity.

Social Networks form a domain (e=virtual - a=human - i=all) where social relations are manifested. It is the facebook / twitter environment in which virtual space is abstracted into a (dynamic) network of relationships. Social reality might be combined with synthetic environments or analyzed with simulated environments. Yet it is something clearly different from virtual environments as it maps explicit real relations ("follows", "friend-of") into a artificial structure and provides meeting opportunities that are potentially decoupled from concurrent behavior/interaction. It could be seen as a manifestation of social interactions.

4   Levels of Support by the Environment

In the global picture built in the previous section showing the importance of the environment in each of the analyzed domain, the level of support of this environment as a first-class entity can be different depending on the specific point or subspace that we consider. In general, three main support levels can be identified [20]:

- *deployment support level*, which is the simplest level in which the environment just introduces a notion of action, perception, observability, without any kind of modularisation;
- *abstraction support level*, where the environment introduces first class logical abstraction to modularize actions/perceptions and to encapsulate functionalities;
- *interaction mediation support level*, where the environment has a role in enabling and ruling/governing/*mediating* the interaction and communication among the agents.

4.1   Levels of Support for Digital Agents or Robots

In literature, these levels have been identified and used to analyse mostly systems considering only artificial agents on the agent type dimension. In our picture, relevant examples for that case are:

- *pure virtual environment, digital agents only* — This is the case of agent-based and MAS-based simulation. Here the virtual environment has the fundamental role of modelling the space of interaction among agents, at the proper level of abstraction.
- *physical + virtual environment, digital agents + robots* — This is the case of *situated MAS*, which is one of the reference cases on which the levels in [20] have been defined. As widely discussed in literature, the integration of physical and virtual environment can be effectively exploited to support in particular agent coordination.

4.2   Levels of Support for Human Agents

The role of the environment support for systems considering only human agents on the agent type dimension has been discussed in the context of cognitive sciences and human socio-psychological fields. Relevant examples in our picture are:

- *physical environment, human agents* — This is the *pure physical reality case*. In this case, Activity Theory and Distributed Cognition focus the importance of physical objects and tools in supporting human activities and problem solving. Even if it is not about the agent environment, the three levels can be adopted as well. The deployment levels refer to those cases in which the physical environment is not specifically designed in order to support human activities; it is just used as the neutral place where some activity takes place. The abstraction support level occurs when the physical environment is specifically conceived and designed to mediate and support human activities; an example is given by any kind of *tool* (e.g. a hammer) used to do some kind of job. The interaction mediation support level happens when the design is explicitly conceived to help the cooperation and communication of humans. Examples include blackboards, cell phones, post-its, etc.
- *virtual environment, human agents* — This is the case of *Social Networks*, for instance. In this case, the tools depicted in the previous point are greatly enhanced by the availability of the information technology, that makes it possible to create more powerful social media that allow to augment human communication and interaction besides time-space barriers. As a distinguishing feature, these tools implement mechanisms to make communication indirect and persistent, so as to create emergent/self-organizing/stigmergic form of coordination and cooperation.
- *physical + virtual environment, human agents* — This is the case of *Augmented Reality*. The integration of the physical environment has the effect to strongly couple and ground the first-class environment abstraction layer with physical artifacts of the reality, augmenting their functionalities. Or, to situate the virtual entities defined in the virtual environment in some physical location. This can be exploited to define a whole new space of spatially-based functionalities and services, as those that are typically provided by mobile augmented reality applications [16].

4.3   Levels of Support for Human, Digital or Robot Agents

Finally, a less explored subspace – in particular in the environments for MAS literature – concerns those cases in which human and artificial agents (robot or digital ones) are both characterising the agent type dimension. Two main cases are the following:

- *virtual environment, human + digital agents* — This includes *Virtual Reality* as well as Intelligent Virtual Environments [5], where virtual environments are inhabited by both humans – represented by some kind of avatars – and artificial agents, both perceiving and acting on the same shared environment. The virtual environment in this case provides functionalities in terms of abstraction, by allowing human users to physically represent and perceive virtual entities, which may be designed to encapsulate different kinds of functionalities, services. Besides, these entities can be exploited also to ease the communication/coordination among avatars, in particular with other human users that may be physically located in a different place, as well as with purely digital agents part the same world.

- *physical + virtual environment, human + digital agents* — This is the case of *Mirror Worlds* and the environment support can be conceived by integrating synergically what discussed for Augmented Reality and situated MAS. In this case, the abstraction support level provided by the environment is twofold: from the artificial agents point of view, it provides a way to represent, perceive and interact with physical things, represented and abstracted by artifacts; from the human agents point of view, the virtual environment provides a way to *augment* the physical world with further functionalities, as well as to empower humans with further cognitive/sensing/acting capabilities. The interaction mediation support level in this case allows for designing environment-meditated coordination and cooperative strategies – possibly self-organising, emerging – that exploit both the physical and digital layer, towards new forms of *Behavioural-Implicit Communication* and stigmergy [6,19].

5   Conclusions or What is Waiting Ahead of Us

In the last years, there has been a growing importance of the environment as a first class entity in the developing of MAS. The increasing maturity of more and more feasible and advanced technology in the area of Virtual Reality has lead to a growing interest in Virtual Environments in both, society and research. As a reflection of this, one can also observe an increasing number of applications of MAS using this technology creating and enabling new environments for the different forms of MAS.

In this chapter, we have extended the idea of the environment as a first class entity for explicitly integrating Virtual Environments and as a consequence mixing the context that they may provide with other types of environments, physical, simulated or synthetic. Before discussing what the explicit treatment can offer for those application areas, we had to locate them clearly in an overall conceptual framework widening the perspective beyond the original environment for multiagent systems idea. From that point of view we analysed environments in different forms together with the overall system application context. We characterized the latter in terms of types of agents and richness and intensity of interaction. We classified various examples of application domains along those dimensions indicating how the environment impacts the overall setup. The contribution of this chapter can be seen in the clear characterization of systems with a wider perspective beyond environments for agents. In the same way software agents, robots and humans can interact in one environment also environments for those diverse and heterogeneous multiagent systems can be of different (also mixed) types. Having a look at science fiction literature and the environment concepts authors have foreseen, may serve as a source of inspiration for setups that once were visionary, but now become more and more reality.

Starting from our discussion in Sect. 4 on what level of support can be expected from the environment in the relevant coordinates/cases, future work in this research area will focus on developing not only frameworks for implementing these kind of applications. Formalized, unifying meta-models, methodologies, and eventually developing toolkits to support the designer to create and manage these applications will clearly help to enable future useful applications beyond what we are able to realize now.

Acknowledgments. This work is partially supported by the Spanish government grant MINECO/FEDER TIN2012-36586-C03-01 and Valencian Government Project PROMETEOII/2013/019.

References

1. Aggarwal, J.K., Ryoo, M.S.: Human activity analysis: a review. ACM Comput. Surv. **43**(3), 16:1–16:43 (2011)
2. Argente, E., Boissier, O., Carrascosa, C., Fornara, N., McBurney, P., Noriega, P., Ricci, A., Sabater-Mir, J., et al.: The role of the environment in agreement technologies. AI Rev. **39**(1), 21–38 (2013)
3. Barreteau, O., et al.: Our companion modelling approach. J. Artif. Soc. Soc. Simul. **6**(1), 1–6 (2003)
4. Boissier, O., Bordini, R.H., Hübner, J.F., Ricci, A., Santi, A.: Multi-agent oriented programming with jacamo. Sci. Comput. Program. **78**(6), 747–761 (2013)
5. Burdea, G., Coiffet, P.: Virtual Reality Technology. Wiley, New York (2003)
6. Castelfranchi, C., Pezzullo, G., Tummolini, L.: Behavioral implicit communication (BIC): communicating with smart environments via our practical behavior and its traces. Int. J. Ambient Comput. Intell. **2**(1), 1–12 (2010)
7. Castelfranchi, C., Piunti, M., Ricci, A., Tummolini, L.: AMI systems as agent-based mirror worlds: bridging humans and agents through stigmergy. In: Bosse, T. (ed.) Agents and Ambient Intelligence, Ambient Intelligence and Smart Environments, pp. 17–31. IOS Press, Amsterdam (2012)
8. Ferber, J.: Multi-Agent Systems: An Introduction to Distributed Artificial Intelligence. Addison Wesley Longman, Harlow (1999)
9. Gelernter, D.: Mirror Worlds - or the Day Software Puts the Universe in a Shoebox: How it Will Happen and What it Will Mean. Oxford University Press, New York (1992)
10. Gibson, W.: Neuromancer. Ace, New York (1984)
11. Klügl, F., Fehler, M., Herrler, R.: About the role of the environment in multi-agent simulations. In: Weyns, D., Van Parunak, H.D., Michel, F. (eds.) E4MAS 2004. LNCS (LNAI), vol. 3374, pp. 127–149. Springer, Heidelberg (2005)
12. Krueger, M.: Artificial Reality II. Addison-Wesley, New York (1991)
13. Luck, M., Aylett, R.: Applying artificial intelligence to virtual reality: intelligent virtual environments. Appl. Artif. Intell. **14**(1), 3–32 (2000)

14. Dorigo, M., Floreano, D., Gambardella, L.M., et al.: Swarmanoid: a novel concept for the study of heterogeneous robotic swarms. IEEE Robot. Autom. Mag. **20**(4), 60–71 (2013)
15. Milgram, P., Kishino, A.F.: Taxonomy of mixed reality visual displays. IEICE Trans. Inf. Syst. **E77–D(12)**, 1321–1329 (1994)
16. Olsson, T., Salo, M.: Online user survey on current mobile augmented reality applications. In: Proceedings of the 2011 10th IEEE International Symposium on Mixed and Augmented Reality, ISMAR 2011, pp. 75–84. IEEE Computer Society, Washington, DC, USA (2011)
17. Saunier, J., Balbo, F., Pinson, S.: A formal model of communication and context awareness in multiagent systems. J. Logic Lang. Inform. **23**(2), 219–247 (2014)
18. Stephenson, N.: Snow Crash. Bantam Books, New York (1992)
19. Tummolini, L., Castelfranchi, C.: Trace signals: the meanings of stigmergy. In: Weyns, D., Van Parunak, H.D., Michel, F. (eds.) E4MAS 2006. LNCS (LNAI), vol. 4389, pp. 141–156. Springer, Heidelberg (2007)
20. Weyns, D., Omicini, A., Odell, J.: Environment as a first class abstraction in multiagent systems. Auton. Agent. Multi-Agent Syst. **14**(1), 5–30 (2007)
21. Weyns, D., Schelfthout, K., Holvoet, T., Lefever, T.: Decentralized control of e'gv transportation systems. In: Proceedings of the Fourth International Joint Conference on Autonomous Agents and Multiagent Systems, pp. 67–74. ACM (2005)
22. Weyns, D., Schumacher, M., Ricci, A., Viroli, M., Holvoet, T.: Environments in multiagent systems. Knowl. Eng. Rev. **20**(2), 127–141 (2005)

Organizational and Holonic Modelling of a Simulated and Synthetic Spatial Environment

Stéphane Galland[(✉)] and Nicolas Gaud

Université Bourgogne Franche-Comté, UTBM, IRTES EA7274,
90010 Belfort, France
{stephane.galland,nicolas.gaud}@utbm.fr
http://www.multiagent.fr

Abstract. Multiagent-based simulations enable us to validate different use-case scenarios in a lot of application domains. The idea is to develop a realistic virtual environment to test particular domain-specific procedures. This paper presents a holonic model — hierarchy of agents — of a simulated physical environment for the simulation of crowds in virtual 3D buildings. The major contributions of this paper are the agentization of the environment model to support multilevel simulation, and the definition of energy-based indicators to control the execution of the model. Finally, the application of the model inside an airport terminal is presented. It permits to validate the principles of the models and the corresponding computational gains.

Keywords: Multi-agent simulation · Holonic multiagent systems · Multilevel simulation · Simulated environment · Physic environment · Virtual environment · SARL language

1 Introduction

The models for urban simulation may be classified in four main families: macroscopic, mesoscopic, microscopic and multilevel simulation models. Macroscopic simulation models are based on the deterministic relationships of the flow, speed, and density of population (peoples or traffic stream) [23]. The simulation in a macroscopic model takes place on a region-by-region basis rather than by tracking individuals. Macroscopic simulation models were originally developed to model traffic into distinct transportation networks, such as freeways, corridors (including freeways and parallel arterials), surface-street grid networks, and rural highways. This approach enables the simulation of very large population with a small relative computational cost. However, due to its high-level of representation, the results are not very accurate and strongly related to masses of population. Microscopic simulation models are concerned with the movement of people on the basis of dynamic individual behaviors. Behaviors may be based on a large scope of models such as the intelligent driver and the lane changing models to

© Springer International Publishing Switzerland 2015
D. Weyns and F. Michel (Eds.): E4MAS 2014 – 10 years later, LNAI 9068, pp. 147–169, 2015.
DOI: 10.1007/978-3-319-23850-0_10

represent the drivers, or a force-based model for the pedestrians [10,17,35,36,46]. These models are effective in assessing the conditions of congestion and saturation, the study of the topological configuration, and evaluating the impact of individual behavior on the system. However, these models are difficult to implement and costly in term of computation time, and they can be difficult to calibrate. Mesoscopic models combine the properties of the microscopic and macroscopic models. For example, they may focus on the entities in the system by using models that do not distinguish the individuals from each other, such as particle models [44], by grouping the individuals within higher-level entities such as groups of pedestrians [19], or by using a discrete model of the simulated environment, such as the cellular automata [25]. Multilevel models support different levels of simulation (macro, meso, micro). Different points-of-view exist on the means to integrate these different levels into a single multilevel model. Two models, one micro and one macro for instance, may be run in sequence, and the output of one is the input of the other [5]. The multilevel model may also be able to select the best simulation level dynamically, according to specific indicators: the more the computer has available resources, the more the selected level tends to be the micro one [20]. This paper is related to this last type of multilevel simulation.

In this paper, authors focus on multiagent-based simulation, and more specifically on the modeling of the simulated environment. As stated by [51], the environment is an important part of a multiagent system that should be studied in details. In the rest of this paper, we focus on the *simulated physical environment* for the microscopic and multilevel multiagent-based simulation of crowds, as illustrated by Fig. 1. The pedestrians' behaviors are not detailed in this paper. Two main common problems may occur during the execution of the simulated environment model: (i) the computational cost may be too huge, and thus incompatible with efficient response constraints; and (ii) many times the executed algorithm is too complex and too expensive according to the topology of the crowd and obstacles; simpler and faster algorithms could be used in place with an equivalent accuracy. Several models and platforms were proposed to address these issues: GAMA [22], Breve [26], FLAME, etc. According to our knowledge, none of them is providing a holistic multilevel model of the simulated environment including the hierarchical spatial decomposition, the management of the transitions between levels, the interrelationships among the environmental components and their associated dynamics.

This paper introduces an agent-oriented multilevel model of the environment for a multiagent-based simulation. Note that in the rest of this paper, the term "agent" refers to the agents, which are supporting the environment model; in opposition to the "application agents," which represent the pedestrians (in our airport simulation, or the vehicles in traffic simulation). Why is an agent-oriented model used for the simulated environment? It permits to adapt the overall simulated environment's behavior dynamically, during its execution. *The use of agents enables to evaluate and to predict the computational costs of the algorithms locally, and to select the one, which is fitting the constraints in time*

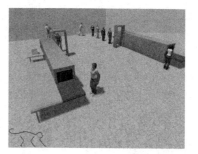

Fig. 1. Screenshots of the Airport simulation, provided by the Simulate® commercial tool.

and in quality. A specific type of agent is considered: the holon[1] [8,41]. Why are the holons used for the simulated environment model? They enable to support the intrinsic hierarchical nature of the simulated physical environment and its dynamics. This agent-oriented model is qualified of holonic, and defined according to the CRIO metamodel and the associated holonic framework[2] [8]. CRIO is an organizational metamodel enabling the hierarchical modeling of a system in terms of organizations and roles.

This paper is structured as follows: Sect. 2 presents the organizational model of the simulated environment. Section 3 describes the agents/holons that are supporting the environment model. Section 4 presents the energy-based indicators that are involved in the multilevel simulation. Section 5 introduces a basic implementation of the holonic environment model using the SARL programming language. Section 6 describes the application of our environment model on the simulation of an airport. Section 7 relates the content of this paper to existing works. Section 8 links our works to the identified challenges related to the environment. And finally, Sect. 9 concludes this paper, and provides perspectives of this work and new challenges.

2   Organizational Model of the Simulated Environment

Urban systems are typical examples of complex systems. Urban simulations quickly require important computational resources if the user want to maintain a high level of accuracy. As shown in [7], the simulated environment is often distributed into a collections of places to easily distribute computational costs. A place is a semi-closed spatial area bounded by static objects (usually walls). Each place may have connections called portals, with its neighbor places. They are used to ease the interaction between two adjacent spaces. They also permit to use structural simulated environment models such as Potentially Visible

---

[1] Holon: an agent composed of agents, which can be seen as an atomic entity from its outside, and an entity composed by sub-holons from its inside, at the same time.

[2] The CRIO metamodel and the holonic framework are outside the scope of this paper. See http://www.aspecs.org or [8] for details.

Set [7] for improving the computation of the visual perceptions of the application agents. Places are basically defined a priori by the designer of the simulation. They generally correspond to the structural decomposition of the simulated environment with connected graphs [12,48]. Entities are objects inside the simulated environment, and are located in a single place through a dedicated data-structure (usually a spatial tree or a spatial grid, see Fig. 2).

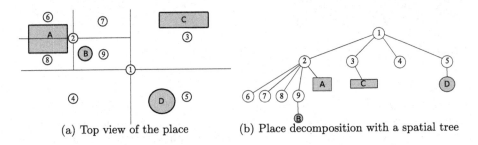

(a) Top view of the place   (b) Place decomposition with a spatial tree

Fig. 2. Decomposition of a place in areas with a spatial tree

To simulate large and complex worlds, it is important to support unbalanced places in terms of entities they are containing. Indeed, the difference of population coverage by the places may cause lower global performances to the simulator. To overcome this problem, places are decomposed in turn into a collection of dynamically built zones. In contrast to the statically defined decomposition, these zones are built during the simulation process according to the population density in each zone.

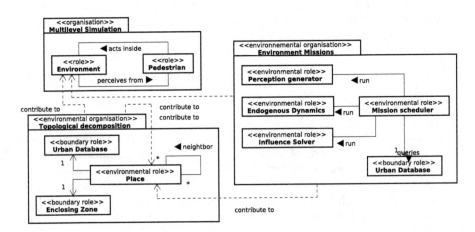

Fig. 3. Organizations and roles of the simulated environment, using the formalism defined in [8], and on http://www.aspecs.org.

Figure 3 shows the various organizations that compose the proposed environment model. In a global point of view, the `Multilevel Simulation` organization defines the overall simulation system according to two main roles. The `Pedestrian` role is played by the agents, which are participating in the simulation, *i.e.* the pedestrians, and describes their corresponding behaviors. The `Environment` role is played by any agent or group of agents that is responsible for the overall behavior of the simulated physical environment. Interactions between them are based on the influence-reaction model [29]; and on the computation of the pedestrian's perceptions [17]. Each player of the `Environment` role must have the capacity [8] to compute the perceptions for each pedestrian usually, by exploring a spatial data-structure (see Fig. 2). The `Environment`'s players must also have the capacity to gather influences — wishes of actions — from each pedestrian.

The `Topological decomposition` organization focuses on the structure of the simulated physical environment itself. This organization provides the capacities that are required by the `Environment` role in the previous organization. The `Topological decomposition` organization can contribute to the behavior of this higher-level role. The `Topological decomposition` organization is composed of interconnected places. Each of them is responsible for the environment's missions [51] in the considered geographical space. It also manages the objects inside the zone. To realize its behavior, a `Place` role must interact with the role `Urban Database` to obtain and to update the information related to the objects inside the simulated environment.

The role `Enclosing zone` supports the multilevel modeling of the simulated environment. The organization `Topological decomposition` represents a level within the hierarchy of composition of the simulated environment. It is necessary that each level in this hierarchy has access to information dedicated to the multilevel dynamics. As a *boundary role*, the role `Enclosing zone` is responsible for providing to a place the state of the considered zone, as well as transferring the indicators and the constraints given by the upper level to the various places, which compose it, if any. All these information will be detailed later in this paper.

The organization `Environment Mission`, inspired by [51], defines the roles that are required to satisfy all the missions of the simulated environment for a specific place. An instance of this organization is supported as a group in the agents, which are playing the role `Place`. This link between the two organizations is represented by the relationship "`contribute to`" in Fig. 3.

The next step is the identification of the agents, and their behaviors, in order to obtain the agents' society, which exhibits the expecting behaviors of the organizations, that are described above.

3   Agents of the Simulated Environment

Figure 4 illustrates an instance of a society of agents, which may execute the simulated environment behavior. The key point is to determine, for each role,

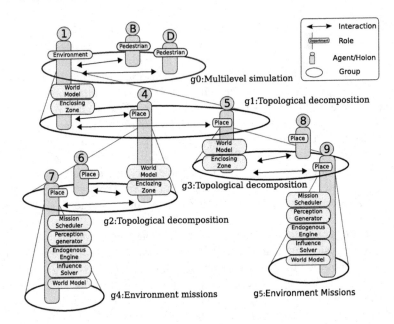

Fig. 4. Example of an agent society, which manages the simulated environment.

if a standalone agent or a group of agents[3] is playing it. When a single agent is managing an entire place, it is playing the role Place in the Environment Model. When a place needs to be split and managed by a group of agents, one of them must play the role Place in the Topological decomposition, and Mission scheduler in the Environment Mission organizations. The decision to decompose or not a place is the responsibility of the agent playing the role Place. It depends on: (i) the individual indicators, which are specific to an agent playing the role Place; and (ii) the indicators shared in the context of a group of agents, which is an instance of the organization Topological decomposition. Each agent playing the role Place can access to these indicators by interacting with the role Enclosing zone. These indicators are detailed in Sect. 4.

Figure 5 illustrates the state machine of the agents of the simulated environment. This state machine describes the composition (resp. decomposition) behavior of the agents. Events isCollapsable and isDecomposable correspond to the detection of a change from the agent situation according to the indicators described in the next section. They correspond respectively to the events of composition and decomposition.

When an agent H decides to decompose the place z associated to it, it applies the algorithm for creating sub-holons that are managing the different sub-zones of z (see Algorithm 1). A group topological decomposition is created and populated by agents playing the role Place, one for each sub-zone. The function

---

[3] Note that a holon may represent either an atomic agent or a composed agent [41].

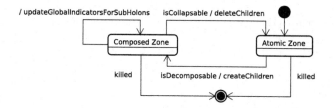

Fig. 5. State machine for the hierarchical behavior of each agent of the simulated environment

updateGlobalIndicatorsForSubAgents updates the indicators that are used by the sub-agents for their own decomposition decisions.

```
1   g := getGroup(H,"Environment missions")
2   if g ≠ nil then
3       releaseRole(H, "Mission scheduler", g)
4       releaseRole(H, "Perception generator", g)
5       releaseRole(H, "Endogenous Dynamics", g)
6       releaseRole(H, "Influence Solver", g)
7       releaseRole(H, "Urban Database", g)
8   end if
9
10  S := computeSubZonesOf(z)
11  g := createGroup("Topological decomposition")
12  requestRole(H, "Urban Database", g)
13  requestRole(H, "Enclosing Zone", g)
14  updateGlobalIndicatorsForSubAgents(H,S)
15  foreach zone in S do
16      agent := createAgentIn(H)
17      requestRole(agent, "Place", g, zone)
18  done
19  E_z := ∅
```

Algorithm 1. Algorithm for the decomposition of an agent associated to a zone of the simulated environment.

When an agent H decides that the place z should not be split, it destroys its sub-holons (see Algorithm 2). The group Topological decomposition is destroyed. A group associated to the organization Environment Missions is then created to enable the super-agent to reach its main two goals: determining the perceptions of the agents, and managing the influences from them.

Both algorithms can build, level by level and during the run-time, the hierarchical model of the simulated environment. The evaluation of the indicators

```
1   g := getGroup(H, "Topological decomposition")
2   if g ≠ nil then
3       foreach agent in getPlayers(g," Place") do
4           kill(agent)
5       done
6       releaseRole(H, "Enclosing Zone", g)
7       releaseRole(H, "Urban Database", g)
8       E_z := createSuperBodies()
9   end if
10
11  g := createGroup("Environment Missions")
12  requestRole(H, "Mission Scheduler", g)
13  requestRole(H, "Perception Generator", g)
14  requestRole(H, "Endogenous Dynamics", g)
15  requestRole(H, "Influence Solver", g)
16  requestRole(H, "Urban Database", g)
```

Algorithm 2. Algorithm for the composition of an agent associated to a zone of the simulated environment.

is performed continuously during the simulation process. The holarchy[4] of the simulated environment may change dynamically, while being influenced by the movements of the pedestrians, and by the resources (machine memory, processing resource, etc.) that are available for the simulation.

The proposed algorithms assume that the super-agent group, which is participating in the organization **Environment Missions**, has all the necessary capacities required by this organization. Each of these capabilities is the realization of one of the missions of the simulated environment. In other words, the super-agent offers a service (a capacity according to the CRIO metamodel) to simulate these missions. An alternative is the definition of sub-agents dedicated to the support of each mission of the simulated environment. The super-agent always plays the role **Mission scheduler**. However, it delegates the other missions to its sub-agents. Thus, each mission could be implemented natively by a service in each agent, or by a whole group of interacting agents. This last possibility is not detailed in this paper.

4   Indicators for the Multilevel Simulation

In this paper, authors propose three main classes of indicators for triggering the events isCollapsable and isDecomposable:

- The **mass of a zone** indicates the relative importance of a place of the simulated environment for the whole simulation. This value obviously depends

---

[4] Holarchy: a hierarchy of holons that may intersect other holarchies by sharing holons together.

on the considered scenario. For example, it may be proportional to the density of pedestrians in the place, or depends upon the presence of an immersed human user in this place.

- The **structural depth** describes the minimum or the maximum depth of the decomposition of a zone. Thus, it is possible for a role Place to restrict the depth of its topological decomposition.
- The **resource constraint** describes the limits of the available resources for a place to achieve its simulation. This constraint allows considering low-level information, close to the operating system, such as the computation time. It is possible to impose a time constraint for approaching a real-time execution. A resource constraint can also describe the limits for any type of low-level resource (memory, network bandwidth, etc.).

The mass of the object e describes the importance of e at a given instant of the simulation. More massive an object is, the more it influences the simulation results, and it consumes resources. This mass, denoted M_e is defined by Eq. 1, where w_e is the constant mass of e.

$$M_e = \begin{cases} w_e & \text{if } e \text{ is an atomic object} \\ \sum_{a \in e} w_a & \text{if } e \text{ is a composed object} \end{cases} \tag{1}$$

The mass of a zone z describes the importance of z during the simulation. It is defined by Eq. 2. More massive a place is, the more it is involved, and it influences the results for the simulation. The mass of z is proportional to the mass of the sub-places and the objects therein.

$$M_z = \alpha_z.w_z + \sum_{a \in D_z} \alpha_a.M_a + \sum_{e \in E_z} \alpha_e.w_e \tag{2}$$

D_z is the set of sub-places of z. E_z contains the objects located on z. w_z is the constant mass of z, given by the designer of the simulation model. It represents the importance of the place in the scenario. w_e is the constant mass of the object e. α_i is the weight of i (z, a and e) when it contributes to M_z. The set of weights is constrained by $\sum_{i \in \{z\} \cup D_z \cup E_z} \alpha_i = 1$.

The resource constraint R_α is imposed by the super-agent to its sub-agents. It represents the amount of available resources for the sub-agents. Its computation is based upon the use of a weight-based function, and is depending upon the mass of the sub-places. The resource constraint for a sub-agent a of the agent z is defined by:

$$R_a = (R_z - k_z) \times \frac{M_a}{\sum_{b \in D_z} M_b} \qquad \forall a \in D_z \tag{3}$$

k_z is a constant, which estimates the consumption of resources by the super-agent to run its decision-making algorithms.

4.1   Dynamics of the Simulated Environment Agents

At every instant of the simulation, the simulated environment agents evaluate the indicators described above. This evaluation determines if they should change of state: either being a manager of a decomposed place, or the manager of an atomic place.

As shown in the state machine presented in Fig. 5, each agent is facing with one of the following decisions:

Case 1: If the agent manages an atomic place, must it decompose this place and create sub-agents?
Case 2: If the agent manages a decomposed place, must it combine the sub-places, and destroy the sub-agents managing these sub-places?

In case 1, the agent can be decomposed if there are enough resources for the execution of its sub-agents. Equation 4 describes the condition that triggers the change of state of the agent (isDecomposable becomes true). A super-agent must decompose when it has sufficient resources at its disposal, or the evaluation of the consistency between simulations at the levels n and $n+1$ indicates that the super-agent does not approximate correctly the behaviors of its sub-agents, any more.

$$\left[\left(\exists a \in D_z, \left|Eg_z - Eg_a\right| > \epsilon\right) \vee \left(\forall R, R_z \geq \sum_{p \in D_z} g_R(p) + k_z\right)\right] \wedge$$
$$\left(\max_z < i \vee \min_z > i_z\right) \wedge \tag{4}$$
$$\left(E_z \neq \emptyset\right)$$

The first member of the equation evaluates the consistency of the simulation. The energies of the sub-agents are computed and compared with the energy of the super-agent. If the difference between the energies of two levels exceeds the threshold ϵ, then the super-agent's behavior does not approximate accurately its sub-agents' behaviors. The energy terms Eg_z and Eg_a are application-dependent, and are illustrated later in this paper. The second member of Eq. 4 is based on the use of the function $g_R : D_z \rightarrow \mathbb{R}$, for estimating the amount of resources that are needed for executing the simulated environment missions by the sub-agent p. This function g_R depends upon the target application. Each super-agent consumes resources for computing the various multilevel indicators, and applying the decomposition policy. This amount of consumed resources is given by the constant k_z. The constants $\min_z$ and $\max_z$ represent the minimum and maximum depths in the hierarchical decomposition of the simulated environment.

In case 2, the agent is decomposed into a set of sub-agents managing the sub-places of z, the place associated with the super-agent. This determines whether to retain its sub-agents or destroy them. This last case corresponds to a change of the state of the super-agent. A super-agent can destroy its members when it does not have enough resources at its disposal for carrying out the simulation,

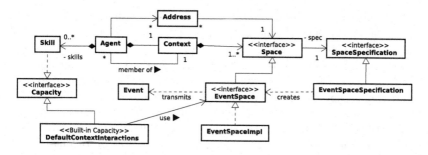

Fig. 6. Major concepts in the SARL metamodel.

and the evaluation of the consistency between the simulation results at the levels n and $n + 1$.

$$\left(\forall a \in D_z, \left| Eg_z - Eg_a \right| \leq \epsilon \right) \wedge \left(\forall R, R_z < \sum_{p \in D_z} g_R(p) + k_z \right) \wedge \min{}_z < i \quad (5)$$

If the simulation has all the required resources, it is done at the most accurate level. In other words, the agents of the level n (the deepest level in the holarchy) are always executed. However, if resources become insufficient, the simulator can identify the places that require a priority allocation of the available resources. The indicators in each super-agent are used for identifying the sub-agent's behaviors that are too approximated.

5 Implementation with SARL

In this section, the implementation with the SARL programming language of the proposed holonic environment model is discussed.

SARL[5] is a general-purpose agent-oriented programming language [40]. This language aims at providing the fundamental abstracts for dealing with concurrency, distribution, interaction, decentralization, reactivity, autonomy and dynamic reconfiguration. These high-level features are now considered as the major requirements for an easy and practical implementation of modern complex software applications. The main perspective that guided the creation of SARL is the establishment of an open and easily extensible language. Such language should thus provide a reduced set of key concepts that focuses solely on the principles considered as essential to implement a multi-agent system. In this paper, two elements of the metamodel of SARL are extensively used: Agent and Space. These two concepts are illustrated on Fig. 6.

In order to take into account heterogeneous interaction models, SARL proposes the **Space** concept, which is an *interaction space*. Space is the abstract to define *an interaction space between agents or between agents and their environment*. This concept is used for defining the interaction between an agent

---
[5] http://www.sarl.io.

and the physical simulated environment. In the SARL toolkit, a concrete default space, which propagates events, called `EventSpace` (and its implementation `EventSpaceImpl`), is proposed.

An agent is an autonomous entity having a set of skills to realize the capacities it exhibits. An agent has a set of built-in capacities considered essential to respect the commonly accepted competences of agents, such autonomy, reactivity, proactivity and social capacities. Among these capacities, the agent can incorporate a collection of behaviors that will determine its global conduct. An agent has also a default behavior directly described within its definition. *A Behavior maps a collection of perceptions represented by Events to a sequence of Actions.* In the default configuration of SARL, the various behaviors of an agent communicate using an event-driven approach. *An Event is the specification of some occurrence in a Space that may potentially trigger effects by a listener* (e.g. agent, behavior, etc.).

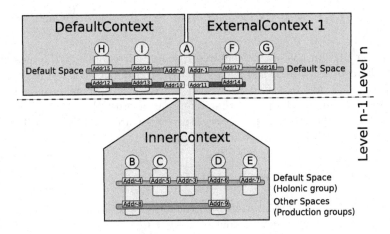

Fig. 7. A holon or a recursive agent in SARL.

In SARL, agents can be composed of other agents. Therefore, SARL agents are in fact holons that can compose each other to define hierarchical or recursive MAS, called holarchies. In order to achieve this, SARL agents are self-similar structures that compose each other via their Contexts. Each agent defines its own Context, called *Inner Context* and it is part of one or more *External Contexts*. For instance in Fig. 7, agent A is taking part of two *External Contexts* (i.e. Default Context and External Context 1) and has its own *Inner Context* where agents B, C, D, and E evolve.

6   Experiments

This section describes several experiments with the proposed simulated environment model in the simulation of an airport halls (illustrated by Fig. 1).

The airport terminal is composed of two halls, which are separated by gates. Each of these gates is a check point between the public area and the boarding area.

The behavior of the agents is decomposed on three majors activities: (i) going to check-in desk, 2/3 of the passengers need to check-in their baggages, and 1/3 have only hand-baggages; (ii) passing the check points; and (iii) boarding. Figure 8 illustrates the evolution of the number of passengers at the check points, and the average waiting time of these passengers. The first peaks correspond to the passengers that are not going at the check-in desks. The second/highers peaks corresponds to the passengers that were at the check-in desks. Figure 9 shows the evaluation of the energy according to different levels of available computational resources. When this resource critera is at 100 %, it means that the computer has enough resources to run the simulation at the finest level. When the resource is down at 60 %, it means that only 60 % of the micro-simulation may be run at the finest level. As explained in the previous section, the energy evaluation depends on the application. Equation 6 details a simple evaluation of this energy for the airport application. Intuitively, this energy assesses the quality of the generated perceptions by the simulated environment: more objects are not included in the perception, compared with the more precised possible perception, less is the quality of the perception. $p^\odot$ is the set of the perceived objects that are found when it is computed at the lowest level. $p^\ominus$ (resp. $p^\oplus$) represents the objects that are lost (resp. added) at a higher level in the holarchy. α_{po} and β_{po} are calibration variables. Our experiments shows that $\alpha_{po} = 1$ et $\beta_{po} = \frac{1}{|E|}$, where $|E|$ is the total number of entities in the airport, may be used by default.

$$
Eg_\alpha = \begin{cases} \dfrac{\alpha_{po}|p^\ominus| + \beta_{po}|p^\oplus|}{|p^\odot|} & \text{if } p^\odot \neq \emptyset \\ \alpha_{po}|p^\ominus| + \beta_{po}|p^\oplus| & \text{else} \end{cases}
\tag{6}
$$

The tests are performed with a set of 2,000 entities in the entry hall and 1,000 entities in the boarding area. Four check points are assumed to be available. The

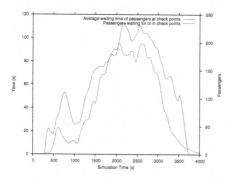

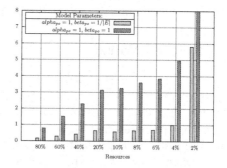

Fig. 8. Average waiting time and passenger density at the check points.

Fig. 9. Evaluation of the average energy

average computation time for one simulation step of the object-oriented model of
JASIM (the original one [17]) is 25.9 s, the equivalent agent-oriented model (proposed in this paper) takes 41.5 s with a single place for the entire area, and 8.1 s
with two places. Figure 10 illustrates a comparison of the running time of the
agent-oriented model and the original object-oriented model. The two curves have
a similar shape, due to the use of the same low-level algorithms (perception and
action computations) on the same types of data-structures (quadtree). The agent-
oriented approach provides a curve nearest to the linear curve than the original
approach. This is mainly due to a better balancing of the nodes of the two trees,
one for each place, than the balancing of the single tree of the original model.

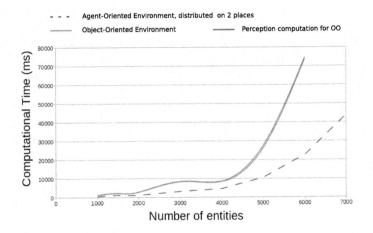

Fig. 10. Running time of the object-oriented and the agent-oriented models.

Figure 11 illustrates the running time of the agent-oriented model when the
computational resources are limited. When this resource critera is at 100 %, it
means that the computer has enough resources to run the simulation at a the
finer level. When the resource is down at 60 %, it means that only 60 % of the
micro-simulation may be run at the finer level.

7   Related Works

Our inspirations for the simulated physical environment are the models for the
simulation of crowds and traffic into virtual environments [2,11,18,31,45]. The
Artifact [37], CArtAgO [38] and smart object [46] models are also an inspiration. They propose similar interaction models between agents and objects in the
environment, and the definition of the latter.

A taxonomy of virtual environments is provided by [6]. A virtual environment
is synthetic and simulated. It may be classified according to three dimensions.
The first dimension is the type of environment: access directly to real environments, or virtual environment. The second dimension characterizes the nature

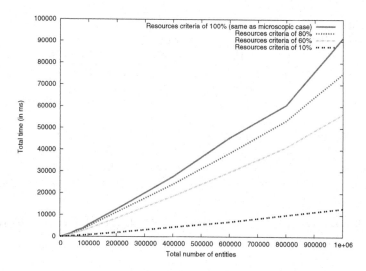

Fig. 11. Running time according to the simulated environment's levels (available resources).

of the agents interacting in the system environment: Human, physical agents (robots), or virtual agents (animats, virtual characters). The third dimension describes the models of interactions that are used by the agents. A wide range of models may be considered from stigmergy [32] to social and organizational interactions. Your model is designed for representing a simulated physic environment. It provides the mechanisms for computing the perception and managing the actions of the agents according to physic laws (gravity, collision avoidance, etc.). Our model is related to the domains "multiagent-based simulation" that is defined by [6]. In our application (including our holonic environment model), the environment and the agents are simulated. The interaction is based on the stigmergy principles. Additionally, our environment model is related to the "interactive simulation" domain [6]. Indeed, the body concept that is used in our model enables to replace any virtual agent associated with a body by a Human, who is controlling this body with the same interaction principles: the body that is controlled by the Human must emit influences [29] as the ones controlled by the virtual agents.

The problems related to the interaction between an agent, and the physical environment have been treated with different perspectives. One of the models used in our approach is the Influence-Reaction model [29]. It supports the simultaneity of the actions in an environment by considering the interactions initiated by agents as uncertain, and detecting and resolving the conflicts between the interactions. This approach can be compared to the artifact concept [37], which proposes to model the objects in the environment. They provide a set of actions that can be applied on each of them. A similar model named smart object is proposed for virtual environments [46]. In your approach, the influences related to spatial traveling, and those dedicated to trigger actions are distinct for enabling a detailed specification of the parameters for each of them. The IODA model [27] and its extension PADAWAN [28] allow modeling the interactions between the agents and the environment by assuming that every entity in the environment is an agent. Our model is partially incompatible with this vision in the context of the physical environment modeling. Indeed, the bodies of the agents are not agents.

Several organizational approaches consider the environment [14,21,33]. In the context of this paper, the key element is the modeling of the environment with a holarchy. The space concept that is provided by the SARL programming language serves as an abstract for organizational groups and spatial areas.

8   Links to Research Challenges Related to the Agent Environment

Since 10 years, research challenges are identified for the environment in multiagent systems. This section provides several links and possible answers to a couple of these challenges.

The first research challenge concerns the **difference between the agent environment and the agents that inhabit it** [51]. Based on the principle that agents are autonomous entities, and the environment does not contain autonomous entities, the question of defining what is an agent and what is not arisen. The model presented in this paper is based on the principle of separation between the mind and the body. This distinction in the context of artificial intelligence was mainly proposed in robotics [3]. Its application to multiagent systems, where there is not necessarily a physical body, has not been examined in detail in the literature [42]. However, this concept has been used occasionally to model and constrain the interactions between the agents and the environment [1,2,9,29,39,43,47]. In these works, the body is an object of the environment, with a dynamic that cannot be controlled directly by the agent. The agent environment controls the dynamics' properties of the body (position, orientation, etc.), and ensures that these properties follow the rules and laws of the Universe [30,34]. Nevertheless, every agent is able influencing its body using a mechanism such as the Influence-Reaction model [29]. Consequently, in our model, *every entity that physically exists is an object of the environment, including the bodies of the agents. Agents become the autonomous entities that control the bodies.* They are able to perceive and acts in the agent environment through their bodies. The major mode of interaction that is considered in our model is the stigmergy.

The second research challenge is related to the **taxonomy of the agent environments** [51]. In previous works, we have considered different dimensions of the agent environment: *the physic dimension, communication dimension, and social/organizational dimension* [15,16]. The first dimension concerns the environments that are represented the physical world. The second dimension contains the communication tools and infrastructures. The third dimension defines the

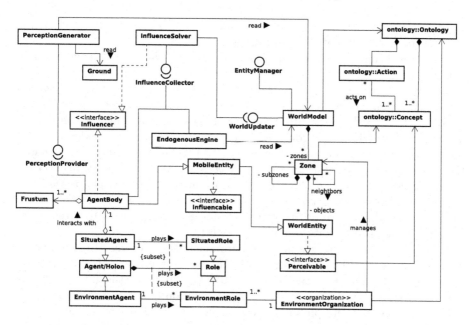

Fig. 12. Concepts for the definition of an agent environment, and the relationship between the agents and this environment [2,9,17]

social and organizational relationship between the agents. This paper treats only of the agent environments that are related to the first category. Moreover, since the agent environment is a model of the real world, it is simulated and synthetic.

The third challenge concerns **the definition of the abstracts and concepts that may be used for defining an agent environment** [24,49]. The model presented in this paper is based on a meta-model that provides abstracts for defining the topology of the agent environment, and the objects that are located in this environment [2,9,17]. Figure 12 provides an overview of the concepts that are at the heart of the holonic model presented in this paper. The physical agent environment is intrinsically hierarchical [13]. The zone concept is proposed for supporting the decomposition of this environment into interconnected sub-zones, that could be decomposed in turn. The objects (`WorldEntity`) are located in a zone of the environment. All these objects could be perceived by the agents (`Perceivable`). And, several of them could have their state changed by agent actions (`Influencable`), according to the Influence-Reaction model [29]. The agent body is an object that could be controlled by an agent (`Situated-Agent`), contains a field-of-view (`Frustum`) that could be used for computing the perception, and provides the functions for emitting influences in the agent environment. In the context of this paper, the dynamics of the agent environment are managed by specific agents (`EnvironmentAgent`), including the internal processes related to the physical agent environment (`EndogenousEngine`). These agents are responsible for supporting the missions of the environments defined in [50,51]. They are members of a holarchy (see Sect. 2) for supporting the hierarchical nature of the physical environment.

The **handling of the interferences between the agents' actions** is a research challenge [24]. In the context of a simulated agent environment, *the Influence-Reaction model* [29] *provides the framework for detecting and solving the conflicts among the influences – uncertain actions – given by the agents.* Unfortunately, the Influence-Reaction model does not give a detailed model for detecting and solving these conflicts. In our agent environment model, the laws of the Universe are known, and correspond to the Newtow laws. Consequently, the *influences are forces when they describe a motion, and action triggers for executing specific actions on the objects,* e.g. pushing a button. *A physic engine is used for computing the reactions of the agent environment related to the motion of the objects* [4]. This approach enables our agent environment to preserve its integrity, which is one of its responsibilities [51].

The second responsibility of the environment is **ensuring the locally of the perception and the actions** [51]. *The perception mechanism is based on a field-of-view* (named `Frustum` in Fig. 12). The shape of the field-of-view is defined by geometrical elements that have a position relative to the position of the agent's body in the physical environment. This definition ensures a local perception for the agents. In our model, *the actions are local since they are always related to an object of the physical agent environment: move the object, do an action on the object.*

The environment includes a broad diversity of logical functionalities. The **3-layer model** was proposed for structuring them [51]. The first layer is dedicated

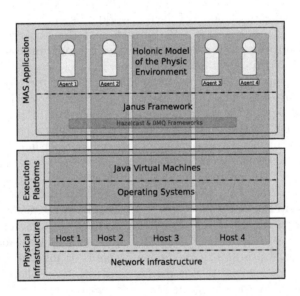

Fig. 13. The 3-layer model with the holonic environment model, and the JANUS framework

to the MAS application. It is composed by the agents, the agent environment, and the MAS framework. The second layer contains the middleware and the operating system. The third layer is related to the infrastructure definition (hosts, network infrastructure, etc.). The works presented in this paper focus of the first layer, as it is illustrated by Fig. 13. Indeed, a model of the agent environment is proposed. This model is implemented in the SARL language[6]. And, the resulting MAS runs on the JANUS framework[7]. This framework supports the distribution of the MAS application over a computer network by using the Hazelcast and 0MQ libraries. According to the specifications of the SARL language, the agents are naturally distributed, and are designed accordingly. The agents are not aware of the means that are used for implementing the distribution by the MAS framework.

The last challenge is related to the **need of a specific language for describing the agent environment** [24]. In the context of this paper, no answer is given to this challenge. However, our experiences in the modeling of the dimensions of the environments with the SARL language give a partial answer [15,16]. It is possible to describe the dynamics of the physic and communication dimensions of the agent environment. Unfortunately, it is still difficult to describe the topology of this environment. *We consider that a specific language is still needed for describing the agent environment.* This language may be based on the works done for Artifact [37] and CArtAgO [38], for instance.

9 Conclusion

Multiagent-based simulations enable us to validate different use-case scenarios in a lot of application domains. The idea is to develop a realistic virtual/simulated environment to test particular domain-specific procedures. This paper presents an agent-oriented and multilevel model of a situated simulated environment for the simulation of a crowd in a virtual $3D$ building. The major contributions in this paper are, in one hand, an agent-oriented model of the simulated physical environment, based on the holarchy, and on the other hand, a collection of energy-based indicators for evaluating the accuracy of the multilevel simulation. The model is successfully applied to the simulation of two airport halls. These experiments permit to evaluate the impact of the multilevel simulation on the simulation results, and the gain in terms of computational cost.

The energy formula presented within this paper may be generalized to become application-independent. One possible direction is to provide formula for classes of simulated environments, which may be used to build applications. We consider that the energy indicators may be interesting to distribute the agents other a computer network also. In this paper, we propose to use energy-based indicators. Other types of indicators may be used in place to obtain accurate evaluations: $\mathbb{Z}$ function... Finally, the proposed model may be applied on large-scale systems to evaluate the approximation introduced by our multilevel model.

---

[6] http://www.sarl.io.

[7] http://www.janusproject.io.

Our model must also be compared to existing multiagent simulation frameworks (GAMA, MatSIM, FLAME, etc.).

Our holonic model of the physic agent environment provides answers to specific research challenges that are identified during the past 10 years (see Sect. 8). Concepts that are used for describing the objects, and the topology of the physical agent environment are proposed: zone, environmental object, body, etc. The use of the CRIO organizational approach enables to define the behaviors related to the environment modules for supporting the agent environment responsibilities. The dynamics of this environment are supported by holons, which also mimic the intrinsic hierarchical nature of the environment. In our opinion, two major challenges are still under research activities: How to handle large-scale systems with a physical environment in multiagent-based simulations? What is the language for defining the elements, the topology, and the dynamics of the agent environment that could be a simulated environment or the Reality?

Acknowledgments. The airport screenshots were produced, in conjunction with the platform JANUS (http://www.janusproject.io), by the commercial tool SIMULATE of the VOXELIA SAS (http://www.voxelia.com) company, France. The views and conclusions contained in this document are those of the authors, and should not be interpreted as representing the official policies, either expressed or implied, of the Voxelia SAS.

References

1. Barella, A., Ricci, A., Boissier, O., Carrascosa, C.: MAM5: multi-agent model for intelligent virtual environments. In: 10th European Workshop on Multi-Agent Systems (EUMAS 2012), pp. 16–30 (2012)
2. Behe, F., Galland, S., Gaud, N., Nicolle, C., Koukam, A.: An ontology-based meta-model for multiagent-based simulations. Int. J. Simul. Model. Pract. Theory **40**, 64–85 (2014). http://authors.elsevier.com/sd/article/S1569190X13001342
3. Brooks, R.A.: Intelligence without representation. Artif. Intell. **47**(1), 139–159 (1991)
4. Buisson, J.: An environment model for the multi-agent simulation of mobility in urban areas. Ph.D. thesis, Universit de Technologie de Belfort-Montbliard, Belfort, France (in French), December 2014
5. Burghout, W., Koutsopoulos, H.N., Andréasson, I.: Hybrid mesoscopic-microscopic traffic simulation. Transp. Res. Rec. J. Transp. Res. Board **1934**, 218–255 (2005)
6. Carrascosa, C., Klügl, F., Ricci, A.: Virtual environments 4 mas. In: International Workshop on Environments for Multiagent Systems (E4MAS 2014). Springer, May 2014
7. Cohen-Or, D., Chrysanthou, Y.L., Silva, C.T., Durand, F.: A survey of visibility for walkthrough applications. IEEE Trans. Visual Comput. Graphics **9**(3), 412–431 (2003)
8. Cossentino, M., Gaud, N., Hilaire, V., Galland, S., Koukam, A.: ASPECS: an agent-oriented software process for engineering complex systems - how to design agent societies under a holonic perspective. Auton. Agents Multi-Agent Syst. **2**(2), 260–304 (2010)

9. Demange, J., Galland, S., Koukam, A.: Analysis and design of multi-level virtual indoor environment. Int. J. Systemics Inform. World Netw. **10**, 145–152 (2010). http://siwn.org.uk/

10. Dey, P., Roberts, D.: A conceptual framework for modelling crowd behaviour. In: DS-RT 2007: Proceedings of the 11th IEEE International Symposium on Distributed Simulation and Real-Time Applications, pp. 193–200. IEEE Computer Society, Washington, D.C. (2007)

11. Donikian, S., Paris, S.: Towards embodied and situated virtual humans. In: Egges, A., Kamphuis, A., Overmars, M. (eds.) MIG 2008. LNCS, vol. 5277, pp. 51–62. Springer, Heidelberg (2008)

12. Farenc, N.: An informed environment for inhabited city simulation. Ph.D. thesis, Lausanne (2001)

13. Farenc, N., Boulic, R., Thalmann, D.: An informed environment dedicated to the simulation of virtual humans in urban context. In: Proceedings of EUROGRAPH-ICS 1999, pp. 309–318 (1999)

14. Ferber, J., Michel, F., Baez, J.: AGRE: integrating environments with organizations. In: Weyns, D., Van Dyke Parunak, H., Michel, F. (eds.) E4MAS 2004. LNCS (LNAI), vol. 3374, pp. 48–56. Springer, Heidelberg (2005)

15. Galland, S., Balbo, F., Gaud, N., Rodriguez, S., Picard, G., Boissier, O.: Contextualize agent interactions by combining social and physical dimensions in the environment. In: Demazeau, Y., Decker, K. (eds.) 13th International Conference on Practical Applications of Agents and Multi-Agent Systems (PAAMS), June 2015

16. Galland, S., Balbo, F., Gaud, N., Rodriguez, S., Picard, G., Boissier, O.: A multidimensional environment implementation for enhancing agent interaction. In: Bordini, R., Elkind, E. (eds.) Autonomous Agents and Multiagent Systems (AAMAS 2015), Istanbul, Turkey, May 2015

17. Galland, S., Gaud, N., Demange, J., Koukam, A.: Environment model for multiagent-based simulation of 3D urban systems. In: The 7th European Workshop on Multiagent Systems (EUMAS 2009), Ayia Napa, Cyprus, paper 36, December 2009

18. Galland, S., Knapen, L., Yasar, A.U.H., Gaud, N., Janssens, D., Lamotte, O., Koukam, A., Wets, G.: Multi-agent simulation of individual mobility behavior in carpooling. Int. J. Transp. Res. Part C **45**, 83–98 (2014).http://www.science direct.com/science/article/pii/S0968090X14000035

19. Gaud, N., Galland, S., Gechter, F., Hilaire, V., Koukam, A.: Holonic multilevel simulation of complex systems: application to real-time pedestrians simulation in virtual urban environment. Simul. Model. Pract. Theory **16**(10), 1659–1676 (2008)

20. Gaud, N., Galland, S., Koukam, A.: Towards a multilevel simulation approach based on holonic multiagent systems. In: UKSIM 2008: Proceedings of the Tenth International Conference on Computer Modeling and Simulation, pp. 180–185 (2008)

21. Gouaïch, A., Michel, F.: Towards a unified view of the environment(s) within multi-agent systems. Informatica **29**(4), 423–432 (2005)

22. Grignard, A., Taillandier, P., Gaudou, B., Vo, D.A., Huynh, N.Q., Drogoul, A.: GAMA 1.6: advancing the art of complex agent-based modeling and simulation. In: Boella, G., Elkind, E., Savarimuthu, B.T.R., Dignum, F., Purvis, M.K. (eds.) PRIMA 2013. LNCS, vol. 8291, pp. 117–131. Springer, Heidelberg (2013)

23. Helbing, D., Treiber, M.: Gas-kinetic-based traffic model explaining observed hysteretic phase transition. Phys. Rev. Lett. **81**(14), 3042–3045 (1998)

24. Helleboogh, A., Vizzari, G., Uhrmacher, A., Michel, F.: Modeling dynamic environments in multiagent simulation. Int. J. Auton. Agent. Multi-Agent Syst. **14**(1), 87–116 (2007)
25. Karafyllidis, I., Thanailakis, A.: A model for predicting forest fire spreading using cellular automata. Ecol. Model. **99**(1), 87–97 (1997)
26. Klein, J.: Breve: a 3D simulation environment for the simulation of decentralized systems and artificial life. In: 8th International Conference on the Simulation and Synthesis of Living Systems. MIT Press (2002)
27. Kubera, Y., Mathieu, P., Picault, S.: Ioda: an interaction-oriented approach for multi-agent based simulations. Auton. Agent. Multi-Agent Syst. **23**(3), 303–343 (2011). http://dx.doi.org/10.1007/s10458-010-9164-z
28. Maudet, A., Touya, G., Duchêne, C., Picault, S.: Representation of interactions in a multi-level multi-agent model for cartography constraint solving. In: Demazeau, Y., Zambonelli, F., Corchado, J.M., Bajo, J. (eds.) PAAMS 2014. LNCS, vol. 8473, pp. 183–194. Springer, Heidelberg (2014)
29. Michel, F.: The IRM4S model: the influence/reaction principle for multiagent based simulation. In: Sixth International Joint Conference on Autonomous Agents and Multiagent Systems (AAMAS 2007). ACM, May 2007
30. Okuyama, F.Y., Bordini, R.H., da Rocha Costa, A.C.: ELMS: an environment description language for multi-agent simulation. In: Weyns, D., Van Dyke Parunak, H., Michel, F. (eds.) E4MAS 2004. LNCS (LNAI), vol. 3374, pp. 91–108. Springer, Heidelberg (2005)
31. Paris, S., Donikian, S., Bonvalet, N.: Environmental abstraction and path planning techniques for realistic crowd simulation. Comput. Anim. Virtual Worlds **17**(3–4), 325–335 (2006)
32. Parunak, H.: Making swarming happen. In: Conference on Swarming and Network Enabled Command, Control, Communications, Computers, Intelligence, Surveillance and Reconnaissance (C4ISR), McLean, Virginia, USA, January 2003
33. Piunti, M., Ricci, A., Boissier, O., Hübner, J.: Embodying organisations in multi-agent work environments. In: IEEE/WIC/ACM International Conference on Web Intelligence and Intelligent Agent Technology (WI-IAT 2009), Milan, Italy (2009)
34. Platon, E., Sabouret, N., Honiden, S.: Environmental support for tag interactions. In: Weyns, D., Van Dyke Parunak, H., Michel, F. (eds.) E4MAS 2006. LNCS (LNAI), vol. 4389, pp. 106–123. Springer, Heidelberg (2007)
35. Razavi, S.N., Gaud, N., Mozayani, N., Koukam, A.: Multi-agent based simulations using fast multipole method: application to large scale simulations of flocking dynamical systems. Artif. Intell. Rev. **35**(1), 53–72 (2011)
36. Reynolds, C.W.: Flocks, herds and schools: a distributed behavioral model. In: SIGGRAPH 1987: Proceedings of the 14th Annual Conference on Computer Graphics and Interactive Techniques, pp. 25–34. ACM, New York (1987)
37. Ricci, A., Viroli, M., Omicini, A.: Programming MAS with artifacts. In: Bordini, R.H., Dastani, M., Dix, J., El Fallah Seghrouchni, A. (eds.) PROMAS 2005. LNCS (LNAI), vol. 3862, pp. 206–221. Springer, Heidelberg (2006)
38. Ricci, A., Viroli, M., Omicini, A.: CArtAgO: a framework for prototyping artifact-based environments in MAS. In: Weyns, D., Van Dyke Parunak, H., Michel, F. (eds.) E4MAS 2006. LNCS (LNAI), vol. 4389, pp. 67–86. Springer, Heidelberg (2007)
39. Rincon, J.A., Garcia, E., Julian, V., Carrascosa, C.: Developing adaptive agents situated in intelligent virtual environments. In: Polycarpou, M., de Carvalho, A.C.P.L.F., Pan, J.-S., Woźniak, M., Quintian, H., Corchado, E. (eds.) HAIS 2014. LNCS, vol. 8480, pp. 98–109. Springer, Heidelberg (2014)

40. Rodriguez, S., Gaud, N., Galland, S.: SARL: a general-purpose agent-oriented programming language. In: International Work on Intelligent Agent Technology (IAT) (2014), to be published

41. Rodriguez, S.A.: From analysis to design of Holonic Multi-Agent Systems: a Framework, methodological guidelines and applications. Ph.D. thesis, Université de Technologie de Belfort-Montbéliard (2005)

42. Saunier, J.: Bridging the gap between agent and environment: the missing body. In: International Workshop on Environments for Multiagent Systems (E4MAS 2014). IFAAMAS, Springer, Paris, France, May 2014

43. Saunier, J., Jones, H.: Mixed agent/social dynamics for emotion computation. In: Proceedings of the 2014 International Conference on Autonomous Agents and Multi-agent Systems, pp. 645–652. International Foundation for Autonomous Agents and Multiagent Systems (2014)

44. Schaefer, L.A., Mackulak, G.T., Cochran, J., Cherilla, J.L.: Application of a general particle system model to movement of pedestrians and vehicles. In: WSC 1998: Proceedings of the 30th Conference on Winter Simulation, pp. 1155–1160. IEEE Computer Society Press, Los Alamitos (1998)

45. Tamminga, G., Knoppers, P., van Lint, H.: Open traffic: a toolbox for traffic research. In: 3nd International Workshop on Agent-based Mobility, Traffic and Transportation Models, Methodologies and Applications (ABMTRANS 2014). Springer, June 2014

46. Thalmann, D., Musse, S.R.: Crowd Simulation. Springer, London (2007)

47. Thiebaux, M., Marsella, S., Marshall, A., Kallmann, M.: Smartbody: behavior realization for embodied conversational agents. In: Proceedings of the 7th International Joint Conference on Autonomous Agents and Multiagent Systems, vol. 1, pp. 151–158 (2008)

48. Vanbergue, D.: Conception de simulation multi-agents: application à la simulation des migrations intra-urbaines de la ville de Bogota. Ph.D. thesis, Université Paris VI, December 2003

49. Viroli, M., Holvoet, T., Ricci, A., Schelfthout, K., Zambonelli, F.: Infrastructures for the environment of multiagent system. Int. J. Auton. Agent. Multi-Agent Syst. 14(1), 49–60 (2007)

50. Weyns, D., Ominici, A., Odell, J.: Environment as a first-class abstraction in multiagent systems. Int. J. Auton. Agent. Multi-Agent Syst. 14(1), 5–30 (2007)

51. Weyns, D., Van Dyke Parunak, H., Michel, F., Holvoet, T., Ferber, J.: Environments for multiagent systems state-of-the-art and research challenges. In: Weyns, D., Van Dyke Parunak, H., Michel, F. (eds.) E4MAS 2004. LNCS (LNAI), vol. 3374, pp. 1–47. Springer, Heidelberg (2005)

Towards a 'Smart' Collaborative Virtual Environment and Multi-agent Approach to Designing an Intelligent Virtual Agent

Nader Hanna[(⊠)] and Deborah Richards

Department of Computing, Macquarie University, Sydney, NSW 2109, Australia
{nader.hanna, deborah.richards}@mq.edu.au

Abstract. Increasing interest in Collaborative Virtual Environments (CVEs) in different applications has imposed new requirements on the design of the CVEs and the resident Intelligent Virtual Agents (IVAs). In addition to cognitive abilities, IVAs in CVEs require social and communication behaviours. The use of a Multi-Agent System (MAS) has been a successful approach to address the variety of evolving abilities needed by an IVA. In this paper, a model of a 'smart' CVE is presented. This CVE model publicizes the properties and the possible events of each entity located in the sensory range of the nearby IVAs. Additionally, this CVE model offers a level of abstraction for the IVAs to interact with the entities in the CVE. This level of the abstraction is distributed within the design of the resident IVAs. Moreover, this paper presents a MAS-based IVA design. This IVA is able to collaborate with humans in CVEs. The proposed model simulates humans by including input, output and processing modules. In addition, the model coordinates the IVA's verbal and non-verbal communication to convey its internal state while achieving a collaborative task.

Keywords: Collaborative virtual environment · Intelligent virtual agent · Human-Agent collaboration · Multimodal communication

1 Introduction

Agents exist in a space that provides the sensors of the agent with inputs and which receives that output or the actions of the agent. This space is the environment, and it contains all the information external to the agent used in the agent's decision-making. In other words, the environment is where the agent receives inputs and affects its environment through its outputs [1]. Moreover, the environment provides a space in which agents interact with the environment and other agents. A number of attempts aimed to define the notion of environment. In many of these definitions, the term environment is either an implicit part of a multi-agent system (MAS) (see [2]) or an explicit element of a MAS [1]; nevertheless, these definitions tend to focus on the environment from the agent's perspective, i.e. the external space, or the design perspective, i.e. means of communication. Additionally, the nature of the agent determined how the environment was defined. For instance, some have considered the environment in the context of spatial distance for continuous space [3], adjacency for grid cells [4],

© Springer International Publishing Switzerland 2015
D. Weyns and F. Michel (Eds.): E4MAS 2014 – 10 years later, LNAI 9068, pp. 170–187, 2015.
DOI: 10.1007/978-3-319-23850-0_11

or connectivity in social networks [5]. Weyns et al. [6] reviewed the literature and listed a wide range of definitions of the environment in a MAS. They extended the concept of the environment to be considered as a level of abstraction *"The environment is a first-class abstraction that provides the surrounding conditions for agents to exist and that mediates both the interaction among agents and the access to resources"* (p. 15). Different roles of the environment in MAS were identified [6] from different perspectives. From an agent's perspective, anything external to the individual agent is considered the environment including other agents, while from a design perspective; the environment is a means of communication that takes place between the agents and a container to resources.

A Collaborative Virtual Environment (CVE) has been defined as "a computer-based, distributed, virtual space or set of places. In such places, people can meet and interact with others, with agents or with virtual objects." p. 5 [7]. CVEs have been used as a mediation tool to facilitate human-human collaboration across disparate spaces. Moreover, the concept of a CVE includes the collaboration between human participants and virtual entities such as Intelligent Virtual Agents (IVAs). IVAs refer to humanoid virtual entities that simulate humans in their abilities and characteristics. CVEs have been used in multiple fields depending on their purpose of use, such as, business [8], entertainment, learning [9, 10], training [11], medicine [12] and dancing [13]. Despite active research to increase the capabilities and application of IVAs, there tends to be little focus or even information provided about the environment the IVA inhabits.

The versatility of CVE usage in various and complex domains requires, on one hand, IVAs to play various roles such as instructing, monitoring, counselling and team working. On the other hand, versatility demands that IVAs have multiple capabilities including reasoning, communication, planning, argumentation and/or negotiation. Owing to the fact that IVAs need to take complex decisions and perform sophisticated actions, there is a need for real-time processing to present satisfactory performance and believable behaviour. While, the use of the Belief-Desire-Intention (BDI) single agent approach [14] has been attractive to researchers because of its simplicity and the ability to trigger the agent's behaviour, the BDI-based single agent approach on its own falls short in handling sophisticated applications that require IVAs to do more than achieve its intentions to reach the determined goal.

Weyns et al. [2] define three levels of support that can be provided by the environment. These levels could be extended to include CVEs. The first level is the basic level. The basic level enables agents to access the resources in the environment (what is called the deployment context). These resources could be hardware, software and external resources. The abstract level bridges the gap between the agents and the low-level details of the environment. In this level, the agent should not access directly the resources of the environment. Instead, an abstract level includes the low-level details of the resources. The third level is the interaction-mediation level that regulates the agent's access to the resources of the environment and mediates the interaction between agents that exist in the environment.

In the previous classification presented in [2], it is the role of the environment to provide an abstraction level for the agent to access the context of the environment (level two) or to provide interaction and mediation control (level three). The agent's role is confined to do the cognitive processing while the environment manages all the interactions external to the agents. This role of the agent may be feasible in situations where the agent needs to perform a well-defined cognitive task. However, in other tasks such as working in a team, which requires not only cognitive but also social and communicative abilities, the role of the agent should go beyond cognitive decisions.

Dynamic environments represent a challenge in designing the environment itself and in designing the agents that will use, exist and interact with this environment [15]. CVEs represent one of these complex dynamic environments, where each partners in the act of collaboration does not know the next action of its partners. Teamwork that combines both humans and IVAs has been a challenging research area. When these heterogeneous team members are involved in a collaborative task, IVAs have to be more aware of the changes in their surrounding virtual environment (VE), take the decision in real-time and be believable in the way they communicate. IVAs may exhibit many types of behaviour including internal and external. Internal behaviour includes reasoning and perception, while external behaviour includes verbal and non-verbal communication. To address the challenge of developing believable IVAs in complex CVEs, the increasing functionality of a BDI-based single agent has been distributed to a group of agents that coordinate their behaviour towards achieving the overall desire (goal state) to form a Multi-Agent System. Over the past decade, MAS has been the subject of AI research as it provides a high level of abstraction in reasoning and modelling [16]. MAS has been used to design Robots [17] and IVAs [18]. MAS have been employed to improve the capabilities of the agents. These capabilities included cognitive skills such as decision-making and planning, or behavioral skills such as animations.

A number of reasons made the MAS approach to designing IVAs for CVE more favorable than a single BDI-agent approach [19]. Among these reasons is simplicity, as the agent can handle part of the processing and not overload the environment with the task of handling all control. Another reason, the distribution of control among multiple agents simplifies the design of each agent. A third reason is parallelism; having multiple agents tends to speed up system overall performance because each agent its own role and part of the abstraction of the environment as well. Another reason is robustness; distributing the responsibilities among interacting agents is more likely to improve fail tolerance of the system. Last but not least, compared to a single agent approach, MAS efficiently control the various components of CVE with different goals and resources.

This paper presents a design of a CVE that distributes the abstraction level across the agents reside in the environment. In this design, the design of the environment will be proposed according to the levels presented in [2]. Novelly, this design will distribute part of the control in the interaction and mediation level to the agents that live in the CVE. As a complement to the design of the CVE, the agent should be adapted to handle the new role as a participant in environment role in interaction control. The IVA will be designed as a MAS. The contributions of the proposed MAS are: first, it couples the human's verbal and non-verbal responses to form input to the agent planner. Human responses represent a dynamic input to the IVA. Second, the MAS manages the cognitive abilities of the collaborative IVA to make a decision about the next step. Finally, the MAS manages the verbal and the non-verbal communication of the IVA to express its internal state and decisions.

The paper is organized as follows. Trends in designing IVA for CVE will appear in Sect. 2. Section 3 introduces the requirements needed in CVE that necessitate a special design for IVAs. Section 4 presents the proposed model of the smart CVE and a MAS-based IVA. Section 5 demonstrates the interaction between MAS-based agent and the proposed CVE. Finally, conclusion of the study and future work come in Sect. 6.

2 Trends in Designing CVEs and the Resident IVAs

Over the last decade, a number of studies have aimed at coupling MAS and IVAs. Within these studies, we can identify three trends of utilizing MASs in IVAs using MAS to manage the physical behaviour of IVAs, MAS to manage the cognitive capabilities of IVAs and Hybrid approaches that combine the cognitive capabilities and the physical behaviour. These trends in utilizing MAS to design IVAs reflects the directions in viewing the role of the environments that host these IVAs [20]. The relationship of the environment to the agent could be categorized as either external or internal to the MAS design, or a mixture of both.

– **External environment**... In one stream of research, the environment was considered as external to the design of the agent system i.e., the environment was not an explicit part of the models or architectures. The environment is viewed as a medium in which the agents live in; nevertheless, this medium is not meant to be considered while engineering the agents. Steels [21], however, states that *"autonomous agents without an internal model of the environment will always be severely limited."*
– **Mixed environment**... For the agents to form a multiagent system they should be situated in a common virtual or physical environment. In this environment the agent interactions with each other and with resources is enabled [22]. In this view, the environment was considered as the medium where the agents live and interact.
– **Internal environment as a first-class abstraction**... In contrast to the external view of the environment, the internal view promotes the role of the environment as a first-class abstraction in the design of multi-agent systems, impacting nearly all stages of multiagent system development: design, implementation, and run-time [2].

These perspectives of an environment can be used to produce alternative IVA designs using a MAS to manage the behaviour of the IVAs. The first (external) perspective considers the CVE as an external surrounding that embraces the *physical behaviour* of IVAs. The second (mixed) perspective of the environment stresses the role of the environment as a medium that facilitates the interaction between the agents to achieve the shared task. This perspective influences the trends in designing the agent where a MAS is used to build the *cognitive capabilities* of the IVA. The third (internal) perspective of the environment is as an explicit element in the MAS. The environment should embrace agent interactions and provide a level of abstraction to the agent behaviour with the resources of the environment. MAS that manage the physical, cognitive and combined elements of an IVA are presented in the following subsections.

2.1   MAS to Manage the Physical Behaviour of IVAs

Studies that fall under the first trend include studies that use MAS for IVA animation and social interaction (e.g., [18]). Grimaldo et al. [23] presented a multi-agent framework to animate a group of IVAs to balance between task-oriented and social behaviour. The presented framework permitted agents to include social tasks to produce realistic behavioural animations. To verify the framework functionally, the authors used a 3D dynamic environment simulating a virtual university bar, where a group of IVAs representing waiters and customers interacted and showed social behaviour. Another study that used a MAS in animating an IVA, Barella et al. [24] separated IVA visualization from intelligence and presented a social-oriented MAS framework to simulate a group of IVAs in a social situation. The agent's beliefs, plans and decision-making were defined in a specification file.

2.2   MAS to Manage the Cognitive Capabilities of IVAs

Following the second trend, in the study of Amo et al. [25] an MAS was integrated into IVAs to create autonomous intelligent agents guided by their own motivations, which live in a virtual world inhabited by other similar agents. The use of MAS concentrated on the cognitive and social role of each individual agent. Another example was the study of Mahdjoub et al. [26] who presented a collaborative design for usability approach, linked with VR tools, and based on a Multi-Agent System for knowledge management in mechanical design projects.

2.3   Hybrid Approaches that Combine the Cognitive Capabilities and the Physical Behaviour

The previous two trends resulted in a gap in the research because the separation of the physical and cognitive aspects of an IVA did not allow coordination between the internal and external behaviours of the IVA. To address this gap in research, Oijen and Dignum [27] proposed a communication model for IVAs. This model tries to balance between being cognitively efficient in managing MAS communication on the one hand and physically believable realizations of human-like interactions on the other hand. The authors found that it was beneficial to middleware to join the reasoning layer of MAS with the physical interaction of the IVA. The result shows a successful agent-agent communication in a dynamic VE; however, the study [27] does not address IVA-Human communication.

As another example of the hybrid approach of using MAS in IVA, Buche et al. [28] proposed a model called MASCARET to organize the interaction between IVAs and an avatar that represents a human. MASCARET aimed to provide the IVA with physical, cognitive and social abilities to collaborate with a human avatar in a virtual training situation. However, the proposed model did not demonstrate the nature of the communication that may exist between the collaborative agents and an avatar. In addition, the agent was not designed using an MAS. In other research that used MAS to manage IVA behaviour, Cai et al. [29] presented a multi-agent framework to design an IVA in an underground coalmine VE. The framework improved the ability of the IVA to interact with the dynamic surroundings of the virtual coalmine. Similar to the study of Buche et al., this study did not include a communication model between the IVA and the other virtual entities or human users.

3   Requirements for a Collaboration in CVEs

The modern sophisticated CVE imposes requirements on designing both the agents and the environment that hosts the agents. These requirements necessitate to design the environment with mediation-interaction mechanisms [30]. In line with these mechanisms embedded in the environment, the agent should be engineered to suit the requirements of the environment. The requirements include multimodal communication exchanged between teammates. Multimodal communication is considered as a catalyst in successful teamwork [31]. Another requirement is the coordination of efforts toward achieving the shared task. This coordination imposes special constraints on the design of the environment and the agent as well.

1. **Perceiving autonomously the teammate's action...** CVE requires IVAs to receive teammates' actions/behaviour autonomously as well as perceive the meaning of the received actions in a specific situation. For instance, moving away from the target spot after taking a decision may mean giving way to the teammate to take his turn, whereas before taking a decision moving away may mean unwillingness to take action at all.
2. **Perceiving autonomously the teammate's requests/prompts...** In addition to perceiving the meaning of teammates' action, IVAs should be able to convert teammates' verbal messages into a meaningful notation that builds on the IVAs' understanding of the teammates' intentions.
3. **Working toward the task...** IVAs' focus need to be directed to achieve the shared task. IVAs should have a main strategy to reach the common task. Despite the dynamic nature of CVE, IVAs have to stay focused on the target task and the best way to achieve it.
4. **Adaptability to changing teammate's decision...** Although IVAs should have a prior plan to achieve the shared task. IVAs have to adapt their plans in real-time to match the changes in teammates' decisions.
5. **Observable non-verbal behaviour...** IVAs need to express the inner state physically through the selection of the appropriate animation to the current situation. The selected animation should be complementary with the verbal communication to convey the IVA's intention.
6. **Believable/Appropriate verbal response...** is another communication channel that IVA should master. The verbal responses should be used either to prompt the human teammate to take certain action or defend IVA's point of view in achieving the task.

4   The Proposed Model of a CVE

To accomplish the collaboration requirements specified in Sect. 3, designs for the CVE and agent are proposed. The proposed design of the CVE is built upon the levels of support in the environment proposed in [2]. The proposed CVE model is created with a distributed abstraction where the agents will not interact directly with the entities in the CVE. The proposed design of the IVA agents uses an MAS architecture that provides this level of abstraction.

In the following section, an introduction to the model of the CVE is presented. The design of an IVA with MAS is presented in Sect. 4.2. In the IVA design, the MAS-approach is used to create the agent with a distributed level of abstraction allowing it to interact with entities in the CVE and with other agents.

4.1   Toward a 'Smart' CVE

A virtual environment is known to be dynamic when the events are not pre-determined, but form a process of interaction [32]. Because the virtual environment is not static, the agent should dynamically reorganize itself to the changes in the environment [33]. Some research work proposed an MAS architecture that can deal with the environment as a black box. For instance, Canedo-Rodriguez [34] presented a multi-agent intelligent system that controls a robot. This MAS can interact with its spatial environment without the need for a map of the environment. However, a lot of computation was required from the MAS and the environment needed to stay simple. One of the proposed solutions to overcome the variability of the environment was to design a middleware [35].

As can be seen in Fig. 1, the environment is a source of inputs to the MAS. These inputs include the objects to identify their properties. Additionally, these inputs include events and actions that require either perception or a response from the agents. The environment could be a medium of communication between two or more agents. In MAS-based agent, it needs to identify whether the input is an object and so a *sensor agent* will be required to recognize this object. Whereas, if the MAS is experiencing an action, then the *receiver agent* will need to identify this action. It is very hard for the MAS to recognise both the object and the actions autonomously unless the environment helps the MAS to identify the environmental inputs. In real life, we identify an object because the object sends a ray to our eye to identify this object. In a virtual environment, the agent is left blind to 'see' the surrounding objects or monitor the events. Researchers used to overcome this problem through coding the information related to the environment inside the agent or externally in a shared repository. Besides the surrounding objects the agent needs to interact with, the virtual environment includes events and actions committed by other virtual agents, conducted automatically or carried out by human participants. These events and actions require the agent to perceive, filter, code and take a decision, if needed.

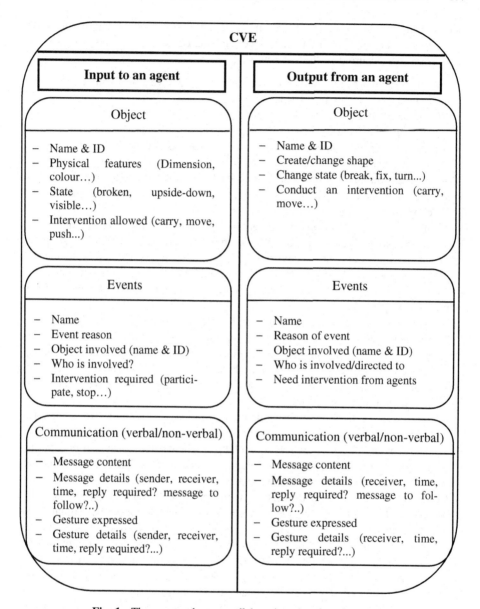

Fig. 1. The proposed smart collaborative virtual environment

As virtual environments get more complex, it becomes more tedious to code all the surrounding objects and events in the agent. Simulating how humans perceive the objects, events and communication in real life, we propose modelling the 'smart' virtual environment. This proposed virtual environment is meant to imitate the physical world that emits stimuli into the physical world and the senses of the human will detect these stimuli as long as it is within the range of the human's senses. Figure 1 shows the model of the proposed virtual environment. The model consists of input and output dimensions. Each dimension has three facets for the objects, the events and the communication that occurred in the environment.

- Object: Any object in the virtual environment should have a profile that it reveals to inhabitant agents. This profile may include:
  - The name and an ID of the object.
  - The physical features such as dimension, shape and colour.
  - The state of this object such as if it is in the normal position, upside-down, visible or invisible.
  - Intervention/interaction allowed with each particular object; for example, tree object can be climbed but not carried, while a small box can be carried but not climbed.
- Event: means any incidence that takes place in the environment in the range of an agent's sensors. Events may or may not require an intervention from the agent. When an event occurs in the environment a profile should be created in the location of this incidence. Any populated agent should be aware of this incidence the moment this incidence becomes in the range of an agent's range of sensing. Event profile may include:
  - Name of this event such as dancing, fighting and playing.
  - Event reason: it is not a must that the virtual environment should reveal the reason of events. In the physical world, the reasons of some events are clearly announced, while others we have to discover the reason ourselves. For example if an agent passes by two other fighting agents, they do not have to announce that they are in disagreement.
  - Intervention required: some incidents may require intervention from populated agents. For example, if an agent falls on a road, the event should be "fallen agent" with a required intervention "help". Whether the agent will conduct the required intervention or not will depend on features in the agent architecture such as personality, priorities and past experience.
- Communication: the third dimension in the proposed virtual environment is the communication. Communication includes any verbal or non-verbal signal in an agent's sensing range. Communication could be incorporated with an event, for example meeting another agent is an event accompanied with communication which is exchanging salutation messages. Communication dimension includes:
  - The verbal or non-verbal messages, either uttered messages from another agent or non-verbal signals from any object in the environment.
  - Message details: such as the ID of the sender, whether the message is directed to a specific receiver or it is undirected and broadcasted to any agent in the surrounding area.

To demonstrate the interaction between an agent and the proposed CVE, an example is proposed. Figure 2 shows an example where an agent (A1) can detect two objects in his sensing range, i.e. a tree (T1) and another agent (A2). Each object has a list of features

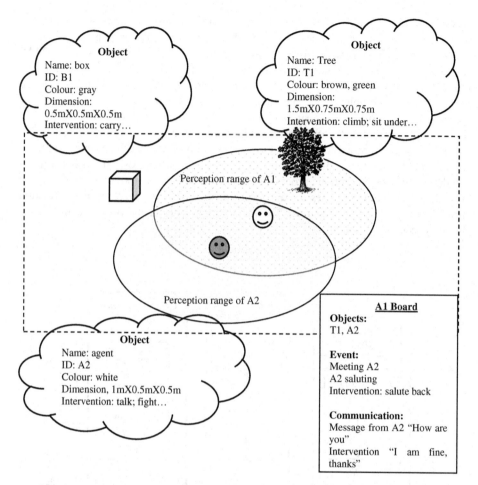

Fig. 2. An example of the interaction between an IVA and the content of the CVE

that can be detected by the agent (A1). Additionally, Agent (A1) can sense an event which is when Agent (A2) is saluting and sending verbal message "how are you?" The event does not require an intervention from the agent (A1); however, the verbal communication detected requires an intervention which is a reply to the salutation. Although the example in Fig. 2 is a simple one, the same strategy will apply to more complex scenarios.

4.2 Designing an Agent with Distributed Abstraction

All of the above requirements need to be embodied and contained within a single IVA; in addition, the IVA should be able to handle parallel processing as the inputs from a

CVE have the characteristics of being variant and dynamic. Creating an IVA that is able to manage its verbal and non-verbal behaviour is a challenging task [36]. To address these challenges, a MAS approach was utilized to design the IVA. MAS consists of a group of autonomous agents that work independently on their own part of the problem towards solving a bigger problem. Therefore, this feature could be used to break down the complex work into smaller tasks that a single agent can achieve. The proposed model used this feature to break down the process of receiving human actions, planning for the next step and coordinating the verbal and non-verbal responses. The proposed MAS model simulates the human brain in receiving stimuli, processing the input data, managing the physical behaviour in VEs. The model consists of three modules: reception, processing and communication modules, as shown in Fig. 3. Each module includes a manager agent to coordinate the flow of information from this module to another one. The main components of the proposed model are briefly described as follows:

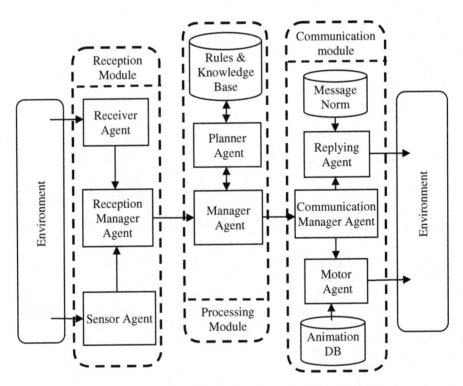

Fig. 3. The proposed MAS approach to design IVA

- The reception module is responsible for receiving both the actions of the human user as well as the verbal messages of the human teammate. It consists of the following agents:
  - *Sensor Agent:* receives the stimuli from the surrounding CVE, filters these stimuli to determine which ones are related to the current task, perceives the meaning of these stimuli based on a rule-based technique and finally passes the filtered action committed by the human to the *Reception Manager Agent*. The *Sensor agent* was proposed to achieve the first requirement of perceiving autonomously the teammate's action.
  - *Receiver Agent:* was presented to fulfil the second requirement of perceiving autonomously the teammate's verbal communication. The *Receiver Agent* was designed to receive the verbal messages from human teammates, encode the possible intention behind that message using a rule-based technique and finally passes the digested message to *Reception Manager Agent*. These messages may include requests from humans to IVA to perform specific actions or replies to the IVA's requests. *Reception Manager Agent*: its role is to couple both verbal and non-verbal responses of the human teammate in order to give the *Planner Agent* in the processing module a picture about the humans' behaviour. A case-based technique is used to couple verbal and non-verbal responses and to deduce a proper conclusion. The case-based technique consists of a group of cases that include both verbal and non-verbal responses of the teammate along with conclusion/label for this case. For instance, if the teammate moves away from the working area and says "be right back", that would be perceived by *Motor Agent* (see below) that the teammate is not interested in completing the shared task; however, coupling the action with verbal responses and matching existing cases, *Reception Manager Agent* would conclude that the teammate is going to be back, hence the processing module should suspend planning for the next step, until the teammate gets back.
  - *Receiver Agent:* was presented to fulfil the second requirement of perceiving autonomously the teammate's verbal communication. The *Receiver Agent* was designed to receive the verbal messages from human teammates, encode the possible intention behind that message using a rule-based technique and finally passes the digested message to *Reception Manager Agent*. These messages may include requests from humans to IVA to perform specific actions or replies to the IVA's requests. *Reception Manager Agent*: its role is to couple both verbal and non-verbal responses of the human teammate in order to give the *Planner Agent* in the processing module a picture about the humans' behaviour. A case-based technique is used to couple verbal and non-verbal responses and to deduce a proper conclusion. The case-based technique consists of a group of cases that include both verbal and non-verbal responses of the teammate along with conclusion/label for this case. For instance, if the teammate moves away from

the working area and says "be right back", that would be perceived by *Motor Agent* (see below) that the teammate is not interested in completing the shared task; however, coupling the action with verbal responses and matching existing cases, *Reception Manager Agent* would conclude that the teammate is going to be back, hence the processing module should suspend planning for the next step, until the teammate gets back.

- The roles of the processing module are to contrast the human's verbal reply along with his/her action in order to figure out the human's commitment to collaborate, plan for the next step the agent should take and pass the result to the communication module.
  - *Manager Agent*: To achieve the requirement of working toward the task, the *Manager Agent* behaves like the brain in humans. It receives responses from the *Reception Manager Agent*, forwards the decision made by the *Planner Agent* to the Communication *Manager Agent* and determines turn-taking in the collaborative activity. *Manager Agent* may manage turn-taking based on succession or through negotiation between collaborators.
  - *Planner Agent*: calculates the next step that the IVA should take. Next step calculation is based on a group of rules and beliefs that are located in the Rules and Knowledge Base. These rules may base on the best time to execute the task, the shortest path, and so on. The rules are continuously updated according to the behaviour of the teammate and the changes in the dynamic CVE. The continuous update to these rules was proposed to achieve the requirement of adaptability to changed teammate's decision.
- The aim of the Communication module is to translate an IVA's internal state and intentions into a physical behaviour. The behaviour includes coordinated verbal and non-verbal communication to give more believability to the IVA's behaviour.
  - *Communication Manager Agent*: works like the hub in the communication module. It receives the message from the *Manager Agent* and decides which agent is more suitable to express the IVA's reaction to the human teammate's behaviour. In addition, the *Communication Manager Agent* will pass the values given in the IVA's responses such as location coordinates, numbers, name agreement/disagreement and so on. The *Communication Manager Agent* works in a similar way to the *Reception Manager Agent* in organizing both the verbal and non-verbal response.
  - *Replying Agent:* when the *Communication Manager Agent* calls it, the *Replying Agent* selects the most appropriate message template from *Message Norm DB* and fills in the template with the values passed by *Communication Manager Agent*.
  - *Motor Agent:* is responsible for the physical behaviour of the IVA. The physical behaviour includes animations, gestures and physical movements. The *Motor Agent* will select a suitable animation from the animation DB, and use the data fed by the *Communication Manager Agent* to generate appropriate responses that are related to the context situation.

5   Interactions of MAS-Based IVA with the Proposed CVE

Figure 4 demonstrates the interactions between the proposed CVE model and the designed MAS-based agent. These interactions could be summarized as follows:

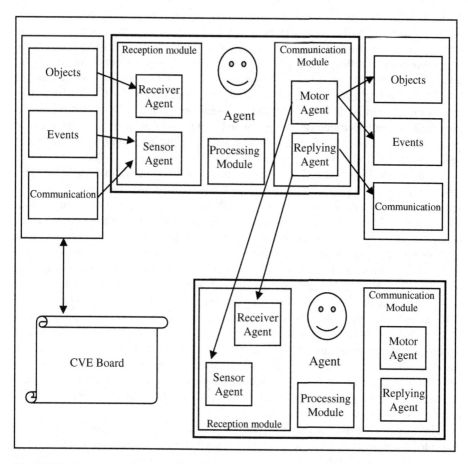

Fig. 4. The interaction between an IVA and the content of the environment and another IVA

- Agent-agent interaction… in this level of interaction, MAS-based agent can receive other agents' verbal messages through the receiver agent, while the non-verbal communication will be received through the motor agent.
- Agent-entity interaction… the MAS-based agent interact with the objects in the CVE. This interaction includes recognizing the surrounding objects within the range of sensing though the receiver agent and sensing the events/communications in the environment that may be caused by another agent.

6 Conclusion and Future Work

According to Aylett and Cavazza [37] the virtual environment is called intelligent when an IVA is placed in it. This perspective of an intelligent virtual environment limits the intelligence to what the agent will do in the environment. A few attempts have been made to add some intelligence to the virtual environment itself; however, these attempts were confined to adding some scripts to make the environment seems smarter (e.g. [38]). In the last decade, the expectations of IVAs are greater. Moreover, virtual environments are getting more complex due to its dynamic nature. Hence, IVAs' interactions with their environment are getting more complex for the environment to handle efficiently. In this paper, we presented a model of a smart CVE. The virtual environment could be described as smart not because it contains IVAs, but because it presented the contained objects and populated agents in a 'smart' manner. One of the benefits of the proposed CVE is that it will guarantee the autonomy of the inhabitant agents without the need to script these agents.

Additionally, in this paper, we have presented a MAS approach to design IVAs that meet a number of requirements specific for CVEs. This design simulates humans in separating input, output and processing modules. On one hand, the input module coordinates verbal and non-verbal responses from the human teammate. One the other hand, the output module coordinates the response of the IVA to express its decisions and requests to the teammate. In addition, the processing module takes into account the teammate's actions and requests before planning for the next step. Furthermore, the proposed MAS-based IVA addresses the issue of coordinating the internal side of IVAs as represented in the intellectual behaviour and the external side of IVAs as represented in the social and animation behaviour. This coordination was the focus of the proposed MAS to develop believable IVA behaviour in a real-time collaborative situation where decisions and communication should be dependent on the teammate's own decisions and communication. Another feature our MAS model focused on was the coordination between the verbal and non-verbal communication in a human-like manner. Because humans use both ways to express their internal state, a MAS-architecture mimicked this property for more believable behaviour.

This paper presented a model to design a smart CVE. Additionally, the paper presented a design of a MAS-based agent that should reside in the proposed CVE. The proposed CVE design exhibited a number of features that included offering an abstract level of interaction between the agents and the CVE object and the interaction among the agents. However, this abstraction level is distributed in the MAS-based agents so that the environment will not become overloaded with agents requesting access. The proposed MAS-based agent exhibited a number of features, including parallel and distributed processing, a manager agent for both verbal and non-verbal communication and balancing between the reasoning capabilities of IVAs and its animated behaviour. Despite the fact that numerous issues still need to be addressed for the system to be used in a more complex situation, the initial implementation shows that the design is practical and the IVA's behaviour is plausible. Besides providing a tool to manage the behaviour of IVAs, MAS could be extended to include further IVA capabilities by adding additional modules each designed as agents. Future work will include re-implementing the proposed MAS using different technologies such as MAS programming languages (e.g. Jason, Jade) with supporting game engine platform (e.g. Unreal Tournament or Unity3D game engines).

References

1. Russell, S., Norvig, P.: Artificial Intelligence: A Modern Approach. Prentice Hall, Englewood Cliffs (2003)
2. Weyns, D., Van Dyke Parunak, H., Michel, F., Holvoet, T., Ferber, J.: Environments for multiagent systems state-of-the-art and research challenges. In: Weyns, D., Van Dyke Parunak, H., Michel, F. (eds.) E4MAS 2004. LNCS (LNAI), vol. 3374, pp. 1–47. Springer, Heidelberg (2005)
3. Giuffra, P., Cecilia, E., Ricardo, A.S.: A multi-agent system model to integrate virtual learning environments and intelligent tutoring systems. IJIMAI **2**, 51–58 (2013)
4. Fenghui, R., Minjie, Z., Soetanto, D., XiaoDong, S.: Conceptual design of a multi-agent system for interconnected power systems restoration. IEEE Trans. Power Syst. **27**, 732–740 (2012)
5. Crooks, A., Heppenstall, A.: Introduction to agent-based modelling. In: Heppenstall, A.J., Crooks, A.T., See, L.M., Batty, M. (eds.) Agent-Based Models of Geographical Systems, pp. 85–105. Springer, Dordrecht (2012)
6. Weyns, D., Omicini, A., Odell, J.: Environment as a first class abstraction in multiagent systems. Auton. Agent. Multi-Agent Syst. **14**, 5–30 (2007)
7. Snowdon, D., Churchill, E., Munro, A.: Collaborative virtual environments: digital spaces and places for CSCW: an introduction. In: Churchill, E., Snowdon, D., Munro, A. (eds.) Collaborative Virtual Environments, pp. 3–17. Springer, London (2001)
8. Nass, C., Fogg, B.J., Moon, Y.: Can computers be teammates? Int. J. Hum. Comput. Stud. **45**, 669–678 (1996)
9. Giraldo, F., María, À., Rojas, J., Esteban, P., Trefftz, H.: Collaborative virtual environments for teaching physics. In: Iskander, M. (ed.) Innovations in E-learning, Instruction Technology, Assessment, and Engineering Education, pp. 89–93. Springer, Dordrecht (2007)
10. Lorenzo, C.-M., Lorenzo, C.-M., Sánchez, M.A., Sicilia, S.: Studying the effectiveness of multi-user immersive environments for collaborative evaluation tasks. Comput. Educ. **59**, 1361–1376 (2012)
11. Holmberg, N., Wunsche, B., Tempero, E.: A framework for interactive web-based visualization. In: The 7th Australasian User Interface Conference (AUIC 2006), pp. 137–144. Australian Computer Society, Inc. (2006)
12. Chee, Y.S., Hooi, C.M.: C-VISions: socialized learning through collaborative, virtual, interactive simulations. In: Proceedings of the Conference on Computer Support for Collaborative Learning: Foundations for a CSCL Community, pp. 687–696. International Society of the Learning Sciences, Boulder (2002)
13. Zhenyu, Y., Bin, Y., Wanmin, W., Nahrstedt, K., Diankov, R., Bajscy, R.: A study of collaborative dancing in tele-immersive environments. In: Eighth IEEE International Symposium on Multimedia (ISM 2006), pp. 177–184 (2006)
14. Bratman, M.E.: Intentions, Plans and Practical Reason. Harvard University Press, Cambridge (1987)

15. Helleboogh, A., Vizzari, G., Uhrmacher, A., Michel, F.: Modeling dynamic environments in multi-agent simulation. Auton. Agent. Multi-Agent Syst. **14**, 87–116 (2007)
16. Anastassakis, G., Ritchings, T., Panayiotopoulos, T.: Multi-agent systems as intelligent virtual environments. In: Baader, F., Brewka, G., Eiter, T. (eds.) KI 2001. LNCS (LNAI), vol. 2174, pp. 381–395. Springer, Heidelberg (2001)
17. Rockel, S., Klimentjew, D., Jianwei, Z.: A multi-robot platform for mobile robots - a novel evaluation and development approach with multi-agent technology. In: IEEE Conference on Multisensor Fusion and Integration for Intelligent Systems (MFI 2012), pp. 470–477 (2012)
18. Rodríguez, S., de Paz, Y., Bajo, J., Corchado, J.M.: Social-based planning model for multiagent systems. Expert Syst. Appl. **38**, 13005–13023 (2011)
19. Stone, P., Veloso, M.: Multiagent systems: a survey from a machine learning perspective. Auton. Robots **8**, 345–383 (2000)
20. Valckenaers, P., Sauter, J., Sierra, C., Rodriguez-Aguilar, J.: Applications and environments for multi-agent systems. Auton. Agent Multi-Agent Syst. **14**, 61–85 (2007)
21. Steels, L.: Exploiting analogical representations. Robot. Auton. Syst. **6**, 71–88 (1990)
22. Viroli, M., Holvoet, T., Ricci, A., Schelfthout, K., Zambonelli, F.: Infrastructures for the environment of multiagent systems. Auton. Agent. Multi-Agent Syst. **14**, 49–60 (2007)
23. Grimaldo, F., Lozano, M., Barber, F., Vigueras, G.: Animating groups of socially intelligent agents. In: International Conference on Cyberworlds (CW 2007), pp. 136–143 (2007)
24. Barella, A., Carrascosa, C., Botti, V.: Agent architectures for intelligent virtual environments. In: IEEE/WIC/ACM International Conference on Intelligent Agent Technology (IAT 2007), pp. 532–535 (2007)
25. Amo, F.A., Velasco, F.F., Gómez, G.L., Jiménez, J.P.R., Camino, F.J.S.: Intelligent virtual agent societies on the internet. In: de Antonio, A., Aylett, R.S., Ballin, D. (eds.) IVA 2001. LNCS (LNAI), vol. 2190, pp. 100–111. Springer, Heidelberg (2001)
26. Mahdjoub, M., Monticolo, D., Gomes, S., Sagot, J.-C.: A collaborative design for usability approach supported by virtual reality and a multi-agent system embedded in a PLM environment. Comput. Aided Des. **42**, 402–413 (2010)
27. van Oijen, J., Dignum, F.: Agent communication for believable human-like interactions between virtual characters. In: Dignum, F., Brom, C., Hindriks, K., Beer, M., Richards, D. (eds.) CAVE 2012. LNCS, vol. 7764, pp. 37–54. Springer, Heidelberg (2013)
28. Buche, C., Querrec, R., De Loor, P., Chevaillier, P.: MASCARET: pedagogical multi-agents systems for virtual environment for training. In: Proceedings of 2003 International Conference on Cyberworlds, 2003, pp. 423–430 (2003)
29. Cai, L., Wang, T., Zhang, J., Luo, Z.: Modeling mine virtual environment based on multi-agent. In: International Conference on Intelligent Human-Machine Systems and Cybernetics, 2009, IHMSC 2009, pp. 257–261 (2009)
30. Platon, E., Mamei, M., Sabouret, N., Honiden, S., Parunak, H.V.: Mechanisms for environments in multi-agent systems: survey and opportunities. Auton. Agent. Multi-Agent Syst. **14**, 31–47 (2007)
31. Smith-Jentsch, K.A., Johnston, J.H., Payne, S.C.: Measuring team-related expertise in complex environments. In: Cannon-Bowers, J.A., Salas, E. (eds.) Decision Making Under Stress: Implications for Individual and Team Training, pp. 61–87. American Psychological Association, Washington, D.C. (1998)
32. van Wissen, A., Gal, Y., Kamphorst, B.A., Dignum, M.V.: Human-agent teamwork in dynamic environments. Comput. Hum. Behav. **28**, 23–33 (2012)
33. Dignum, V.: A Model for Organizational Interaction: Based on Agents, Founded in Logic. Ph.D. thesis, Utrecht University (2004)

34. Canedo-Rodriguez, A., Alvarez-Santos, V., Regueiro, C.V., Pardo, X.M., Iglesias, R.: Multi-agent system for fast deployment of a guiderobot in unknown environments. J. Phys. Agents **6**, 31–41 (2012)
35. Weyns, D., Helleboogh, A., Holvoet, T., Schumacher, M.: The agent environment in multi-agent systems: a middleware perspective. Multiagent Grid Syst. **5**, 93–108 (2009)
36. Gillies, M., Robeterson, D., Ballin, D.: Direct manipulation like tools for designing intelligent virtual agents. In: Panayiotopoulos, T., Gratch, J., Aylett, R.S., Ballin, D., Olivier, P., Rist, T. (eds.) IVA 2005. LNCS (LNAI), vol. 3661, pp. 430–441. Springer, Heidelberg (2005)
37. Aylett, R., Cavazza, M.: Intelligent virtual environments: a state-of-the-art report. In: Eurographics 2001, STAR Reports volume, pp. 87–109 (2001)
38. Luck, M., Aylett, R.: Applying artificial intelligence to virtual reality: intelligent virtual environments. Appl. Artif. Intell. **14**, 3–32 (2000)

Environment Modelling for Spatial Load Forecasting

Ander Pijoan$^{(\boxtimes)}$, Oihane Kamara-Esteban, and Cruz E. Borges

Deusto Institute of Technology – DeustoTech Energy, University of Deusto,
Avda. Universidades 24, 48007 Bilbao, Spain
{ander.pijoan,oihane.esteban,cruz.borges}@deusto.es

Abstract. We present here an autonomous agent-based system tightly coupled with Geographic Information Systems (GIS). Our objective is to model a city's dynamic in order to foresee both its urban evolution and the influence that the appearance of new settlements has on the overall electricity demand. This environment is deployed on a GIS-based Multi-Agent System platform where the geographical and communication components have been abstracted from the agent system onto the environment. The configuration model uses geographical information in order to improve the agents' connection and perception of their surroundings. Based on the agent's choices, we forecast urban evolution and derive the expected increment in electric consumption. We have validated our approach with real data and discuss here our conclusions.

Keywords: Agent-based simulation · Environment modelling · Geographic Information System · Spatial Load Forecasting

1 Introduction

One of the biggest challenges that electrical distribution companies face is the growth in demand for electrical power. Under the current economic conditions, this problematic boosts exponentially: distribution companies aim at getting the most out of the existing infrastructures, especially when their renovation can be really expensive. Thus, long term load forecasts are extremely useful for energy suppliers, Distribution System Operators (DSOs), financial institutions, and other participants in the electric energy generation, distribution, and retail sectors.

The concept of Long-Term Load Forecasting (LTLF) involves social, economic, policy and technical issues to which we must add the problems of having limited amounts of information and the difficulty to operate with the scarce data available [1]. In this sense, LTLF is closely linked to urban evolution since its main models derive from the fields of geography and sociology. Nowadays, these models are being combined with others stemming from Artificial Intelligence (AI). This integration brings together the best qualities of both areas: AI provides the learning ability and the capacity to interpret the available data, while social and spatial models define the natural behaviour and characteristics of the

© Springer International Publishing Switzerland 2015
D. Weyns and F. Michel (Eds.): E4MAS 2014 – 10 years later, LNAI 9068, pp. 188–206, 2015.
DOI: 10.1007/978-3-319-23850-0_12

problem at hand. The technical literature shows a wide range of methodologies and models for LTLF which can generally be classified into two broad categories: statistical methods and artificial-intelligence-based methods. Statistical load forecasting methods comprise approaches mainly based on time series and regression models [2]. In turn, artificial intelligence methods comprise methodologies like networks [3], genetic algorithms [4], support vector machines [5], and fuzzy logic [6].

The growth in demand for electric power can be decomposed into two axes. On the one hand, there is the so-called *vertical growth*, which represents a boost in power demand due to an increment in the electrification of the existing households. On the other hand, the *horizontal growth* involves the appearance of new settlements on an specific area, motivated by the natural evolution of the population. The analysis of these phenomena is crucial since an improper estimation may lead to the saturation of the electrical infrastructure and the loss of power supply, along with the consequent economic losses and social distress.

In this venue, there is a special type of LTLF that deserves a closer look due to its economic importance: Spatial Load Forecasting (SLF). SLF uses a model built over a Geographic Information System (GIS) to get together data related to electric distribution, land use, and development indicators. In this way, urban infrastructure engineers will be able to predict, years in advance, any new load and how it affects the electric system, helping them to determine whether the current infrastructure should be upgraded or not. Failing to do so leads to the inability to cope with load peaks, appearance of brownouts, blackouts and, in general, low-quality supply. Furthermore, there is a lengthy amount of previous research on agent-based simulations using GIS, whether it is a geographic phenomena or a phenomena with an important geographic component, covering several aspects of Urban Modelling [7,8] and Housing [9].

Agent-Based Modelling (ABM) is experimenting a notable boost in new fields lately due to its versatility and ability to model and simulate human behaviour in very diverse disciplines, as seen in [10–12]. Paradoxically, though ABM is a well-known and intensively used tool in related areas SLF remains *terra incognita* for this paradigm. SLF is a crucial task for the majority of the stakeholders in the electric sector due to its capacity to calculate the future evolution of energy demand on a certain zone. So far, the only attempt to bring together ABM and SLF is, to our notice, [13]. Still, ABM and GIS should be coupled tighter in order to improve the quality of forecasts.

We advance the state of the art by describing our experience in integrating an ABM and a GIS along with Volunteer Geographic Information in order to obtain an improved SLF system. The remainder of the paper is divided as follows. Section 2 describes the most relevant research done in the field of agent environments. Sections 3 and 4 give an overview of the Environment definition and its application to SLF. Section 5 describes both the architecture and logic schema of the application. Section 6 discusses the main results obtained. Section 7 introduces new research challenges in the field of SLF. And, finally, Sect. 8 draws the conclusions of the paper and points out our future work.

2   Related Work

Within MAS technologies, the Environment concept has been recognised as an independent and living element which is essential to model dynamic real world problems. Ten years ago, [14] already defined the scope and differences between the agent environment and agents that inhabit it.

Real Environments are inherently dynamic, they change beyond the agents' control, therefore this dynamism must be modelled explicitly as part of the simulated Environment by implementing processes that can change its own state. In this sense, [15] defines the structural parts of the Environment that endow the system with a logical definition and abstraction: entities, properties, activities, states and scenarios. They also propose a domain-specific formalism that provides models and constructs to control dynamism in the simulated Environment and delineates how agents can manipulate such dynamism. The way in which agents interact is conceptualised by *interference laws* which provides a model with explicit means to define what kind of interactions between entities are relevant for the simulation.

[16] defines a suitable software architecture that highlights the core functionalities that should be present in every agent environment such as a deployment context that comprises sensors and actuators with which the MAS interacts, an abstraction level that bridges the conceptual gap between agent abstraction and low-level details, as well as an interaction-mediation level that regulates the access to shared resources and mediates the interaction between agents. [17] establishes a design and implementation of an environment as a first-class entity for a geographically based sgimulation system.

[18] establishes that MAS applications can be heavily influenced by the structure of the environment in which their agents operate. An appropriate environment definition can help and bring together real world scenarios and applications by addressing key issues as time management, sensor processing, augmented reality and virtual actuators. In this sense, Electronic Institutions can be exploited as they provide the means to enforce and monitor the language, behaviour and protocol within agents society, enabling the interaction between the environment and the real world.

Agent environments are an exploitable design element in MAS. [19] defines several mechanisms of the environment that address activities related to the different levels of support that should be available in every agent system, such as, an interaction mediation that enables agent to interact and communicate in a flexible and uncoupled way, a centralised synchronisation that supports the simultaneity of actions for system consistency, an overlay network that represents the relationships between agents, a resource and context manager for representing context information and resources in an efficient way and notification of contextual events for the production and delivery of event notifications to create dynamic agent contexts.

3   Environment Modelling

Following the bibliography, our Environment consists of three main pieces. On the one hand, a Physical Environment and a Social Environment, which come together to form the universe where both passive entities and agents are situated. On the other hand, a Simulation Engine which is in charge of modelling the skills these entities are able to execute (including their communication and perception capabilities).

In fact, the skill sets defined by the Environment are the central point of our vision. Skills are the degree of competence that differentiates and empowers people to perform tasks and do so with agents and passive entities. The skills serve both to characterize Entities in the MAS and are the way to perceive or propagate actions into the Environment and other entities. However, every skill needs to be contained within a context and behave under some restrictions. We believe that the Environment needs to hold the responsibility of ensuring that these constraints are met and limit the capabilities of each entity type. So, in our vision, Entities *use* the skills provided by the Environment.

The Entities are the actors that interfere in the simulation. All of them are derived from a parent skeleton that contains the basic attributes and procedures, even if they do not make use of them. These entities can be categorised in two different groups whether they have their own behaviour or they just react to stimuli.

Autonomous Agents constitute the traditional agents in a MAS. They are scheduled to follow a certain behaviour and can use the already mentioned skills to interact with other Entities or with the Environment. Each agent type is characterised by its set of skills and will have a state given by several private parameters.

On the other hand, Passive Entities are those entities who, although having some *logic* inside, just react to the actions of other Entities. Namely, they provide or receive information from agents and other passive entities. Please note that passive entities can make use of skills as well while honouring their restrictions. Figure 1 shows a more comprehensive diagram of the proposed architecture.

To clarify the previous concepts we will present a toy example. Suppose that we want to make a simulation of a road junction. In this case the Environment would consists on the graph that represents the junction and a routing skill. The simulation would be formed by several autonomous Agents including different vehicles and pedestrians. The environment would provide them with the same routing skill `route(Point A, Point B; Agent Type)` but depending on the agent type it would compute different routes (pedestrian cannot use roads and vehicles cannot use side walks). A traffic light on the road junction which only changes its state from time to time would be a Passive Entity but an intelligent traffic signal, that reacts to the amount of pedestrian and vehicles in the junction, would be an Autonomous Agent.

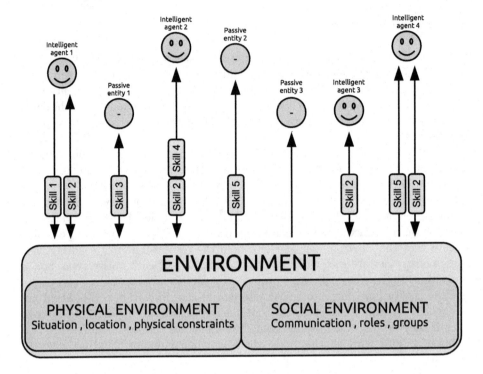

Fig. 1. Architecture of the environment and agents.

4   Environment Modelling for Spatial Load Forecasting

The MAS system presented hereby is able to simulate the variation in the load of the transformers and electrical substations located on a certain city. To this end, we have modelled the behaviour, evaluations and decisions a human takes when choosing a new place to live. Figure 2 describes a simplified class diagram of the code implementation. Our configuration is based on the environmental approach proposed by *Russel and Norvig* [14, 20] being:

Accessible: The agents have access to the whole environment.
Non-deterministic: A change in the state of the environment depends on the management of threads by the Operating System on which the simulation is running.
Dynamic: The environment can change while the agent deliberated.
Discrete: The number of percepts is limited and centralised.

Our Environment is populated by both Passive Entities, used for representing the city infrastructure like substations, transformers and existing buildings, and Autonomous Agents in the form of greenfields and buyers.

In line with this model, the pseudo code can be described as follows:

Procedure. RUN-ENVIRONMENT(state, UPDATE-FN, agents, termination)

Data: Initial state of the environment
while *!termination(state)* **do**
    for greenfield *in* greenfields **do**
        PERCEPT1[*greenfield*] = Get-Around-Facilities(greenfield, state)
        PERCEPT2[*greenfield*] =
        Get-Around-Constructed-Buildings(greenfield, state)
        ACTION1[*greenfield*] =
        Determine-Dwelling-Characteristics[PERCEPT1,PERCEPT2(*agent*)]
        ACTION2[*greenfield*] = Set-Dwelling-Price[ACTION1(*agent*)]
    end
    for agent *in* agents **do**
        PERCEPT[*agent*] = Get-List-Greenfields(agent, state)
        ACTION1[*agent*] = Evaluate-Greenfields[PERCEPT(*agent*)]
        while *!assigned &&greenfields-available* **do**
         | ACTION2[*agent*] = Get-Greenfield[ACTION1(*agent*)]
        end
        ACTION3[*CT*] = Add-Load[ACTION2(*agent*)]
    end
    state = UPDATE-FN(*actions, agent, state*)
end

4.1 Substations and Transformers

Substations and transformers are modelled as Passive Entities as their only function is to receive the power demands of the new households (see Sect. 4.4 below for more details).

Each transformer t and substation s has a nominal power, a demanded power (E_t and E_s) and a simultaneity factor (S_t and S_s). Since the electric grid and its elements need to size their nominal power in order to manage demand peaks, the simultaneity factor is critical. It is calculated comparing the maximum power demand with the contracted power of the clients. In that way, it adjusts the theoretical total consumption of the clients to real conditions. Unfortunately, the dataset we have does not include power measurements for the transformers (for more details see Sect. 5.1). In fact, the lowest level where we had real measures was at substation outputs. Therefore, we had to calculate the simultaneity factor S_t at this level, inheriting the simultaneity factor to all the transformers connected to it. The formula used is:

$$S_t := \frac{r_s}{\sum_{t \in T_s} \sum_{c \in C_t} p_c},$$

where r_s denotes the maximum measure registered at the substations output s, T_s denotes the set of transformers connected to that substation output, C_t

denotes the set of clients connected to transformer t and finally p_c denotes the contracted power of client c.

4.2   Buildings

Buildings are those residential dwellings situated in the environment. Every building has its physical representation, concerning location, area, building levels, and the electrical information regarding the amount of clients, the transformer they are connected to and how much power they demand. Buildings are modelled as Passive Entities, so that greenfields (Autonomous Agents) can ask them in order to forecast which type of construction they will harbour.

4.3   Greenfields

Greenfields are modelled as agents that emulate the land plots where new buildings can be constructed. Local authorities define a location as *accessible to citizens* if it is within 5 min walking. That is, considering that the speed of a pedestrian is 4 km/h, this distance corresponds to 300 m. Therefore, every greenfield has the skill to perceive its surroundings up to 300 m. As a first approximation, these agents will search and calculate the straight-line distance d_i to several public facilities (e.g. green zones, public transports, parking spaces, and the like). Table 1 shows a comprehensive list of these public facilities. One of the problems faced when working with developable land use, is that, though not yet urbanised, some of these areas have already been split into smaller parcels while others comprise a whole rural area. Although clipped greenfields give some clues about the type of buildings they may contain, without such information, it is still hard to determine the type of construction and how many citizens will host each greenfield. So, as next step, in order to overcome this problem the greenfield estimates, using a spatial moving window smoothing [21], the type of building, number of dwellings and building levels expected according to all adjacent buildings within 300 m.

Finally, based on the loaded information, each plot establishes its price per square meter and searches for its nearest transformer substation, which the new settlements will connect to. The process is as follows: first a Voronoi diagram is calculated from the set of transformers that serve more than one client (single-client transformers are owned individually, which means that they are not accessible by the DSO). Then, the plot makes the connection with the transformer whose area of influence presents the largest intersection with its own surface.

4.4   Buyers

The buyers are agents that emulate the people looking for a new house. Since every person has different preferences about the presence of (or distance to) a particular public facility, we have encoded them in a vector a_i that describes how important each infrastructure is to a particular agent i. Moreover, agents

Table 1. Factors considered.

Factor	Infrastructures considered
HEALTH	Hospitals, clinics
EDUCATION	Schools, colleges, kindergardens, universities
SPORTS	Public swimming pools, pitch, stadiums
CULTURAL	Art centres, theatres, community centres, conference centres, museums, libraries, cinemas
FOOD SHOPS	Food and convenience shops, department stores, supermarkets

have an individual budget limit and a degree of greediness depending on which, they will query a different number of greenfield. Further, we have identified three primary target groups sharing a common preference pattern: Elderlies, Families and Singles. The accurate values of the preference vector have been issued using a uniform random variable with the mean described in Table 2 and a 10 % of standard deviation.

Table 2. Agents types and their preferences. Average values.

Type	HEALTH	EDUCATION	SPORTS	CULTURAL	FOOD	AFFORD
ELDERLIES	1	0.2	0	0.7	0.8	€1800
FAMILIES	0.9	1	0.7	0.3	0.5	€1750
SINGLES	0.2	0.2	1	1	0.8	€1700

When the agents have been loaded into the Environment, they select a number of greenfields that will be asked for information. The agent will then select the plot that maximises the following function f:

$$f(a, d) := \begin{cases} -1 & \text{if plot price} > \text{agent budget} \\ \sum_{j \in J} \dfrac{a_{ij}}{d_j} & \text{in other case,} \end{cases}$$

where a_i is the preference vector of the agent i, d_j is the distance from each building to the infrastructure j (see Table 2) and J are the categories in Table 1. Next, the agent will try to buy this plot. In case some other agent has already bought it, the current agent will try to acquire its next preferred option until the plots reach the minimum desired quality set. Please note that it may be possible for an agent not to get a greenfield. Finally, the electrical load generated by each agent is added to the corresponding electrical infrastructure following the function l:

$$l(a, d) := E_t + I_a \cdot S_t \cdot A \cdot P_c,$$

where E_t is the previous load in that particular electrical infrastructure, I_a is the electrical intensity of agent a (i.e. how much power will the new settlement need), S_t is the simultaneity factor (see Sect. 4.1) of the loads in that particular infrastructure, A is the area covered by this plot, and P_c is the power intensity of the area, measured as:

$$P_c := \frac{|B_{300}| \sum\limits_{c \in C_{300}} p_c}{|C_{300}| \sum\limits_{b \in B_{300}} s_b},$$

where B_{300} is the set of buildings within 300 m radius, C_{300} is the set of clients within a 300 m radius, $|\cdot|$ denotes the set cardinality, p_c is the contracted power by client c, and s_b is the total surface of the building (measured as the constructed area times the floor count).

By combining these data, when an agent is assigned to an available greenfield, the system analyses the consumption of the neighbouring parcels and size of the buildings in order to predict how much power this new settlement will need. This amount is then added to the total load of the transformer from which the plot feeds.

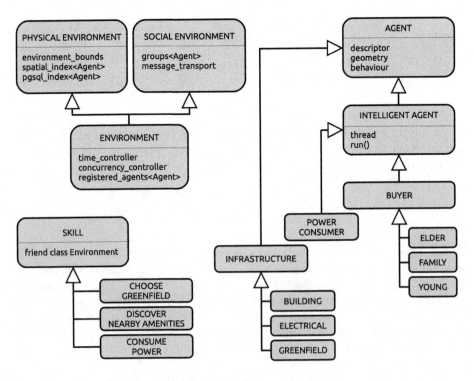

Fig. 2. Simplified class diagram of the environment.

5   Experimental Set-Up

5.1   Data

The experiments have been carried out with real data from Ciudad Real, a Spanish middle-sized city with about 32 thousand power consuming clients and a surface of $400\,km^2$, including the surrounding municipalities of Miguelturra, Carrión de Calatrava and Poblete. A map of the zone can be seen in Fig. 3. Electric infrastructure and clients' measurements were provided by the corresponding utility (Gas Natural Fenosa, a Spanish DSO) while buildings and landuse data was obtained by conflating the Spanish cadastre records with the VGI source OpenStreetMap [22,23]. Both datasets are stored in a PostgreSQL relational database bolstered with the PostGIS geographical extension for manipulating spatial data. Although the Spanish cadastre registers the price for each plot, said information is private and is not provided in their open-data initiative. The most detailed prices found were extracted from recent appraisals performed by the appraiser Tasamadrid [24], which provides average prices per square meter grouped by postcode.

Despite the spatial data being only a snapshot of the city in 2013, all electric power clients are geolocated and have a registration date. So that, we can assume that the date of the building's creation is the same as the first client assigned to that particular building. The information covers the years from 2005 to 2010. Therefore, we get a complete historical map of the evolution of the city and can determine which areas were inhabited between those years. Nevertheless, we cannot ensure the moment in which the rural areas were zoned into greenfields as the status of the plots change by local laws and is not recorded in public databases.

5.2   Implementation

In a first approach, we developed the simulation based on the SPADE platform. Written in Python, SPADE is a free software multi-agent system platform based on the instant messaging XMPP technology [25]. The most noticeable features include support for virtual organisations, presence notifications, compliance with the FIPA standard, P2P communication between agents, remote invocation of services using the standard XML-RPC, inclusion of multiple knowledge-based engines, such as XSB-Prolog, SWI-Prolog, Flora-2, ECLiPse-Prolog and SPARQL.

Although the implementation of agents in SPADE is quite straightforward, we found some difficulties and drawbacks on the real experimentation. While SPADE provides many utilities for the construction of the infrastructure, given that our project does not need distributed agents, the heavy communication protocol that SPADE deploys has become more of a limitation than a facility. As the amount of agents starts to increase, operations like registration and intercommunication between agents become slower. This makes big simulations very heavy or directly unmanageable. Executions in a big server showed that the maximum amount of

Fig. 3. Overview map of the test zone.

agents SPADE could create, while being fully functional, was around 600, including both agents and passive entities which was not an acceptable amount.

In search for a highly abstracted and scalable solution to be used for future simulations as well, we developed a second approach from scratch using C++ programming language. For this purpose, we have gone through Qt [26] which is a widely used cross-platform framework for developing native applications. Qt uses standard C++ with extensions including signals and slots for event handling, metaobject compiler and the ability to detach pieces of code and moving them to another thread.

Using Qt has allowed us to create a complete independent and robust simulation engine based on our understanding of the Environment described in Sect. 3. . Regarding implementation, the main Environment class inherits from two parent classes that correspond to the Physical World, containing location, geometries and geospatial indexes for all entities, and a Social Environment, which is in charge of managing groups, knowledge and messages between entities. Spatial indexing and operations are resolved using a PostGIS spatially extended PostgreSQL database where all entities are situated for 3D measurements, spatial routing, nearest neighbours searches and other. Messaging is built on the Paradigm of Qt signals and slots, one of its central features and probably the part that differs most from the features provided by other frameworks. As alternative to callback techniques, signals are events that any object can connect from 0 to N slots in a loosely coupled way. A class which emits a signal neither knows nor cares which slots receive the signal and it can take any number of arguments of any type.

In addition to the Environment, the wide range of skills is the main bulk of the simulation platform. All skills are implemented by extending an abstract base skill forming a big hierarchy tree grouped by physical and mental abilities. Being the skills embedded in the environment makes it possible for both to ensure all constraints and laws are satisfied.

For parallelisation and queueing management we have used the Threadweaver system library included in KDE Frameworks [27]. By splitting the workload into individual jobs, Threadweaver permits to define relationships, priorities and dependencies between jobs working out the most efficient way to execute them. Complementing parallelisation, Qt's QMutex class provides access serialisation between threads to critical resources and attributes. Both Agents and Passive Entities extend an abstract base Entity class. The main difference between these two is that Agents will extend a Threadweaver job and consequently will have a Run() method for starting their behaviour in an independent thread.

Finally, the described architecture defines the backend of the system for the simulation. But regarding visualisation and interaction, the system implements a real-time light web frontend. Optionally, the backend can deploy an HTTP Server with a RESTFULL API to access and modify from simulation parameters to the entities themselves. Execution is displayed over an interactive map built with LeafletJS [28] light maps library and real time events are pushed from the backend to the frontend through Qt's websockets.

6   Experimental Results

For each independent year which electrical growth we want to forecast, the validation process creates a historical map that describes the status of the buildings of the city. In addition, it creates several distributions of agents in order to contrast the process outcome with the real settlements:

Environment: The validation process identifies the buildings that were registered as such from a given year onwards and marks them as available greenfields, considering the date in which the building was created is the same as the oldest settlement registered.

Agent System: All the scenarios will create the same amount of agents as new possible settlements that may appeared on that year. The main difference will be the amount of agents of each type created at each case.

Greediness: We have validated the system considering agents with and without greediness. Obviously, the experiments that do not consider agent's greediness obtain better results as the agents are aware of the whole environment. We only provide results experiments where the greediness is considered as it is a more realistic scenario.

Plots' price: The unitary price of the plots is estimated using recent appraisals performed by the appraiser Tasamadrid.

We have defined different metrics in order to test the results obtained with this model. The error can be split into two categories: spatial errors and effective errors.

Spatial Errors: Errors related to the spatial component of the forecast. Namely, we measure how many agents correctly select the year y in which a greenfield has been built ($hits_y$), how many agents incorrectly select the year y in which a greenfield has been built ($semi_y$) and how many agents have completely failed by selecting a greenfield that even today has not been built ($fails_y$). Thus, we have measured:

$$hits_y := \frac{a_y}{b_y}, \qquad semi_y := \frac{f_y}{\sum_{j=y+1}^{2010} b_j}, \qquad fails_y := 1 - hits,$$

where a_y denotes the number of agents that correctly select a plot that is built in the year y, f_y denotes the number of agents that incorrectly set on a plot in the year y which in reality was built in the following years, b_y denotes the number of plots that have indeed been built in the year y. The variables $hits$, $semi$ and $fails$ are just mean values over of $hits_y$, $semi_y$ and $fail_y$ respectively.

Effective Errors: In this category we measure the load forecasting error. Traditionally, this error is calculated using the MAPE error [29]:

$$mape := \frac{1}{6|S|} \sum_{s \in S} \sum_{y=2005}^{2010} \frac{|r_y^s - p_y^s|}{r_y^s},$$

where S denotes the set of transformers, $|\cdot|$ denotes the set cardinality operator, p_y^s denotes the model's forecast for the maximum load of substation s at year y and r_y^s denotes the real one.

Please note that, in this model, MAPE is not a reliable source of error as there is a large variability among the experiments. This situation is due to technical or electrical infrastructure exploitation issues that force a building to not be always connected to its nearest transformer. In order to mitigate this problem, a possibility solution is to measure the error one level higher in the electrical infrastructure, that is, at substation level. However, this measurement would blur the results and hinder the possibility to identify zones where the model is not working correctly. Moreover, in terms of performance, the calculation of this value is quite complex due to the number of database queries that would need to be performed which, in turn, increases the execution time of each simulation.

We have tested the forecasting ability of the model in two situations: for one year ahead and five years ahead forecasts. Moreover, as a contrast method we used random assignation of agents to greenfields. In order to calculate an approximated p-value we have used a Monte Carlo approach. Namely, we have repeated 100 times the random assignation for every year to approximate the density function of the random variable $hits + semi$ under the null hypothesis that our method and the random Monte Carlo approach would derive the same results. From the approximate density function we calculate the associated $p-value$ (see $pval$ in Table 3).

In the first case, each year is evaluated independently, and the outcome is not considered for the following evaluation. Figure 4a shows the empirical probability density function constructed with 100 repetitions of the contrast method. Table 3 shows the numerical results for 1 year ahead forecast (mean value of the 5 years). The first three columns represent the percentage of agent of every type that we have created in that particular experiment. Please note that the 0/0/0 row represent the Monte Carlo approach.

On the other hand, for the 5 year forecasting, we use a *rolling forecast* approach [30]. Namely, we will use the foretasted results of the previous years to predict the following year. As for the 1 year ahead case, Fig. 4b shows the empirical probability density function constructed with 100 repetition of the contrast method and Table 3 shows the numerical results of the five years ahead forecast.

Figure 4 shows, as expected, a large difference between the errors of the experiment in the 1 year ahead forecasting and the 5 years ahead forecasting. Not only

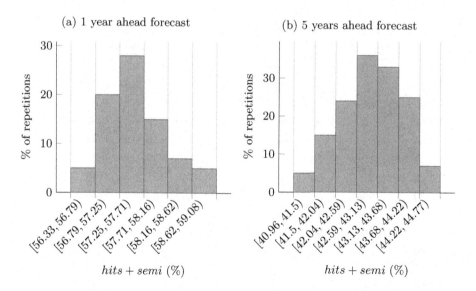

Fig. 4. Probability density function of the random variable $hits + semi$.

do the results of the random assignation are better in the 1 year ahead forecasting, but they also have considerably less variance. Table 3 confirms this expectation. In the case of the 1 year ahead forecasting the mean value of *hits* + *semi* is around 70 %, while in the case of 5 years forecasting it is around 66 %. Please note that this value is quite high considering that the random assignation has achieved 58 and 43 % (respectively) in those experiments. The results of using the proposed MAS model are in all cases significantly better than those corresponding to the random Monte Carlo approach. Take into account that the first row corresponds to the Monte Carlo approach, so in this particular case, we are comparing the same results.

The distribution of *hits* and *semi* in both experiments is also interesting. While in the 1 year ahead forecasting experiment *semi* is quite high (around 50 %) in the 5 years ahead forecasting experiment is near 30 %. The explanation of these results is straightforward: in the 1 year ahead forecasting experiment, the number of greenfields that (if occupied) score a *semi* decrease with every year, while in the case of 5 years ahead forecasting they are constant. Please note that it is impossible to score a *semi* in the last year of the 1 year ahead forecasting experiment since we do not have information of the next year and all the houses of previous years have already been occupied.

The results show how different agent type distributions affect the accuracy of the prediction delivered by our model. As the typical house buyers in Spain are families, it is expected that models with a high percentage of families agents will perform better. The results from the 5 years ahead forecasting confirm that

Table 3. Experimental results for the different agent type composition. All measures are in %.

Elderly	Families	Young	1 year forecast				5 years forecast			
			hits	semi	fails	pval	hits	semi	fails	pval
0	0	0	0.14	0.44	0.42	0.41	0.18	0.25	0.57	0.45
100	0	0	0.17	0.49	0.34	0.00	0.34	0.31	0.35	0.00
0	100	0	0.22	0.50	0.28	0.00	0.34	0.35	0.32	0.00
0	0	100	0.19	0.55	0.26	0.00	0.29	0.37	0.34	0.00
50	25	25	0.17	0.51	0.31	0.00	0.30	0.35	0.35	0.00
25	50	25	0.21	0.49	0.30	0.00	0.33	0.34	0.34	0.00
25	25	50	0.17	0.55	0.28	0.00	0.27	0.37	0.36	0.00
80	10	10	0.18	0.49	0.33	0.00	0.34	0.31	0.35	0.00
10	80	10	0.22	0.49	0.29	0.00	0.34	0.35	0.32	0.00
10	10	80	0.19	0.55	0.26	0.00	0.29	0.36	0.34	0.00
60	20	20	0.17	0.50	0.33	0.00	0.34	0.32	0.35	0.00
20	60	20	0.21	0.49	0.30	0.00	0.33	0.34	0.33	0.00
20	20	60	0.18	0.54	0.28	0.00	0.28	0.37	0.35	0.00

hypothesis. The best agent mix consists of considering only agents of Family type while in the mixed cases, those with high percentage of Family agents perform at least as well as the other. On the contrary, it seems that in the short term (1 year ahead forecasting), the Young are the main variable. This can be explained as Young frequently change their homes, so in the short term, buildings near their favourite places are occupied in a short time.

Qualitatively, we can see that the solutions follow the logic imposed by the vector of preferences in the settlement of the agents. Figure 5 shows the distribution of Elderly, Families and Young agents through three different heatmaps. The first one shows how the final distribution of the Elderly and the localisation of Clinics and Hospitals. In the second one, we present the final distribution of Families and the localisation of Schools. Finally, in the third one, we present the final distribution of Young agents and the localisation of Sport Centres. In the three cases the final distribution loosely approximate to the localisation of the corresponding infrastructures.

7   Open Challenges in SmartGrid Integration

To conclude this paper, we describe research challenges that, in our opinion, are important for the further exploration of spatial load forecasting within MAS environments.

New smart power grids demand a huge effort in redesigning and enhancing current power networks, as well as integrating distributed generation, renewable energies and the electric vehicle. Contrary to the previous centralised and unidirectional model (i.e., from centralised generation via the transmission and distribution grids to the customers), smart grids will change to a bidirectional power flow model that will include distributed generation (mainly from renewable sources) and the electric vehicle.

The power network operation needs to be safe, reliable and, as long as possible, cost effective. The new scenario enabled by the massive adoption of distributed generation and storage and the intensive application of information technologies render the old centralised and static architecture infeasible. The main reason is that gathering the complete information to achieve optimal management, if possible at all, would entail a prohibitive cost in infrastructure and time. Therefore, a trade-off must be found between distributing the intelligence and the costs associated to this decision.

The grid computing paradigm presents inspiring characteristics for modelling agent environments that will help the smart grid vision come true. Indeed, grid computing applications are based on a group of distributed nodes carrying out a task coordinated by a central entity: power networks do have many nodes (e.g., meters and substations) and tasks that require participation and coordination (e.g., invoicing: demands retrieving the consumption data from all clients, applying the corresponding prices, and notifying the clients) among all of the nodes. MAS and agent environments can tackle this challenge by distributing the intelligence all over the grid by means of individual intelligent agents controlling a number of assets.

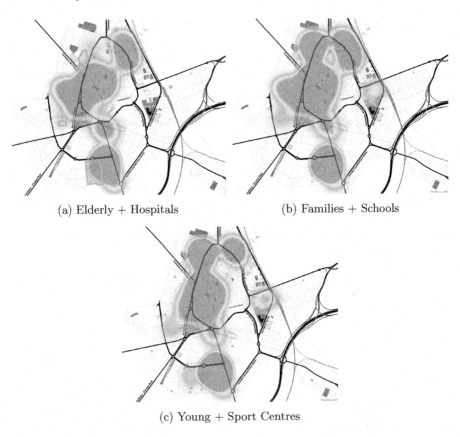

(a) Elderly + Hospitals   (b) Families + Schools

(c) Young + Sport Centres

Fig. 5. Distribution (heatmap) of the new settlement by type.

The management and configuration of power grids is closely linked with urban evolution. Social dynamics dictate the appearance of new settlements as well as the amount of energy demanded depending on the economic availability, the age and preferences of new costumers and the own evolution of the city. The edification of new infrastructures such as hospitals, schools, parks, malls; even the construction of new roads heavily influence the citizens' decisions and mobility.

Proper modelling of the dynamics of human behaviour will help in achieving more accurate simulations. Though simulation of the exact process of human thought is a complex task, the introduction of AI techniques in our system, such as Fuzzy Logic, will allow to mimic human decision making by building a wide range of behavioural rules in response to the stimulus and events of the environment, instead of the fixed decision approach used in our experiments. This modelling would then provide a parametrised sandbox to analyse and classify what kind of infrastructural and social changes in the city influence the most the variation of the electricity demand.

8   Conclusions

This paper presents a novel Spatial Lad Forecasting model for Long Term Load Forecasting based in a proper modelling of the Environment plus the coupling of a MAS system with a GIS software. The use of open data from public administrations, such as Spanish cadastre and Volunteer Geographic Information allows us to validate the model using real world examples. The success rate when issuing 1 year ahead forecast is above 70 % and 66 % when issuing a 5 years ahead forecasting. Although the model is achieving very good results, we are looking forward to adding an evolutionary algorithm in order to train the model with the optimal parameters. This will allow us to issue improved forecast that indirectly will give us a better representation of the process.

Acknowledgments. This research was partially funded by ITEA2 Nemo & Coded (ITI-20110864) and the Ph.D. grant PRE_2013_1_516 given by the Basque Government. The authors would also like to thank the reviewers for their comments and suggestions to improve this paper.

References

1. Willis, H.: Spatial Load Forecasting. Marcel Dekker Inc., New York (1996)
2. Alfares, H.K., Nazeeruddin, M.: Electric load forecasting: literature survey and classification of methods. Int. J. Syst. Sci. **33**(1), 23–34 (2002)
3. Senjyu, T., Takara, H., Uezato, K., Funabashi, T.: One-hour-ahead load forecasting using neural network. IEEE Trans. Power Syst. **17**(1), 113–118 (2002)
4. Lai, L.L.: Intelligent System Applications in Power Engineering: Evolutionary Programming and Neural Networks. Wiley, New York (1998)
5. Pai, P.-F., Hong, W.-C.: Forecasting regional electricity load based on recurrent support vector machines with genetic algorithms. Electr. Power Syst. Res. **74**(3), 417–425 (2005)
6. Farahat, M.: Long-term industrial load forecasting and planning using neural networks technique and fuzzy inference method. In: 39th International Universities Power Engineering Conference, UPEC 2004, vol. 1, pp. 368–372. IEEE (2004)
7. Li, Y., Muller, B.: Residential location and the biophysical environment: exurban development agents in a heterogeneous landscape. Environ. Planning B **34**, 279–295 (2007)
8. Crooks, A., Castle, C., Batty, M.: Key challenges in agent-based modelling for geo-spatial simulation. Comput. Environ. Urban Syst. **32**, 417–430 (2008)
9. Jordan, R., Birkin, M., Evans, A.: Agent-based simulation modelling of housing choice and urban regeneration policy. In: Bosse, T., Geller, A., Jonker, C.M. (eds.) MABS 2010. LNCS, vol. 6532, pp. 152–166. Springer, Heidelberg (2011)
10. Axtell, R.L., Epstein, J.M., Dean, J.S., Gumerman, G.J., Swedlund, A.C., Harburger, J., Chakravarty, S., Hammond, R., Parker, J., Parker, M.: Population growth and collapse in a multiagent model of the kayenta anasazi in long house valley. Proc. Nat. Acad. Sci. **99**(suppl 3), 7275–7279 (2002)
11. Malleson, N., Heppenstall, A.J., See, L.M.: Crime reduction through simulation: an agent-based model of burglary. Comput. Environ. Urban Syst. **34**(3), 236–250 (2010)

12. Crooks, A., Heppenstall, A.: Introduction to agent-based modelling. In: Heppenstall, A.J., Crooks, A.T., See, L.M., Batty, M. (eds.) Agent-Based Models of Geographical Systems, pp. 85–105. Springer, Netherlands (2012)
13. Borges, C., Penya, Y., Pijoan, A.: Agent based spatial load forecasting. In: Proceedings of 3rd International Workshop on Agent Technologies for Energy Systems (ATES 2012) held at the 11th International Conference on Autonomous Agents and Multiagent Systems (AAMAS 2012), Valencia, Spain, pp. 107–108. ACM press, 5 June 2012
14. Weyns, D., Van Dyke Parunak, H., Michel, F., Holvoet, T., Ferber, J.: Environments for multiagent systems state-of-the-art and research challenges. In: Weyns, D., Van Dyke Parunak, H., Michel, F. (eds.) E4MAS 2004. LNCS (LNAI), vol. 3374, pp. 1–47. Springer, Heidelberg (2005)
15. Helleboogh, A., Vizzari, G., Uhrmacher, A., Michel, F.: Modeling dynamic environments in multi-agent simulation. Auton. Agent. Multi-Agent Syst. **14**(1), 87–116 (2007)
16. Weyns, D., Omicini, A., Odell, J.: Environment as a first class abstraction in multiagent systems. Auton. Agent. Multi-Agent Syst. **14**(1), 5–30 (2007)
17. Steiner, R., Leask, G., Mili, R.Z.: An architecture for MAS simulation environments. In: Weyns, D., Van Dyke Parunak, H., Michel, F. (eds.) E4MAS 2005. LNCS (LNAI), vol. 3830, pp. 50–67. Springer, Heidelberg (2006)
18. Valckenaers, P., Sauter, J., Sierra, C., Rodriguez-Aguilar, J.A.: Applications and environments for multi-agent systems. Auton. Agent. Multi-Agent Syst. **14**(1), 61–85 (2007)
19. Platon, E., Mamei, M., Sabouret, N., Honiden, S., Parunak, H.: Mechanisms for environments in multi-agent systems: survey and opportunities. Auton. Agent. Multi-Agent Syst. **14**(1), 31–47 (2006)
20. Russell, S.J., Norvig, P., Canny, J.F., Malik, J.M., Edwards, D.D.: Artificial Intelligence: A Modern Approach. Prentice Hall, Upper Saddle River (2003)
21. Kiesel, J., Wenkel, K.-O.: Spatial generalization methods based on the moving window approach and their applications on landscape analysis. In: Olgierd Hryniewicz, M.R.E., Studzinski J. (ed.), Shaker Verlag, pp. 619–626. Shaker Verlag (2007). ISBN: 978-3-8322-6397-3
22. Pijoan, A., Borges, C.: Tutorial de importación de datos de Catastro a OSM (cat2osm). In: Actas de las vi Jornadas de SIG Libre, Girona 21–23 marzo, España, Servicio de SIG y Teledetección - SIGTE - de la Universitat de Girona (2012)
23. Borges, C., Pijoan, A., Sorrosal, G., Oribe-García, I., González, M., Esteban, O.K.: Uso de fuentes de información geográfica voluntarias en proyectos de ingeniería. In: Actas de las vii Jornadas de SIG Libre, Girona 6–8 marzo, España, Servicio de SIG y Teledetección - SIGTE - de la Universitat de Girona (2013)
24. Tinsa, Precio medio del m^2 por provincia (2013). http://www.elmundo.es/suvivienda/sv/tasaciones/
25. Gregori, M.E., Cámara, J.P., Bada, G.A.: A jabber-based multi-agent system platform. In: Proceedings of the Fifth International Joint Conference on Autonomous Agents and Multiagent Systems, pp. 1282–1284. ACM (2006)
26. Qt Company, Qt cross-platform application framework (2014). https://qt-project.org/
27. KDE e.V, KDE frameworks (2014). https://www.kde.org/
28. Agafonkin, V.: LeafletJS (2014). http://leafletjs.com/
29. Hyndman, R.J., Koehler, A.B.: Another look at measures of forecast accuracy. Int. J. Forecast. **22**(4), 679–688 (2006)
30. Hyndman, R.J., Athanasopoulos, G.: Forecasting: principles and practice. OTexts (2014)

Open Agent Environments
and Interoperability

Towards Organizational Interoperability Through the Environment

Fabio Tsuyoshi Muramatsu[1], Tomas Monteiro Vitorello[1],
and Anarosa Alves Franco Brandão[1,2(✉)]

[1] Computing Engineering and Digital Systems Department, University of Sao
Paulo, Sao Paulo, Brazil
{fabio.muramatsu, tomas.vitorello,
anarosa.brandao}@usp.br
[2] Sorbonne Universités, UPMC Univ Paris 06, LIP6, 75005 Paris, France

Abstract. Although Organization-Centered MAS (OC-MAS) are suitable for developing open systems for distributed and heterogeneous environments, they are still dependent on their underlying Organizational Models and associate Organizational Middleware (or infrastructure) to execute properly. This makes interoperability an issue worthy of consideration since agents must be able to run on different organizational infrastructures in order to interact with several OC-MAS. Such issue is closely related to the distribution of responsibilities over environment technologies and subsystems, which is still under investigation among the researchers on environments for MAS. In this paper we presented a step towards providing an environment where the knowledge of different organizational infrastructures could be available by the definition of organizational artifacts. Such artifacts are distributed throughout the environment in order to provide interoperability among agents that have different underlying organizational models, following the multiagent programming approach from the JaCaMo platform.

1 Introduction

During the last decade, the research related to environments for MAS has evolved considerably, but a variety of issues still remain open [14, 24, 28, 29, 33, 34]. This collection of papers represents the first initiative on achieving some consensus in the area and establishing some challenges for interested researchers. These challenges include (i) the definition of mechanisms for addressing the responsibility of hiding the complexity of coordination issues, to regulate agent activities, and perhaps to support trust management [24]; and (ii) the identification of a general model for environment abstractions [29]. Organizational models [7–9, 11, 18] are tailored for dealing with coordination and regulation issues while modeling groups of agents in MAS; and artifacts are already used to deal with coordination [26] and to describe an organizational model via its associate dimensions along artifact-based environments [16]. This paper is related to the use of artifacts to abstract the knowledge from diverse organizational models in order to provide interoperability between MAS that are designed

© Springer International Publishing Switzerland 2015
D. Weyns and F. Michel (Eds.): E4MAS 2014 – 10 years later, LNAI 9068, pp. 209–231, 2015.
DOI: 10.1007/978-3-319-23850-0_13

according to different organizational models. In such sense, this could be seen as a step towards addressing the aforementioned challenges for artifact-based environments.

Weyns and colleagues [33] stated that environments are first class abstractions while engineering multiagent systems. They presented a definition for environments in MAS, established levels of support they could provide for the MAS as well as a reference model for guiding their design. They classify these levels of support in (i) basic level, where the environment just enables agents with access to the deployment context; (ii) abstraction level, where the environment abstracts from agents the low-level details to access the deployment context as well as some of the system resources; and (iii) interaction-mediation level, where the environment supports access regulation to shared resources and mediation of interaction between agents.

This paper is an integration of results presented at E4MAS 2014 [22] and WES-AAC 2014 [30] with additional extensions related to the description of the models and implementation of the artifacts. It is organized as follows: Sect. 2 presents an overview of our proposal, Sect. 3 presents the background knowledge for understanding the paper idea. Section 4 presents two existent organization models and their respective translations into NPL. Section 5 details the implementation of AGR following an environment-oriented approach. Section 6 discusses about what was done and compares it with some related work followed, in Sect. 7, by the conclusion and further work suggestions on the issue.

2   Overview

Our interest relies in environments that support mediated interaction, which is the case of infrastructures for electronic institutions [9]. Similar to such infrastructures are the ones that allow the execution of Organization-Centered MAS (OC-MAS). In OC-MAS, there is a definition of a set of constraints that a group of agents adopts to achieve their social purposes easily [21]. This set of constraints is usually described by organizational models, such as MOISE [18], AGR [11], and OperA [7] and their associate infrastructures. For instance, S-MOISE [19] or JaCaMo [3] are infrastructures for MOISE and MADKit [13] is for AGR. The same occurs with electronic institutions, being ISLANDER [9] the underlying organizational model for AMELI [10].

The adoption of an underlying organizational model may provide the system adaptability at runtime, whenever exposed to changes on the organizational structure [20, 31, 32] or on the environment the system is situated in [31, 32]. This characteristic makes such approach suitable for developing open systems.

However, the implementation of OC-MAS is usually dependent on organizational infrastructures (OI) tailored to the OC-MAS underlying model, preventing the realization of open systems in their strict sense. In this scenario, to interoperate with several OC-MAS, agents must be able to run on different OI, which is still an open problem. This is an issue closely related to the distribution of responsibilities over environment technologies and subsystems [28], still under investigation among the community that research on environments for MAS. One solution that deals with this is ORA4MAS [16], an approach that transfers to the environment the responsibility of the OI, implementing it through the use of artifacts [23]. In such approach, the environment is considered a software entity composed of artifacts, and agents must be able to interact with organizational artifacts, reducing the problem of joining an organization to simply interacting with the environment. An implementation of that was given considering MOISE and CArtAgO [27], which is an environment-oriented framework to support the development of MAS based on artifacts. Moreover, CArtAgO was integrated with several agent-programming platforms [25], including Jason [4].

Considering that MOISE and CArtAgO had already been integrated with Jason [17, 25], respectively, Boissier et al. recently proposed JaCaMo [3], a platform that integrates Jason, CArtAgO and MOISE by combining agent-oriented, environment-oriented and organization-oriented programming paradigms. Also, JaCaMo adopts a normative programming language (NPL) [15] to describe the organization constraints related to coordination and control originally present in MOISE (the organizational model in charge), through the inclusion of a normative engine within the organizational artifacts. In this approach, the implementation of the organizational artifacts relies on the NPL interpreter.

Therefore, we investigate if the NPL adopted by JaCaMo could be used to describe other organizational models as a first step to address interoperability among agents running on distinct organizations using an environment-oriented approach. This is so because the organizational artifacts responsible for coordinating and controlling the organization constraints only require a translation of the organization specification to the NPL to run. Moreover, responsibility for coordination and control would be abstracted within artifacts in artifact-based environments, described using the NPL, as a step towards defining a mechanism as mentioned in the aforementioned challenge (i). In addition, an environment with organizational artifacts that describe existing organizational models should be general enough considering the interaction-mediation support the environment should provide, as a step towards addressing the aforementioned challenge (ii).

3   Background Concepts and Technologies

In this section we briefly describe background concepts and technologies that are used along the proposed step towards achieving interoperability among agents that run on different organizations in open systems.

3.1   Artifacts

An artifact is the main component of a working environment. It can be defined as a passive entity, which can be managed by agents in order to perform a function [23]. Basically, it consists of an interface that agents use either to send commands or to receive information. An agent requests the artifact's functionality by triggering an operation defined in it, which is similar to a method in an object. The artifact, in turn, communicates with the agents by updating its observable properties (analogous to attributes in an object) or by sending signals. The CArtAgO framework implements artifact-based working environments through an environment-oriented approach using Java.

One of the main advantages in this approach, especially when dealing with multi-agent systems, is that agents can now rely on the environment to get resources and tools to promote their activities. For instance, because artifacts are easily accessible by any agent in a workspace, they can be of great importance when coordinated teamwork is necessary [27].

3.2 Organizational Models

Ferber [12] argues that organization is one of the basic concepts of any MAS, being such organization a predefined unit or emerging from interactions occurring during system execution. Lemaitre and Excelente [21] proposed a categorization for MAS as organization-centered (predefined unit) or agent-centered (emergent from interactions) according to the type of organization they present. Several authors [9, 21] had argued that the adoption of an organization-centered approach is tailored for developing Open MAS and, in order to realize such approach several organizational models were defined [7, 11, 18, 31].

In this paper we advocate that, although organizational models were tailored for developing Open MAS, their realization is dependent of dedicated OIs, while the responsibility about the OI knowledge is left to the agent. Usually, organizational models provide means for designing the way MAS should coordinate and control the behavior of its agents, specifying constraints in a number of dimensions. Structural constraints, for instance, define the roles and groups that will form the MAS, and functional ones specify the way agents that play such roles within some group should behave in order to achieve goals. Furthermore, some models provide rules and norms for rewarding and/or punishing agents, depending on their behavior in an organization. A study categorizing organizational modeling dimensions is presented in [6] and the associated dimensions are: functional, structural, normative, dialogical and ontological.

Therefore, leaving the agents responsible for the organizational knowledge may hamper the strict realization of open systems. In this context, organizational knowledge refers to the knowledge of the organizational model and the OI. A proposal for moving the responsibility of such knowledge to the environment was given by ORA4MAS, considering MOISE as the underlying organizational model. Our proposal is using a similar approach to move the knowledge of the AGR and OperA OIs to an artifact-based environment, as a step towards providing interoperability among Open MAS. To do so, a normative programming language must be introduced as common language to describe organizational models.

3.3 Normative Programming Language

A Normative Programming Language (NPL) is, as the name implies, a programming language based on norms. In general, a norm is a statement that describes an expected pattern of behavior and the consequences of disregarding it. In addition, the language also utilizes facts, which are statements of information, and inference rules.

Usually these norms can be one of three types: obligation, permission or prohibition and are enforced by either sanctions or regimentations [15]. An obligation constitutes a behavior that must be complied; permission refers to an allowed behavior and, of course, a prohibition is a disallowed behavior.

In the case a violation to a norm occurs, the appropriate enforcement strategy should activate. Regimentations are strategies to prevent a norm infringement in the first place; therefore, no actions that would result in regiment infraction are possible. Meanwhile sanctions are punitive strategies that become effective after an infraction, so actions that fall under a sanctioned norm are indeed possible. Regimented norms are primarily designed as means to preserve the system from otherwise harmful actions. Sanctioned norms, on the other hand, should encourage desired behavior without effectively compromising autonomy of the concerning party.

$$
\begin{aligned}
np & \ ::= \ \text{"np"} \ atom \ \text{"\{"} \ (\ rule \mid norm \ )\text{*} \ \text{"\}"} \\
rule & \ ::= \ atom \ [\ \text{":-"} \ formula \ ] \ \text{"."} \\
norm & \ ::= \ \text{"norm"} \ id \ \text{":"} \ formula \ \text{"->"} \ (\ fail \mid obl \ ) \ \text{"."} \\
\\
fail & \ ::= \ \text{"fail("} \ atom \ \text{")"} \\
obl & \ ::= \ \text{"obligation("} \ (var \mid id) \ \text{","} \ atom \ \text{","} \ formula \ \text{","} \ time \ \text{")"} \\
\\
formula & \ ::= \ atom \mid \text{"not"} \ formula \mid atom \ (\ \text{"\&"} \mid \text{"|"}) \ formula \\
time & \ ::= \ \text{"'"} \ (\ \text{"now"} \mid \\
& \qquad number \ (\ \text{"second"} \mid \text{"minute"} \mid ...)) \\
& \qquad \text{"'"} \ [\ (\ \text{"+"} \mid \text{"-"} \ ) \ time \ ]
\end{aligned}
$$

Fig. 1. NPL syntax (source [15]) - non-terminals *atom*, *id*, *var* and *number* corresponds, respectively, to *predicates*, *identifiers*, *variables*, and *numbers*, as used in Prolog.

A program described in the NPL consists of (i) a set of facts and inference rules and (ii) a set of norms. Norms have unique identifiers, activation condition and consequence. Consequence could be of types *fail* or *obligation*. Figure 1 shows the syntax of the NPL, where *np* is a program in NPL.

A successful implementation of MOISE by means of translating it to a simplified NPL containing only two constructs, *obligation* and *regimentation*, is described in [15]. This approach used the aforementioned ORA4MAS platform and had the NPL engine embedded in the organizational artifacts, as shown in Fig. 2. It was further integrated with Jason, originating JaCaMo.

In conclusion, the NPL serves to regulate behavior and, specifically in the case of MAS, it may be used to regulate agent behavior as prescribed by organizational models. Nevertheless, to make this possible, it is necessary [15]: (i) an interpreter capable of running the NPL; and (ii) the translation of the organizational specification into a normative specification.

The possibility of running distinct organizational models using the same interpreter, just by making adequate translations, led us to investigate the adoption of NPL as a step to address the interoperability problem. The NPL, in this context, would be a common language to describe organizations.

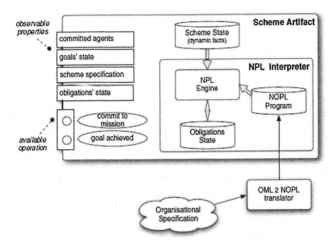

Fig. 2. General view of the organizational Scheme Artifact in MOISE (source [15])

Two organizational models are described in Sect. 4, with their respective translations into NPL. They were chosen from a list of models analyzed by Coutinho et al. [6] which was used to identify common organizational dimensions.

4   Translating Organizational Models to the NPL

4.1   AGR

Description. The AGR (Agent/Group/Role) model [11] was developed aiming at providing a simple and concise way to describe multiagent organizations. As its acronym suggests, it is based on three primitives: agents, groups and roles. Agents are proactive, autonomous and communicative entities that populate these organizations by assuming certain roles within groups. Groups can be defined as sets of agents that have some similarities. Lastly, roles are abstract representations of agent functionalities in a group.

In this model, a group is described by a group structure. Such structure contains all the characteristics that define a group, for example its name and the roles agents are allowed to play in it. Thus, it is possible to conceive groups as instances of group structures.

In AGR, two types of constraints between roles are defined, namely correspondence and dependence. If there is a correspondence constraint between two roles A and B, it means that an agent who plays A will automatically play B. In its turn, a dependence constraint between A and B means that playing A is a prerequisite to play B. This model also specifies that, in order to adopt a role, an agent should be member of the group where it is defined.

Finally, the description of this model states that it is possible to define interaction relationships between roles, in order to constrain the communication performed by agents. Moreover, communication is allowed only if the involved agents are in the same group. However, no detailed explanation about the nature of these interactions is provided, leaving it as an open aspect for implementation.

There are two organizational dimensions in AGR according to the study presented in [6]. First, the notions of groups and roles compound the structural dimension. Furthermore, the definition of interactions between agents forms the dialogical dimension. The translation will organize facts, rules and norms according to their corresponding dimension, in a similar way as done in MOISE (see Sect. 5.2).

Translation to NPL. In order to describe the AGR model in terms of normative language, it is necessary first to obtain facts and rules that are inherent to the model, and then define the correspondent norms in terms of them.

Facts. The following facts describe the structural dimension of AGR. Some of the notations used here are suggested in [11].

- member(x,g) : represents that agent x is member of group g;
- plays(x,r,g) : agent x plays role r in group g;
- GStruct(g,gs) : group g is described by group structure gs;
- roleIn(r,gs) : r is a role defined in group structure gs;
- correspondence(role1, gs1, role2, gs2) : there is a correspondence constraint between role1 defined in gs1, and role2 defined in gs2, meaning that an agent who plays role1 will be obligated to play role2;
- dependence(role1, gs1, role2, gs2) : there is a dependence constraint between role1 in gs1 and role2 in gs2, meaning that playing role2 is a prerequisite for assuming role1.

The next facts relate to the dialogical dimension of AGR.

- interact(role1,role2) : role1 has an interaction relationship with role2, meaning that an agent playing role1 can send messages to another agent playing role2. Thus, an interaction is a directed relation;
- msg(x,y,content) : agent x has sent to agent y a message content. It is assumed content is of the form achieved(g), meaning that x told y to achieve g;
- achieved(a, g) : indicates that goal g was achieved by agent a.

Next, inference rules that help describe the state of the organization will be presented. Both rules shown here relate to the structural dimension of AGR.

Rules. The first rule tells whether a certain role is defined in a group instantiated in the organization. Remember that roles are described directly in a group structure.

    rdefined(G,R) :- Gstruct(G,GS) & roleIn(R,GS).

The second one informs if two agents are members of the same group, i.e. whether there is a group g in which both agents participate.

    samegroup(X,Y) :- member(X,G) & member(Y,G).

Finally, it is possible to define the set of norms that characterize this model.

Norms. At first, we start with the norms related to the structural dimension.

- Norm role_member: if an agent X plays a role R in a group G, he must be a member of this group.

  ```
  role_member: plays(X,R,G)& not member(X,G)-> fail
  (role_member).
  ```

- Norm role_def: a role must be defined in a group structure for an agent to adopt it.

  ```
  role_def: plays(X,R,G) & not rdefined(G,R) -> fail
  (role_def).
  ```

- Norm role_corresp: implements the correspondence constraint between roles.

  ```
  role_corresp: plays(X,Role1,G1)& GStruct(G1,GS1)& GStruct
  (G2,GS2)&
  correspondence(Role1,GS1,Role2,GS2)->
  obligation(X,role_corresp,plays(X,Role2,G2),now + t).
  ```

- Norm role_dep: implements the dependence constraint between roles

  ```
  role_dep: plays(X,Role1,G1)& not plays(X,Role2,G2)&
  GStruct(G1,GS1)& GStruct(G2,GS2)&
  dependence(Role1,GS1,Role2,GS2)->
  fail(role_dep).
  ```
  The next norms are related to the dialogical dimension of AGR.

- Norm group_comm: two agents can communicate with each other only if they are members of at least one group in common.

  ```
  group_comm: msg(X,Y,C)& not samegroup(X,Y)-> fail
  (group_comm).
  ```

- Norm inter_comm: two agents may communicate only if there is an interaction defined between them.

  ```
  inter_comm: msg(X,Y,_) & play(X,R1,_) & play(Y,R2,_) & not
  interact(R1,R2)-> fail(inter_comm).
  ```

- Norm msg_obl: this norm interprets messages as a means of delegating obligations. In this view, if an agent X can send messages to Y, then X has authority over Y.

  ```
  norm msg_obl: msg(_,Y,C) -> obligation(Y, msg_obl, C,
  now + t).
  ```

4.2 OPERA

Description. OperA is a model devised to describe open MAS using formal logical semantics and aims to ensure interaction and collaboration among its members while maintaining autonomy between society design and agent design [7]. The structure of the model is split into three separate sub models: the Organizational Model, the Interaction Model and the Social Model.

The Organizational Model is a description of the system itself, that is to say, it describes how the system is organized. This description is further segmented into four components: social, communication, interaction and normative structures. The Social Structure specifies the existing roles, as well as the goals and relations associated with them. The Communication Structure defines the ontology and communication language used in the system. The Interaction Structure contains the possible system states (interaction scenes) and describes the allowed transitions between them. Finally, the Normative Structure describes norms imposed upon the roles and interaction scenes' norms.

The two remaining sub models regulate behavior within the MAS. The Social Model manages agents' enactment of roles whereas the Interaction Model serves to adjust role-enacting agents' actions during interaction scenes.

The analysis done in [6] identified five different modeling dimensions in OperA model. They are the structural dimension, encompassed by the social structure and social model; the functional dimension, represented by the interaction structure and the interaction model; the dialogical and ontological dimensions, both housed within the communication structure; and the normative dimension, associated with the normative structure.

Translation to NPL. In the following, we describe OperA model using the normative programming language, beginning with the facts and rules related to its structural dimension.

Facts.

- plays(x,r): indicates that agent x plays (enacts) role r;
- objective(obj,r): indicates that objective obj is an objective of role r;
- sub-objective(sobj,obj): indicates that objective sobj is a sub-objective of objective obj;
- contains_sub-objectives(obj): indicates that objective obj has sub-objectives;
- right(rt,r): indicates that rt is a right of role r;
- completed(obj): indicates that requirements of objective obj have been fulfilled.

Rules. This rule indicates whether an objective has been achieved. An objective is achieved if all of its sub-objectives are achieved or if, in the case it has no sub-objectives, it has been completed.

```
achieved(Obj):-contains_sub-objectives(Obj) &
.findall(Sobj,sub-objective(Sobj, Obj),L) &
allAchieved(Sobj) |
completed(Obj) & not contains_sub-objectives(Obj).

allAchieved([H|T]) :- achieved(H) & allAchieved(T).
allAchieved([]).
```

The .findall procedure is defined in Jason. In the code presented above, the method populates L with instances of Sobj that makes sub-objective(Sobj,

Obj) be a logical consequence of the set of system facts. The `allAchieved` rule takes a list as argument, and splits it in the first element H and the remaining items T. It checks if every element of the list is achieved in a recursive fashion. The `allAchieved([])` is the base case of the recursion, specifying it to stop with the empty list.

In sequence, the facts, rules and norms related to the OperA functional dimension are presented.

Facts.

- `in_progress(s)`: indicates that scene s is in progress;
- `finished(s)`: indicates that scene s has finished;
- `start(s,x)`: indicates that agent x has initiated scene s;
- `end(s,x)`: indicates that agent x has terminated scene s;
- `scene_manager(x)`: indicates that agent x may initiate and terminate scenes;
- `from(t,s)`: indicates that scene s transits from transition t;
- `to(s,t)`: indicates that scene s transits to transition t;
- `and(t)`: indicates that scene transition t is an AND operator;
- `or(t)`: indicates that scene transition t is an OR operator;
- `xor(t)`: indicates that scene transition t is a XOR operator;
- `part(l,s)`: landmark l is part of scene s;
- `order(l1,l2)`: landmark l1 is ordered before landmark l2;
- `state_requirement(obj,l)`: landmark l requires that objective obj is achieved.
- `state_negative_requirement(obj,l)`: landmark l requires that objective obj is not achieved.
- `scene_requirement(l,s)`: scene s requires that landmark l has been reached for before starting.

Rules. Scene transitions are valid when the transition requirement is satisfied. The requirement depends on the transition type: AND transitions require that all scenes leading to the transition be finished, OR transitions require that at least one scene leading to the transition be finished and XOR transitions require that one, and only one, scene leading to the transition be finished.

```
Valid(T)  :- and(T) & .findall(S,to(S,T),L) &
  allFinished(S) |
  or(T) & (to(S,T) & finished(S) |
  xor(T)&.findall(S,to(S,T),L) & oneFinished(S).

allFinished([H|T])  :- finished(H) & allFinished(T).
allFinished([]).

oneOrMoreFinished([H|T]):- finished(H) |
  oneOrMoreFinished(T)

oneFinished([H|T]):-finished(H) & not
  oneOrMoreFinished(T) |
  not finished(H) & oneFinished(T).
```

A landmark is considered reached if all state requirements and state negative requirements are met, and all previous landmarks have also been reached.

```
reached(L) :-
.findall(Obj,state_requirement(Obj,L),ListObj) &
allAchieved(ListObj) &
(.findall(Obj,state_negative_requirement(Obj,L),ListObj)&
noneAchieved(ListObj)
& .findall(PL,Order(Pl,L),ListPL) & allReached(ListPL).

noneAchieved([H|T]) :- not achieved(H) & noneAchieved(T).
noneAchieved([]).

allReached([H|T]) :- reached(H) & allReached(T).
allReached([]).
```

Norms.
```
ended_without_permission: end(S,X) & not scene_manager(X)
-> fail(ended_without_permission)

started_without_permission: start(S,X) & not sce-
ne_manager(X) -> fail(started_without_permission)

started_at_inappropriate_time: start(S,X) & from(S,T) &
not valid(T) -> fail(started_at_inappropriate_time)

and_transition: valid(T) & from(S,T) & and(T) &
scene_manager(X) ->
obligation(X,and_transition,start(S,X), now+Ts)

xor_transition: xor(T) & ( in_progress(S1) | finished(S1)
& from(T,S1)) & ( in_progress(S2) | finished(S2) &
from(T,S2)) -> fail(xor_transition)

started_without_requirements: start(S,X) &
scene_requirement(L,S) & not reached(L) ->
fail(started_without_requirements)
```

Finally, the model's explicit norms are described. Each of these explicit norms has a unique id and can either be active or inactive depending if the activation and termination conditions are met or not. They also have a maintenance condition that refers to the behavior regulated.

Norms.

```
obligation_norm_id: (activation condition) &
not(termination condition) & (maintenance condition(R))
-> obligation(X, obligation_norm_id, action, deadline)

permission_norm_id: (activation condition) &
not (termination condition) & (maintenance condition(R))
& not right(RT,R) -> fail(permission_norm_id)

prohibition_norm_id: (activation condition) &
not (termination condition) & (maintenance condition(R))
-> fail(prohibition_norm_id)
```

The following assumptions were made in the OperA's translation to the normative language:

- Group notion was not included in this description.
- Links existing between roles have also not been included here as they can be expressed through explicit norms.
- An action constitutes of any behavior that causes an observable change in the system (such as choosing to enact a role, achieving an objective or initiating/terminating a scene).
- The requirements for a scene to be initiated are represented by a list of landmarks.

Having described the models using the NPL, we are able to analyze if existing organizational artifacts could be reused by simply feeding them with NPL descriptions, or if extra modifications are required. The development for AGR is presented in the next section.

5   Work on AGR Implementation

5.1   Overview

One of the main reasons that makes the adoption of NPL interesting on the translation is the possibility of reusing the normative engine of ORA4MAS, used to implement an OI for MOISE, on the implementation of an infrastructure to run AGR. This process involves making minor modifications on the interface of the organizational artifacts, in order to reflect the particularities of the model.

The scheme presented in Fig. 3 illustrates the required adaptations on ORA4MAS to allow it to run the presented AGR translation. First, it is necessary to define a set of dynamic facts, which are used to describe the state of the organization (e.g., which agents are playing a role). Then, a set of operations must be specified on the artifacts to allow agents to interact with the organizational infrastructure, generating dynamic facts that may trigger the activation of norms. If this scheme is compared to the one depicted in Fig. 2, it is possible to notice that the AGR artifact receives the NPL file directly as input, whereas the MOISE version gets a specific OML file, and internally translate it to NPL. This modification was essential to remove the dependency of the artifacts with MOISE.

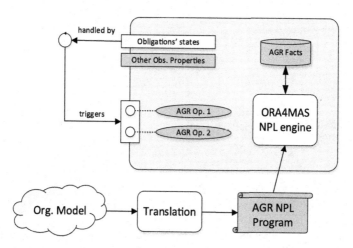

Fig. 3. Adaptations performed on ORA4MAS to allow compatibility with AGR's NPL translation

It is important to point out that these adaptations do not change the requirements over the agents. Since the NPL language remains unmodified, an agent that understands obligations, running in a MOISE organization, should run with this AGR implementation.

Since the artifacts for AGR will be heavily based on existing ones used in MOISE, it is convenient to explain briefly how they are originally implemented.

5.2   MOISE's Organizational Artifacts Implementation

As explained previously, ORA4MAS is an artifact-based solution, implemented on top of the CArtAgO framework. Thus, it basically consists in an object-oriented implementation of a set of organizational artifacts. The class diagram shown in Fig. 4 presents relevant classes of ORA4MAS, as found in JaCaMo.

The main class in this diagram is `OrgArt`, which contains the normative interpreter `NPLInterpreter` and is responsible to parse the OML file and initialize the organizational artifacts with static facts, rules and norms. The `CollectiveOE` class is responsible to keep track of the state of the organization, defining dynamic facts and providing them to the normative engine through the `DynamicFactsProvider` interface (this is detailed in the next section). The `GroupBoard` and `SchemeBoard` classes implement the actual artifacts, each of them with an associated `CollectiveOE` instance (`Group` and `Scheme`, respectively). It is interesting to notice that each of these artifacts deal with a specific dimension of MOISE [6] (structural and functional, respectively). When instantiating a GroupBoard, for instance, the artifact loads facts, rules and norms related to the structural dimension, labeled as "group" in the NPL file.

Analyzing the code of the artifacts, it is possible to infer what actions are taken to update the state of the organization when an operation is triggered by an agent. Figure 5 shows a sequence diagram with the methods called by `GroupBoard` when an agent triggers its `adoptRole` operation. First, the `addPlayer` method on `CollectiveOE` is called to add the dynamic fact `plays(a,r,g)`, meaning that agent a

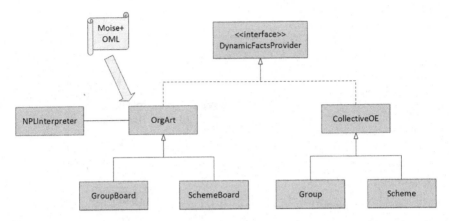

Fig. 4. Class diagram of MOISE artifacts in JaCaMo, showing relevant classes only [30]

adopted role r in group g. These facts are stored in lists either in the CollectiveOE class or in one of its children. Then, verifyNorms is called to check if the addition of the fact violated a norm or triggered an obligation. If no violation occurs, GroupBoard notifies any linked artifacts about the change with notifyObservers and the dynamic fact is made visible by agents by defining it as an observable property. However, if a violation is detected, the state of the organization is reverted, and a failure signal is emitted.

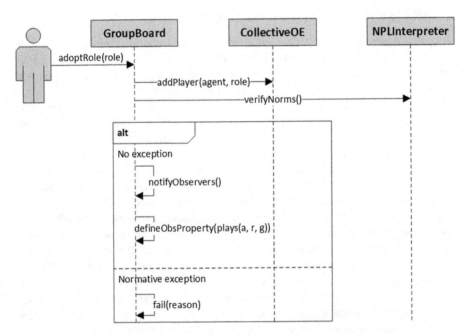

Fig. 5. Sequence diagram illustrating the main operations taken by the GroupBoard when the adoptRole operation is triggered

This analysis makes it possible to use MOISE artifacts as a starting point for implementing the ones for AGR, as explained in the next section.

5.3 Implementation of AGR Artifacts

The first step in designing artifacts for AGR is to define how many of them are necessary to represent an AGR organization. For instance, MOISE adopted `Group-Board` and `SchemeBoard` to represent its structural and functional dimensions [6], respectively. Likewise, it seems natural to adopt a `GroupBoard` for AGR, since it models essentially the structure of the organization. The dialogical dimension of this model is implemented into the `GroupBoard` artifact as well, since communication constraints are strongly dependent on the definition of roles. Then, in order to remove dependency with MOISE, the initialization procedure of `OrgArt` must be modified, removing the parser and making it accept an NPL file directly. This is quite straight-forward if we compare Figs. 2 and 3. The only necessary modification is to feed the NPL engine directly, bypassing the OML to NPL parser.

The following operations were defined in the `GroupBoard` artifact.

- `enterGroup`: this operation is responsible to generate the fact `member(x,g)`, which is related to an agent's membership to a group;
- `adoptRole`: reflects the adoption of a role, generating the fact `play(x,r,g)`;
- `sendMessage`: implements the dialogical part of the organization. Generates a fact `msg(x,y,c)`, where `c` should be in the form `achieved(g)`;
- `achieved`: this operation is triggered by an agent when it achieves the obligation expressed in a message. Generates the fact `achieved(g)`.

Each of these operations behave in a similar way as shown in Fig. 5, dealing with the corresponding dynamic facts and checking the normative constraints when triggered.

Now, it is necessary to deal with the definition and storage of the dynamic facts, allowing them to be supplied to the normative engine when necessary. This is done exactly as in MOISE: the `GroupBoard` has a `Group` class associated, where the dynamic facts `play`, `member`, `gstruct`, `msg` and `achieved` are defined and the corresponding lists are created for their storage.

Lastly, it is necessary to provide a way for the normative engine to know where each dynamic fact is generated and stored. This is trivial for this implementation of AGR, which has only one organizational artifact, but is essential for more complex models. To solve this issue, the authors of ORA4MAS defined the `DynamicFactsProvider` interface, which specifies two methods: `isRelevant` and `consult`. The first one informs whether an artifact is responsible to hold a given fact, while the second one returns the list corresponding to the fact. Thus, for AGR, it was enough to enumerate the dynamic facts generated in `GroupBoard` and map each fact to its list.

5.4 Example: Write Paper Organization

In order to test this implementation, a simple organization was instantiated, consisting of only one group with two roles. The role "Editor" has authority over "Writer", meaning that an editor can send messages delegating tasks to a writer. This example was inspired by the writing paper example using MOISE, presented at [16]. The organization structure is represented in Fig. 6, using the same notation as suggested in [11].

The input NPL file corresponding to this organization is presented below.

```
scope group(writePaperGr) {

  //Facts for the write paper group
  roleIn(editor, writePaperGr).
  roleIn(writer, writePaperGr).
  interact(editor, writer).

  //Rules
  //Those are the same for any AGR group
  rdefined(G,R) :- gstruct(G,GS) & roleIn(R,GS).
  samegroup(X,Y) :- member(X,G) & member(Y,G).

  //Norms
  //These are the same for any AGR group
  norm role_member:
  play(X,R,G) & not member(X,G) -> fail(role_member).

  norm role_def:
    play(_,R,G) & not rdefined(G,R) ->  fail(role_def).

  norm role_correspondence:
    correspondence(Role1, Gs1, Role2, Gs2) &
    play(X, Role1, G1) & gstruct(G1, Gs1) &
    gstruct(G2, Gs2) ->
    obligation(X, Role_correspondence, play(X, Role2,
    G2),`now`+`30 minutes`).

  norm role_dependence:
    dependence(Role1, Gs1, Role2, Gs2) &
    play(X, Role1, G1) & not play(X, Role2, G2) &
    gstruct(G1, Gs1) & gstruct(G2, Gs2) ->
    fail(role_dependence).

  norm inter_comm:
      msg(X,Y,_) & play(X,R1,_) & play(Y,R2,_) &
      not interact (R1, R2) -> fail(inter_comm).

  norm group_comm:
      msg(X,Y,_) & not samegroup(X,Y) -> fail(group_comm).

  norm msg_obl:
      msg(_,Y,C) & play(X,R1,_) & play(Y,R2,_) & interact
  (R1, R2) ->
      obligation(Y, msg_obl, C, `now`+`30 minutes`).
}
```

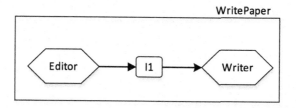

Fig. 6. Organizational structure used for testing AGR's infrastructure

The next step is to design two Jason agents to interact in this group, called *Alice* and *Bob*. *Alice* will create a CArtAgO workspace and instantiate one AGR `GroupBoard` artifact, specifying the above NPL file. Then, she will join the group she has just created and adopt the role editor (if she did not join the group, norm role_member would fail). After that, she waits for *Bob* to adopt role writer, and sends him a message to achieve the goal of writing a section. The code for *Alice* is shown below.

```
/* Initial goals */
!create_org.

/* Plans */
//Create a CArtAgO workspace and the write paper group
+!create_org
  <- createWorkspace("ora4mas");
   joinWorkspace("ora4mas", _);

   //instantiate the GroupBoard, and point to the NPL
   //file
   makeArtifact("wpaper", "agr.ora4mas.nopl.GroupBoard",
     ["src/AGR.npl", "writePaperGr", false, false],
     GrArtId);
   focus(GrArtId);

   //wait for Bob and send him the message to write
   .wait(+play(bob, writer, "wpaper"));
   sendMessage("bob",
     "achieved(write_section)")[artifact_id(GrArtID)].
```

Bob tries to enter the workspace and group created by *Alice*, and when he succeeds to do so, he adopts role writer. Then, he waits for *Alice* to send her order. Bob's Jason code is shown below.

```
/* Initial goals */
!join.
!enter_org.

/* Plans */
+!join
 <- joinWorkspace("ora4mas",_).

+!enter_org
 <- lookupArtifact("wpaper", ArtID);
    //enter the group created by Alice, and adopt role
    //writer
    enterGroup[artifact_id(ArtID)];
    focus(ArtID);
    adoptRole("writer")[artifact_id(ArtID)].

+!write_section
 <- //do some work...
    //tell the organization that the goal is achieved
    achieved(write_section)[artifact_id(ArtID)].
```

The code below is necessary for any agent intending to participate in the organization. They define plans that handle the correspondence constraint, which is the obligation to play a certain role, and the obligation resulting from a message. Therefore, they are included in both agents.

```
//plans to deal with role correspondence
+obligation(Ag,Norm,play(_, Role, Group),Deadline)
      : .my_name(Ag)
    <- !adopt_role (Role, Group).

+!adopt_role (Role, Group)
<-  lookupArtifact(Group, GroupID);
    adoptRole(Role)[artifact_id(GroupID)].

//plan to deal with obligation from messages
+obligation(Ag,Norm,achieved(Goal),Deadline)
      : .my_name(Ag)
    <- !Goal.
```

Notice that this code is the only knowledge of AGR that agents are required to have (apart from knowing what type of artifact to instantiate), and even so, they are merely checking the content of obligations for AGR-specific constructs. This is very similar to what is found in the code of agents used to run the MOISE write paper example[1]. The difference is that they check for contents specific to MOISE in the obligations.

---

[1] Available at http://moise.sourceforge.net/.

Figure 7 shows *Bob*'s beliefs after running the agents for a few reasoning cycles. It is clear that his beliefs reflect the state of the organization, which both agents get from focusing on the organizational artifact. Also, notice that *Alice*'s message triggered the norm `msg_obl`, generating the obligation directed to *Bob*, who in turn responded accordingly.

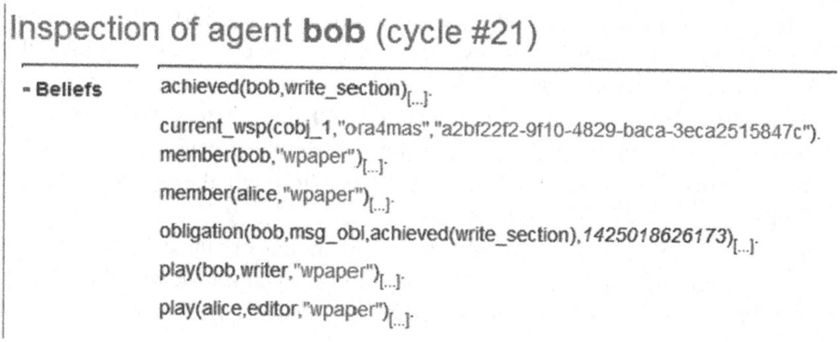

Inspection of agent **bob** (cycle #21)

· Beliefs	achieved(bob,write_section)$_{[...]}$
	current_wsp(cobj_1,"ora4mas","a2bf22f2-9f10-4829-baca-3eca2515847c").
	member(bob,"wpaper")$_{[...]}$
	member(alice,"wpaper")$_{[...]}$
	obligation(bob,msg_obl,achieved(write_section),*1425018626173*)$_{[...]}$
	play(bob,writer,"wpaper")$_{[...]}$
	play(alice,editor,"wpaper")$_{[...]}$

Fig. 7. Bob's beliefs after running the agents

6 Discussion

The results of the work done in [15] suggest that the adoption of the proposed normative programming language and its artifact-based interpreter is a viable solution for transferring the responsibility of one OI to the environment. We advocate that this could be generalized for existing OIs as a step towards the interoperability problem for organizational models. The key idea is to investigate the possibility of translating different organizational models other than MOISE to the NPL, that was left open in [15], and analyze whether the implemented infrastructure for the interpreter fits with the translation. Our initial work consisted in understanding the main aspects of two organizational models, namely AGR and OperA, and describing them in terms of facts, rules and norms. The results presented in Sect. 4 shows that this translation is feasible, at least for these two models.

The next step was checking whether the artifact-based interpreter for MOISE, as implemented in JaCaMo, could be used with our translation in order to effectively run the organization. Preliminary results presented in Sect. 5 for AGR suggests that it is possible to manipulate the existing artifacts to accept a general NPL file and, with a number of adaptations, it is also possible to allow the execution of the organization.

For OperA, analyzed in Sect. 4.2, which incorporates both the functional and structural dimensions, but also dialogical, normative and ontological ones, an additional artifact may be required to deal with the dialogical dimension. In addition, the existing structural and functional artifacts may suffer modifications to incorporate elements not present in other organizational models. Moreover, since the ontology is directly translated into NPL facts, there is no need of an artifact dedicated to the ontological dimension. Finally, we presume that there is no need for a normative artifact, since the normative engine embedded in the artifacts already represents this dimension.

Arcos et al. [1] presented EIDE, an integrated environment which includes a set of technologies to develop electronic institutions where all the institution regulation mechanisms are implemented in the environment. They argue that their approach is tailored for developing a-open systems, which require an agent to adscript to the institution conventions in order to enter in the system. As AMELI and ISLANDER are among the technologies it encompasses, adscripting to the institution conventions implies to be modeled according to ISLANDER or, at least, have the knowledge of how to interact with institutional governors [2]. In our proposal, we advocate that including organizational artifacts with embedded NPL interpreters in the environment could be used by agents modeled according different organizational models to understand the organization/institution conventions (through the artifacts observable properties) in order to commit to them.

Esparcia et al. [8] defined a set of artifacts to model organizational mechanisms within MAS environments, adding to the Virtual Organization Metamodel (VOM) an environmental dimension. Their approach only suggests transferring the responsibility of regulating organizations to the environment, since it is devoted to modeling and no implementation was provided until now. Nevertheless, they do not address the problem of using such artifacts to deal with agents modeled according to organizational models diverse from VOM.

At the best of our knowledge, Coutinho et al. [5] is the only work that explicitly addresses the organizational interoperability problem. They defined a model-driven approach to build an integrated organizational model that can be mapped to existing ones and used as a common model as a means to provide interoperability among different organizational models.

7   Conclusion and Future Work

Environments play an important role for developing MAS. Whenever we think about electronic institutions or other systems that relies on organizational models, an issue to be considered is the distribution of responsibilities related to the coordination and control of their agents. Currently, such systems run in dedicated environments, also known as organizational infrastructures (OI).

In this paper, we presented a step towards providing an environment where the knowledge of different OIs could be available through the definition of organizational artifacts, and distributed throughout the environment in order to provide interoperability among agents that have different underlying organizational models.

To accomplish this, we analyzed the use of a NPL to describe organization specifications from two organizational models: AGR and OperA. The analysis showed that the NPL proposed by Hübner et al. could, in fact, be used as is to describe organization specifications from the aforementioned models. Also, the results from the infrastructure implementation for AGR were encouraging, since it reinforces the possibility of adopting ORA4MAS as a model to build generic organization infrastructures within artifact-based environments.

As mentioned, the description of different organizations in a common language and running on a homogeneous framework is a first step to achieve interoperability. This solution allows interaction with distinct organizations, but does not provide a means to enable agents to reason about the organizational characteristics. This matter should be further explored to provide better support for open systems. Moreover, the translation of OperA into NPL should be tested in order to ensure correctness, which is left as future work. Finally, performance issues related to CArtAgO regarding the instantiation of multiple organizational artifacts must be considered and is a subject that requires further investigation.

Acknowledgements. Fabio T. Muramatsu and Tomas M. Vitorello were partially supported by grant #013/17948-7, São Paulo Research Foundation (FAPESP), and #013/17973-1, São Paulo Research Foundation (FAPESP). Anarosa A. F. Brandão is supported by grant #014/03297-7, São Paulo Research Foundation (FAPESP).

References

1. Arcos, J.L., et al.: Engineering open environments with electronic institutions. Eng. Appl. Artif. Intell. **18**(2), 191–204 (2005)
2. Arcos, J.-L., Noriega, P., Rodríguez-Aguilar, J.-A., Sierra, C.: E4MAS through electronic institutions. In: Weyns, D., Van Dyke Parunak, H., Michel, F. (eds.) E4MAS 2006. LNCS (LNAI), vol. 4389, pp. 184–202. Springer, Heidelberg (2007)
3. Boissier, O., et al.: Multi-agent oriented programming with JaCaMo. Sci. Comput. Program. **78**(6), 747–761 (2013). M. Mernik, et al., (eds)
4. Bordini, R.H., Hübner, J.F., Wooldridge, M.: Programming Multi-agent Systems in AgentSpeak Using Jason, vol. 8. Wiley, New York (2007)
5. Coutinho, L.R., Brandão, A.A.F., Sichman, J.S., Hübner, J.F., Boissier, O.: A model-based architecture for organizational interoperability in open multiagent systems. In: Padget, J., Artikis, A., Vasconcelos, W., Stathis, K., da Silva, V.T., Matson, E., Polleres, A. (eds.) COIN@AAMAS 2009. LNCS, vol. 6069, pp. 102–113. Springer, Heidelberg (2010)
6. Coutinho, L.R., Sichman, J.S., Boissier, O.: Modelling dimensions for agent organizations. In: Virginia, D. (ed.) Handbook of Research on Multi-Agent Systems: Semantics and Dynamics of Organizational Models, pp. 18–50. IGI Global, Hershey (2009)
7. Dignum, M.V.: A model for organizational interaction: based on agents, founded in logic. SIKS (2003)
8. Esparcia, S., et al.: Artifacting and regulating the environment of a virtual organization. In: 2011 23rd IEEE International Conference on Tools with Artificial Intelligence (ICTAI 2011), pp. 547–554. IEEE (2011)
9. Esteva, M., de la Cruz, D., Sierra, C.: ISLANDER: an electronic institutions editor. In: Proceedings of the First International Joint Conference on Autonomous Agents and Multiagent Systems: part 3, Bologna, Italy. ACM, New York (2002)
10. Esteva, M., et al.: AMELI: an agent-based middleware for electronic institutions. In: Proceedings of the Third International Joint Conference on Autonomous Agents and Multiagent Systems, vol. 1. IEEE Computer Society, New York (2004)
11. Ferber, J., Gutknecht, O., Michel, F.: From agents to organizations: an organizational view of multi-agent systems. In: Giorgini, P., Müller, J.P., Odell, J.J. (eds.) AOSE 2003. LNCS, vol. 2935, pp. 214–230. Springer, Heidelberg (2004)

12. Ferber, J., Perrot, J.-F.: Les systèmes multi-agents: vers une intelligence collective. InterEditions (1995)
13. Gutknecht, O., Ferber, J.: MadKit: a generic multi-agent platform. In: Proceedings of the Fourth International Conference on Autonomous agents, Barcelona, Spain, pp. 78–79. ACM, New York (2000)
14. Helleboogh, A., et al.: Modeling dynamic environments in multi-agent simulation. Auton. Agent. Multi-Agent Syst. **14**(1), 87–116 (2007). Kluwer Academic Publishers-Plenum Publishers
15. Hübner, J.F., Boissier, O., Bordini, R.H.: A normative programming language for multi-agent organisations. Ann. Math. Artif. Intell. **62**(1–2), 27–53 (2011). Springer, Netherlands
16. Hubner, J.F., et al.: Instrumenting multi-agent organisations with organisational artifacts and agents. Auton. Agent. Multi-Agent Syst. **20**(3), 369–400 (2010). Springer US
17. Hübner, J.F., Bordini, R.H., Picard, G.: Using Jason and Moise + to develop a team of cowboys. In: Hindriks, K.V., Pokahr, A., Sardina, S. (eds.) ProMAS 2008. LNCS, vol. 5442, pp. 238–242. Springer, Heidelberg (2009)
18. Hübner, J.F., Bordini, R.H., Picard, G.: A model for the structural, functional, and deontic specification of organizations in multiagent systems. In: Bittencourt, G., Ramalho, G. (eds.) SBIA 2002. LNCS, vol. 2507, pp. 118–128. Springer, Heidelberg (2002)
19. Hübner, J.F., Sichman, J.S., Boissier, O.: S-Moise(+): a middleware for developing organised multi-agent systems. In: Boissier, O., Padget, J., Dignum, V., Lindemann, G., Matson, E. (eds.) ANIREM and OOOP 2005. LNCS, vol. 3913, pp. 64–77. Springer, Heidelberg (2006)
20. Hübner, J.F., Sichman, J.S., Boissier, O.: Using the MOISE + for a cooperative framework of MAS reorganization. In: Bazzan, A.L.C., Labidi, S. (eds.) SBIA 2004. LNCS (LNAI), vol. 3171, pp. 506–515. Springer, Heidelberg (2004)
21. Lemaitre, C., Excelente, C.B.: Multi-agent organization approach. In: Lemaitre, G.A. (ed.) Proceedings of II Iberoamerican Workshop on DAI and MAS, Toledo, Spain (1998)
22. Muramatsu, F.T., Vitorello, T.M., Brandao, A.A.F.: Towards organizational interoperability through artifacts. E4MAS (2014). http://homepage.lnu.se/staff/daweaa/events/E4MAS/2014/4.pdf
23. Omicini, A., Ricci, A., Viroli, M.: Artifacts in the A&A meta-model for multi-agent systems. Auton. Agent. Multi-Agent Syst. **17**(3), 432–456 (2008). Springer US
24. Platon, E., et al.: Mechanisms for environments in multi-agent systems: Survey and opportunities. Auton. Agent. Multi-Agent Syst. **14**(1), 31–47 (2007). Kluwer Academic Publishers-Plenum Publishers
25. Ricci, A., et al.: Integrating heterogeneous agent programming platforms within artifact-based environments. In: Proceedings of the 7th International Joint Conference on Autonomous Agents and Multiagent Systems, vol. 1, pp. 225–232. International Foundation for Autonomous Agents and Multiagent Systems, Estoril, Portugal (2008)
26. Ricci, A., Viroli, M.: Coordination artifacts: a unifying abstraction for engineering environment-mediated coordination in MAS. Informatica (Slovenia) **29**(4), 433–443 (2005)
27. Ricci, A., Viroli, M., Omicini, A.: CArtAgO: a framework for prototyping artifact-based environments in MAS. In: Weyns, D., Van Dyke Parunak, H., Michel, F. (eds.) E4MAS 2006. LNCS (LNAI), vol. 4389, pp. 67–86. Springer, Heidelberg (2007)
28. Valckenaers, P., et al.: Applications and environments for multi-agent systems. Auton. Agent. Multi-Agent Syst. **14**(1), 61–85 (2007). Kluwer Academic Publishers-Plenum Publishers

29. Viroli, M., et al.: Infrastructures for the environment of multiagent systems. Autonomous Agents and Multi-Agent Systems **14**(1), 49–60 (2007). Kluwer Academic Publishers-Plenum Publishers

30. Vitorello, T.M., Muramatsu, F.T., Brandao, A.A.F.: Extending JaCaMo for organizational interoperability. In: Silva, V.T., Bordini, R.H., Meneguzzi,F. (eds.) 2014 Proceedings of the WESAAC 2014. PUCRS, Porto Alegre, Brazil, pp. 143–148 (2014)

31. Weyns, D., Haesevoets, R., Helleboogh, A.: The MACODO organization model for context-driven dynamic agent organizations. ACM Trans. Auton. Adapt. Syst. **5**(1), 1–29 (2010). ACM, New York

32. Weyns, D., et al.: The MACODO middleware for context-driven dynamic agent organizations. ACM Trans. Auton. Adapt. Syst. **5**(1), 1–28 (2010). ACM, New York

33. Weyns, D., Omicini, A., Odell, J.: Environment as a first class abstraction in multiagent systems. Auton. Agent. Multi-Agent Syst. **14**(1), 5–30 (2007). Kluwer Academic Publishers-Plenum Publishers

34. Weyns, D., Van Dyke Parunak, H., Michel, F., Holvoet, T., Ferber, J.: Environments for multiagent systems state-of-the-art and research challenges. In: Weyns, D., Van Dyke Parunak, H., Michel, F. (eds.) E4MAS 2004. LNCS (LNAI), vol. 3374, pp. 1–47. Springer, Heidelberg (2005)

Infrastructures to Engineer Open Agent Environments by Means of Electronic Institutions

Dave de Jonge[✉], Juan A. Rodriguez-Aguilar, Bruno Rosell i Gui,
and Carles Sierra

Artificial Intelligence Research Institute, IIIA,
Spanish National Research Council, CSIC,
08193 Bellaterra, Spain
{davedejonge,jar,rosell,sierra}@iiia.csic.es

Abstract. Electronic institutions provide a computational analogue of human institutions to engineer open environments in which agents can interact in an autonomous way while complying with the norms of an institution. The purpose of this paper is twofold. On the one hand, we lightly survey our research on coordination infrastructures for electronic institutions in the last ten years. On the other hand, we highlight the research challenges in environment engineering that we have tackled during this journey as well as promising research paths for future research on the engineering of open environments for multi-agent systems.

1 Introduction

As the complexity of actual-world applications increases, particularly with the advent of the Internet, there is a need to incorporate organisational abstractions into computing systems that ease their design, development, and maintenance. Electronic Institutions (EIs) are at the heart of this approach [3]. Just like any human institution, an EI is a place where participants come together and interact according to some pre-defined norms. An EI warrants that the norms of the institution are enforced upon its participants, and thus prevents them from misbehaving. Therefore, an EI provides the *environment* in which agents can interact in an autonomous way within the norms of the institution.

From a computational point of view, an EI realises an environment for agents in the sense proposed in [22], namely it provides "the surrounding conditions for agents to exist and that mediates both the interaction among agents and the access to resources". Considering the levels of support, as defined in [22], which an environment may provide, EIs focus on two particular levels of support: (i) an abstraction level that shields agents from the low-level details of deployment, and (ii) mediated interaction between agents. With this aim, EIs provide a computational infrastructure for agent environment design, as discussed in [21], and the mechanisms to enforce and monitor the norms and laws that apply to a multi-agent system in a given environment. More precisely, an EI is implemented itself

D. Weyns and F. Michel (Eds.): E4MAS 2014 – 10 years later, LNAI 9068, pp. 232–254, 2015.
DOI: 10.1007/978-3-319-23850-0_14

as a multi-agent system composed of two types of (internal) agents, the so-called staff agents and governor agents. While governor agents mediate the interactions of (external) agents within the environment, staff agents manage the norms in the institution. The dynamics of the environment is restricted to those external agents that satisfy the social laws represented by the norms and enacted by the coordinated actions of governors and staff agents. With this aim, governors and staff agents employ synchronisation mechanisms for interaction mediation, along the lines of [17].

EIs have been under development for almost 20 years, which has resulted in a large framework consisting of tools for implementing, testing, running and visualizing them [3]. Therefore, research on EIs has strongly focused on contributing with infrastructures and tools that support systematic engineering support of environments for multi-agent systems, which has been identified as one of the challenges in environment engineering [20].

Since their inception, EIs have focused on computationally realising environments for multi-agent systems. The purpose of this paper is to show the evolution of the infrastructures that we have employed over these years to engineer *open* agent environments by means of electronic institutions. We aim at illustrating the way the surveyed infrastructures deal with different degrees of openness.

With this aim, we survey the four generations of coordination infrastructures for EIs developed so far. For each generation, we dissect: (i) the features of the coordination infrastructure running an EI; (ii) the facilities provided to support human participation; and (iii) a case study illustrating some application built with the aid of EIs. Furthermore, after introducing each generation of the corresponding EI infrastructure, we provide a critical analysis that motivates the need to move from one generation to the next one.

First, we lightly touch upon first generation (1G) EIs, whose tremendous development complexity and effort motivated the subsequent introduction of AMELI [13], a general-purpose coordination infrastructure for second generation (2G) EIs. 2G EIs represented a very significant advance with respect to 1G EIs because they provided MAS engineers with well-founded tools that significantly eased development. Thus, the development of 2G EIs consists of two main stages: the specification of institutional rules by means of ISLANDER [12], a graphical specification tool; and their subsequent execution by AMELI, a general-purpose coordination infrastructure. Hence, instead of programming an EI, as it was the case with 1G EIs, 2G EIs allow a MAS engineer to focus on *specifying* the rules of an EI.

Nonetheless, some drawbacks hinder the applicability of 2G EIs. On the one hand, 2G EIs cannot be designed and enacted on-line. Consider, for instance, a business scenario where manufacturers are allowed to meet on-line and arrange collaborations on the fly to produce the goods requested by customers. These companies do not know beforehand neither what customers will request, nor the partners to collaborate with, nor the rules of their collaborations. In this setting, if a group of manufacturers aim at employing an EI to structure their collaboration, this must be designed and enacted on-line upon request. On the other hand, human participation in 2G EIs is highly complex, since it forces users to learn about the inner formal languages employed by EIs.

Third-generation (3G) EIs were conceived to support the on-line enactment of EIs. This facility is provided in the realm of the Agreement Technologies Environment (ATE) [1], an OSGi-compliant [2], open environment that provides the seamless interplay of agents and services. An EI is offered as an organisation service within the ATE. Thus, during the run-time operation of the ATE, agents participating in the environment are allowed to start and run an EI at any given time. In other words, EIs can be started on-line, during the run-time operation of the ATE, depending on agents' needs. And yet, notice that 3G EIs do not offer any facilities for the on-line design of EIs, though this is an important requirement for applications requiring the on-line enactment of collaborations (e.g. crowdsourcing, supply chain formation).

Indeed, some open environments may require that communities of participants design electronic institutions on-line. The fourth generation of tools for EIs is completely web-based, the tools allow users to specify EIs using a graphical editor that is much simpler than ISLANDER, and less expressive as well. There are no free lunches. Specifications can include web services and agents. Users can search specifications and launch them, participate in them through a web browser and enjoy an automatically generated web interface. The programming effort has been reduced enormously in this generation of tools. Finally 4G EIs are implemented as a P2P network of nodes that allows to exploit the benefits inherent to P2P systems (e.g. self-organisation, resilience to faults and attacks, low barrier to deployment, privacy management, etc.).

The paper is organised as follows. Sections 2, 3, 4, and 5 review the features of the first, second, third, and fourth generations of EIs. Section 6 further analyses the relationship between EIs and environments, and Sect. 7 draws some conclusions and sets paths to future research.

2   First Generation: Electronic Institutions Enacted by Ad-Hoc Coordination Infrastructures

First-generation (1G) EIs are represented by the early developments reported in [10,18]. Each of those EIs implemented an electronic auction house inspired on the fish market described in [16] with different focuses. First, [10] is a proof-of-concept, PVM-based implementation of the fish market. The use of PVM [15] was intended to support and ease the distributed execution of agents and communication protocols. As reported in [18] (see Sect. 5), further prototype development of the fish market followed using PVM and MPI for inter-networking and C and EU-Lisp. All of these implementations focused on low-level communication aspects and shared the commonality of being rather costly. Finally, the implementation in [18], thanks to the use of the Java language, allowed us to focus on modularity and search for the core objects required to implement structured interactions in an EI.

All in all, the EIs implemented from [10] to [18] focused on developing each their own, ad-hoc coordination infrastructure. Furthermore, in all cases, support for human interaction was provided by means of tailored graphical user interfaces. However, notice that all of them realised open, distributed environments that supported the remote participation of trading agents.

3   Second Generation: Electronic Institutions Enacted by a General-Purpose Coordination Infrastructure

The experience during the implementation of the above-described first-generation electronic institutions taught us that the design and development of open MAS is a highly complex task. This motivated research on tools that ease MAS engineers' development effort. Thus, in [4], we introduced EIDE, an integrated development environment for electronic institutions that supports all the stages of the design and development of an open MAS as an electronic institution. EIDE clearly differentiates two main stages: the specification of institutional rules; and their subsequent execution by a coordination infrastructure. In this way, instead of programming an electronic institution, as it was the case for first-generation electronic institutions, a MAS engineer can focus on *specifying* the rules of an electronic institution.

In this section we describe the key features of AMELI, the coordination infrastructure provided by EIDE to run electronic institutions. Moreover, we also comment on the tools provided by EIDE to support human interaction. Finally, we analyse the drawbacks of second-generation electronic institutions.

3.1   AMELI: A Core Infrastructure for Electronic Institutions

The infrastructure (i.e. set of institutional agents) that enables the execution of EIs is called AMELI [13]. AMELI enables agents to act in an electronic institution and controls their behaviour. Its main functionalities are:

- to provide a way for different agents with different architectures to communicate with one another without any assumption about their respective internal architectures; and
- to enforce a protocol of behaviour as specified in an institution specification upon the agents. This means that AMELI makes sure that the agents can only do those actions that the protocol allows them to do.

AMELI was conceived as a general-purpose platform in the sense that the very same infrastructure can be used to deploy different institutions. With this purpose, agents composing AMELI load institution specifications as XML documents generated by ISLANDER, a graphical editor for EI specifications. Thus, the implementation impact of introducing institutional changes amounts to the loading of a new (XML encoded) specification. Therefore, it must be regarded as domain-independent, and it can be used in the deployment of any specified institution without any extra coding. During an EI execution, the institutional agents composing AMELI keep the execution state and they use it, along with the institutional rules encoded in the specification, to validate agents' actions and to enforce their consequences.

AMELI is composed of three layers: a communication layer, which enables agents to exchange messages, a layer composed of the external agents that participate in an EI, and in between a social layer, which controls the behaviour of the participating agents. The social layer is implemented as a multi-agent system whose institutional agents are responsible for guaranteeing the correct execution of an EI according to the specification of its rules.

The participation of each agent in an EI through AMELI is handled by a special type of institutional mediator, the so-called governor. An agent must be able to communicate with its governor, but this only requires that the agent is capable of opening a communication channel. Since no further architectural constraints are imposed on external agents, we can regard AMELI as agent-architecture neutral.

The current implementation of AMELI can either use JADE (Bellifemine et al., 2001) or a publish-subscribe event model as communication layer. When employing JADE, the execution of AMELI can be readily distributed among different machines, permitting the scalability of the infrastructure. From the point of view of the participating agents in an EI, AMELI is communication neutral, since they are not affected by changes in the communication layer.

3.2 Human Participation

Instead of providing a domain-dependent graphical user interface for human interaction as first-generation electronic institutions did, EIDE provides a general-purpose interface, the so-called *dummy agent*. Figure 1 depicts a screenshot of the dummy agent as displayed to a user. On the left-hand side, the interface shows a tree-like structure that displays the run-time structure of an electronic institution together with the agents participating in the institution. Such run-time structure is composed of the on-going activities (scenes) in an electronic institution. On the right hand side, the figure shows the events, including the speech acts exchanged between agents, occurring within a particular scene selected by the user. Notice that the dummy agent offers a user the possibility of building speech acts to interact with the rest of agents within an institution. In other words, humans interact using the same language employed by software agents. Therefore, in order to participate in an electronic institution by means of a dummy agent, a user must know: (i) how an electronic institution is formally represented; and (ii) the formal language employed by EIDE to represent speech acts.

3.3 Case Study

EIDE was employed in the development of an actual-world application: the Multi-Agent System for FIsh Trading (MASFIT) [9]. MASFIT allows buyers to remotely participate in several wholesale fish auctions simultaneously with

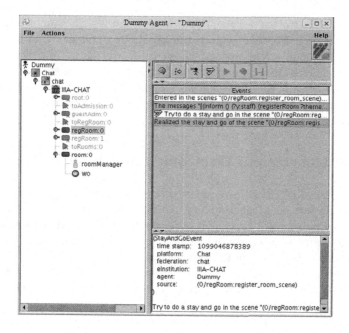

Fig. 1. Dummy agent user interface.

the help of software agents, while maintaining the operation of traditional auctions. The participation of buyer agents in actual-world auctions is mediated by an electronic institution run by AMELI. MASFIT's institution controls buyers' access to the auctions, provides them with information, and collects their bids during the auctions. To permit this, the actual auction systems running at different auction houses were connected to the developed institution. MASFIT interconnects multiple auction houses, and thus provides structure to a federation of auction houses. MASFIT guarantees equal conditions for both human buyers physically participating at the auction and software buying agents participating through the Internet.

3.4 Analysis

2G EIs represent a significant advance with respect to 1G EIs. Very importantly, notice that the tools developed to design and run 2G EIs are general-purpose. That means that the very same tools can be employed to design and run different EIs. In this new context, MAS engineers do not have to cope any longer with low-level implementations of communication and coordination protocols, as it was the case for 1G EIs. Instead, they can only concentrate on *specifying* the rules for EIs. Therefore, 2G EIs allow to shift the development effort from programming to specifying.

Nonetheless, several drawbacks may hinder the applicability of 2G EIs. First, notice that the design of the rules of the institution is carried out off-line by a single user, the institution designer. That means that 2G EIs cannot be employed in application domains that require the on-line enactment of an EI. Second, AMELI enacts open environments whose rules are static, and hence cannot change over time. Third, human interaction is highly intricate, since it forces human users to learn the inner formal languages of EIs. This is too heavy a burden for human users, and clearly motivates the need for more user-friendly EI interfaces.

4   Third Generation: Electronic Institutions

Third generation (3G) EIs were conceived to allow agents the on-line enactment of EIs. To support such functionality, we developed the so-called Agreement Technologies Environment (ATE) [1], a service-oriented, open environment that provides the seamless interplay of agents and services. Then, an EI is offered as an organisation service within the ATE. Thus, during the run-time operation of the ATE, agents participating in the environment are allowed to start and run an EI at any given time. In other words, EIs can be started during the run-time operation of ATE depending on agents' needs.

Next, in Sect. 4.1 we describe the implementation of Agreement Technologies Environment. As part of this description, we detail how EIs are offered within the environment as organisation services. Thereafter, in Sect. 4.2 we describe a case study that shows how EIs are designed and enacted on-line, namely during the operation of the ATE. Finally, Sect. 4.3 explains how 3G EIs simplify human participation with respect to 2G EIs, while Sect. 4.4 provides a critical analysis.

4.1   Agreement Technologies Environment

The Agreement Technologies Environment (ATE) [1], formerly introduced in [1], is an environment that provides the seamless interplay of agents and services. We chose to implement the ATE as a service-oriented environment based on the OSGi [2] technological framework.

The OSGi technology is a *de facto* industry standard that defines a dynamic component system for Java. OSGi reduces complexity by providing a modular architecture for today's large-scale distributed systems as well as for small, embedded applications. Therefore, the OSGi programming model is called to fulfill the promise of component-based systems and beyond, since OSGi is intended to allow an application to emerge from dynamically assembling a set of components.

Modularity is at the core of the OSGi specifications and embodied in the *bundle* concept. Bundles are the OSGi components built by developers. AN OSGi bundle is like a Java JAR file, but it hides everything unless explicitly exported. The OSGi architecture offers a service model whose aim is to have bundles collaborate. The services layer connects bundles in a dynamic way. This is feasible because a bundle can register a service, it can get a service (from another bundle), and it can listen for a service (from another bundle) to appear or disappear. Furthermore, services are dynamic: bundles can register and withdraw their services at any time.

To summarise, OSGi provides a very powerful architecture to support the dynamic collaboration of services offered by bundles. We developed the ATE to be OSGi-compliant. However, in order to turn it into an environment were also agents were able to participate, it was endowed with bundles providing three types of agent support services: (i) agent-to-service interactions; and (ii) agent-to-agent interactions; (iii) multi-agent collaborations. Figure 2 shows the architecture of the ATE developed on top of OSGi. The agent support services mentioned above correspond to the following groups of services (bundles):

Service Tools. They allow agents, as well as services, to discover and call remote services in a distributed environment.

Agreement Services. They are intended to help agents to reach agreements (by means of argumentations), and monitor and manage agreements (by means of the use of trust and reputation ratings provided by the trust/reputation service, which in turn may require the use of the ontology service).

Organisation Services. They provide services to enact collaborations between agents. For instance, an EI is offered as a service. In fact, notice that all the services provided by EIDE, the development environment for 2G EIs, are provided as organisation services.

Figure 2 also shows environment and user interface services. On the one hand, environment services ensure that dependencies between modules are met and facilitate collaborations in a distributed environment. On the other hand, user interface services provide interfaces to the ATE and define an interface to help ATE services to implement interactions with human users.

As mentioned above, EIs are offered as organisation services. In the example that follows, we illustrate the on-line design and enactment of EIs by groups of agents taking part in the ATE.

4.2 Case Study

In [1] we describe the *Assembling Business Collaborations for Multi-agent System* (ABC4MAS) platform, a collaboration environment to support the rapid

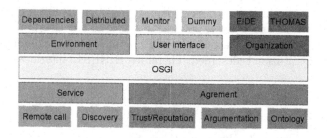

Fig. 2. ATE services and tools.

assembly of agent-oriented business collaborations. ABC4MAS allows: (i) to set up a collaboration environment as a virtual organization; (ii) to reach agreements within the collaboration environment to form short-term business collaborations to manufacture customer-requested goods; (iii) to enact business collaborations to produce goods; and (iv) to track the performance of agents within business collaborations to build their trust and reputation. ABC4MAS was built as an application running on the Agreement Technologies Environment described in Sect. 4.1 above.

Figure 3 shows the architecture of the ABC4MAS platform. First, the platform counts on a collaboration environment enacted as a virtual organisation thanks to the THOMAS Platform [5]. When a customer within this collaboration environment issues an order, a new virtual organisation is spawned to service the request. This virtual organisation contains all business parties that may take part in the production of the requested good together with an auctioneer. The auctioneer is in charge of assessing an optimal supply chain by means of a mixed auction [8], an auction protocol aimed at solving supply chain formation problems. Hence, after clearing the auction, the auctioneer obtains the specification of a supply chain that it translates into an EI specification. Thereafter, the auctioneer launches an EI by means of the AMELI service, which is fed with the EI specification generated by the auctioneer. AMELI then tracks each and every action as defined in the supply chain, allowing the auctioneer to monitor: (1) which entity is performing each task, (2) that all the agreements are being fulfilled, and (3) that no task is overdue. When AMELI detects that the production process has finished, both the EI and the virtual organization started to serve the customer request are terminated. At production time, during the execution of an EI, there is a service, the Supplier Relationships Management (SRM) service [14] is in charge of collecting information about the agents taking place in the supply chain to keep up to date the trust and reputation values of the agents participating in the collaboration environment.

4.3 Human Participation

In Sect. 3.2 we argued that the interaction of a user with a dummy agent is intricate. 3G EIs try to overcome this problem. Thus, they offer a methodology, the so-called *human interaction within hybrid environments regulated through electronic institutions* (HIHEREI) [6], to help an institution designer produce a more user-friendly interface to electronic institutions. Unlike a dummy agent, which was conceived as a general purpose interface to any electronic institution, an interface produced by means of HIHEREI is tailored to the domain for which the electronic institution is designed. Therefore, HIHEREI interfaces are domain-specific.

4.4 Analysis

Although 3G EIs allow to dynamically start EIs as services, they do not offer any facilities to support the on-line design of EIs, neither by a single designer

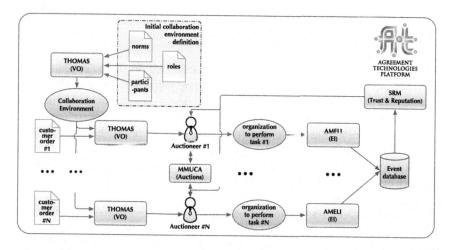

Fig. 3. ABC4MAS platform architecture.

nor by a group of designers. And yet, this feature is particularly interesting in some application domains. For instance, consider a social network that lets its users form their own communities and choose and enact their own rules. Furthermore, although 3G EIs ease human participation by means of the HIHEREI methodology, this new approach still suffers from some drawbacks. First, it is now the designer, and not the end user, the one who must know about the formal languages used by EIs. Furthermore, HIHEREI does offer a methodology, but the designer is responsible for programming users' interfaces. In other words, HIHEREI shifts the burden from the end user, as it is the case in 2G EIs, to the EI designer. Second, the interface produced by HIHEREI is as static as the dummy agent offered by 2G EIs. More precisely, such an interface starts out with a single EI specification that cannot change at run time. Consider again a social network like the one mentioned above. In that setting, the interface of a user may need to change depending on the different communities where the user participates. In the next section we show how fourth generation EIs have successfully tackled these issues.

5 Fourth-Generation: Peer-to-Peer Electronic Institutions

In a recent document by IBM, "Device Democracy: Saving the future of the Internet of Things"[1] a case is made about the uncertain future of centralised approaches in the context of networks composed of billions of interconnected devices. Centralised approaches would become prohibitively expensive, would not protect privacy and would not make business models endure.

It is our ambition that electronic institutions become a pervasive mechanism to co-ordinate very large networks of humans and devices and thus a centralised

---

[1] ibm.biz/devicedemocracy.

approach seems a bad solution for the future. We thus wanted to recover the spirit of the implementations of the first generation using libraries like PVM or MDI but with modern technologies.

Peer-to-peer (P2P) networks appear as the natural option to implement distributed electronic institutions nowadays as they provide a number of desirable properties. They are very robust in that there is no single point of failure. If a node fails, the other nodes may continue the computation, in many cases without any loss or with minimal loss of information. P2P networks scale very well as a new node increases the overall amount of computation requests but it also brings in resources in the form of e.g. memory or CPU cycles. Nodes are equally privileged and the quality of service they receive does not depend on whether they can afford expensive cloud servers.

In the last decade many applications and technologies have been built using this approach: file sharing (e.g. Gnutella or BitTorrent), distributed storage (e.g. Symform, Freenet, Yvi), or web search engines (e.g. Yaci, Faroo). P2P platforms (i.e. set of interconnected nodes over TCP/IP protocols) provide different features: trust, authentication, data persistency, state guarantee, anonymity, etc.

In this section we will describe an implementation of a P2P software node, named PeerFlow, that extends AMELI (of the second generation) with a number of P2P features. Thus, the fourth generation grows out of the second generation incorporating an improved human interface over HIHEREI from the third generation and leaving out the Agreement Technologies toolbox structuring the third generation. We may however incorporate some of these tools in the near future.

5.1   PeerFlow Basic Infrastructure

We have built PeerFlow on top of the *Freepastry*[2] library. A free and open-source Java library that implements Peer-to-Peer network [7,11,19]. Freepastry provides a number of useful features such as the routing of messages, or the possibility to create broadcast messages.

5.2   P2P Electronic Institution Internal Agents

A running institution is managed by a number of agents called *scene managers* and *governors*. On a Peer-to-peer system one needs to decide on which node in the network each of these agents will be running. For this reason we have added another type of agent to the framework called the *device manager*. Each node in the network runs exactly one device manager. Whenever a new agent needs to be launched, the device managers determine where that agent is going to be launched. In the current implementation this is decided randomly, but in future implementations the device managers will apply negotiation to make such decisions, taking into account the capacity of each node (e.g. bandwidth and CPU power).

---

[2] http://www.freepastry.org/FreePastry/.

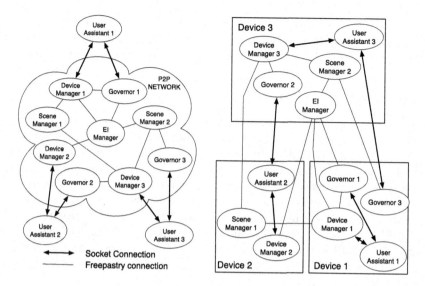

Fig. 4. Diagram of the Peer-to-Peer Electronic Institutions topology

Note that the agents participating in the EI are not directly inside the P2P network. Instead, they are connected to a governor through a direct socket connection, which is inside the P2P network. We have chosen this model for security reasons, because messages in a P2P network do not always go straight from sender to receiver, but may make several 'hops' between nodes of the network before arriving at the receiver. This means that agents participating in the institution would be able to intercept those messages and manipulate them.

5.3 Peerflow Distributed Database

Peerflow also provides a distributed database where users can publish their EI-specifications, search for existing specifications, and search for running instances of electronic institutions. This is implemented using the indexer/search library *Apache Lucene.*[3] Each node in the network has its own repository which is maintained by the device manager. When a query to the database is made, this query is sent to all the device managers in the network, and each of them sends back a reply, if possible.

5.4 Building Software Agents. What's Different?

Programming an agent that interacts in a P2P EI can be done in two ways. One way consists of extending an existing Java agent that abstracts away all the underlying communication protocols. The other way is to make use of a *rest governor*. The intended actions of the agent are then sent as http requests to the

---

[3] http://lucene.apache.org/.

rest governor. The advantage of the second method is that one can use any kind of programming language or technology that allows making web requests, but has the disadvantage that one has to deal with the http protocol on a lower level.

5.5   Human Participation

Earlier versions of EIDE, in the second and third generations, where intended as a framework for software agents and did not provide significant support for humans to participate in Electronic Institutions. For many purposes, however, it is desirable to have both humans and agents participating. One can for example imagine an auction house in which bids are made by humans, but in which the tasks of the auction house, such as registration of participants and leading the auction are taken care of by automated agents. Therefore, we have extended the existing EI framework with a Graphic User Interface (GUI) that allows humans to enter into an EI and interact with other users or software agents. This new extension is called GENUINE, which stands for GENerated User INterface for Electronic institutions.

We think that this extension could be especially useful for the development of a new type of social network, where users can set up sub-communities, each with its own rules and protocols. We think that the fact that many social networks are nowadays existing next to each other is inefficient and is due to the fact that users are not able to adapt norms and protocols to their own needs. Electronic Institutions would provide a solution to this problem. Another advantage of allowing human users to interact in an EI is that it enables developers of institutions to test an institution during its development, without having to program any agents. While the EI is under development human users can take the place of the software agents that would later participate in it, for testing purposes. This can highly increase the speed of development.

Our tool automatically generates a default user interface based on the EI specification, without the need for extra programming. But, on the other hand, if one does require a more case-specific user interface, it still provides an API that enables any web designer to easily design a custom GUI without the need for much knowledge of Electronic Institutions or Java programming. Our approach is completely web-based, meaning that the GUI is in fact a website, implemented using standard web-technologies such as HTML5, Javascript and AJAX. In short, we have developed our framework with the following goals:

– To allow people to interact in an EI through a web browser.
– To have a generic GUI that is generated automatically.
– To allow any web designer to easily design a new GUI, if desired.
– To allow testing of an EI under development, before having implemented its agents.

Our Framework. A human user would interact in an EI by clicking buttons in a browser window. To allow these actions to have effect in the EI, we have

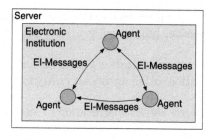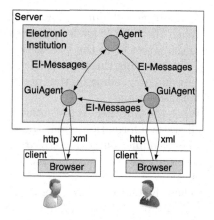

Fig. 5. Left: a 'classic' EI with only software agents. Right: an EI with one software agent and two users. In these images the agents are located on a server, but they may just as well run on a P2P node.

implemented a software agent that represents the user inside the EI and that executes the actions requested by the user. This agent is called the *GuiAgent*. Its current implementation does not do anything autonomously, but, if necessary, it can be extended with more sophisticated capabilities, such as giving intelligent strategic advice to the user.

When developing the framework we took into account that, on one hand, one may want to have a good-looking GUI that is specifically designed for a given institution. But, on the other hand, one may not want to develop an entirely new GUI for every new institution, or one may want to have a generic GUI available to test a new EI during its development, so that one can postpone the design of its final GUI until the EI is finished. Therefore, our framework allows for both. It generates a GUI automatically from the EI-specification, but at the same time provides an API that enables web designers to easily create a custom GUI for every new EI. The framework is used on top of the existing EI-framework and consists of the following components:

- A Java agent called *GuiAgent* that represents the user in the EI.
- A Java component that encodes all relevant information the agent has about the current state of the institution into an xml file.
- A Javascript library called *GenuineConnection* that translates the xml file into a Javascript object called *EiStateInfo*.
- A Javascript library called *GenuineDefaultGUI* that generates a default Graphic User Interface (as html) based on the EiStateInfo object.

How It Works. In order for a user to participate in an institution, there must be an instance of that EI running on a server or in the P2P network. To join the institution, the user then needs to open a web browser and navigate to the institution's URL. The process then continues as follows:

1. A web page including the two Javascript libraries is loaded into the browser.
2. When the page is loaded, GenuineConnection library sends a login request to the server or to the P2P network.
3. Upon receiving this request the server or network starts a GuiAgent for the user and, depending on the specific institution, other agents necessary to run the institution.
4. When the GuiAgent is instantiated it analyzes the EI-specification to retrieve all static information about the institution.
5. The GenuineConnection library starts a polling service that periodically (typically several times per second) requests a status update from the GuiAgent.
6. When the GuiAgent receives a status update request it asks its Governor for the dynamic information about the current status of the institution.
7. The GuiAgent converts both the static and the dynamic information into xml which is sent back to the browser.
8. The GenuineDefaultGUI Javascript library then uses this information to update the user interface (more information about this below).
9. The user can now execute actions in the institution or move between its scenes by clicking buttons on the web page.
10. For each action the user makes, the GenuineConnection library sends a HTTP-request to the GuiAgent.
11. The GuiAgent uses the information from the http-request to create an EI-message which is sent like any other message in a standard EI.

As explained, the GuiAgent uses two sources of information: static information from the EI-specification stored on the hard disk of the server and dynamic information from the Governor. The static information consists of:

- The names and protocols of the scenes defined in the institution.
- The roles defined in the institution.
- The ontology of the institution.

While the dynamic information consists of:

- The current scene and its current state.
- The actions the user can take in the current state of the scene.
- For each of these actions: the parameters to be filled out by the user.
- Which agents are present in the current scene
- Whether it is allowed to leave the scene and, if yes, to which other scenes the user can move.

Generating the GUI. Every time the browser receives information from the GuiAgent, it updates the GUI. This takes place in two steps, respectively handled by the two Javascript libraries. In the first step the GenuineConnection library converts the received XML into a Javascript object called EiStateInfo, which is composed of smaller objects that represent the static and dynamic information as explained above.

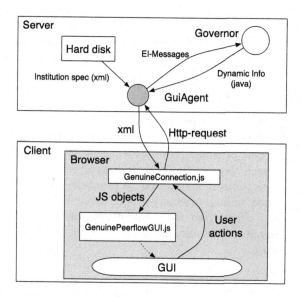

Fig. 6. The components necessary to generate the GUI. Solid arrows indicate exchange of information. The dashed arrow indicates that the GUI is created by the GenuineDefaultGUI library

In the second step the EiStateInfo-object is used by the GenuineDefaultGUI library to draw the GUI. This GUI is completely generic, so it looks the same for every institution. If one requires a more fancy user interface tailored to one specific EI, one can write a new library that replaces the GenuineDefaultGUI.

The fact that these two steps are handled by two different libraries enables designers to reuse the GenuineConnection when designing a new GUI, without having to worry about how to communicate with the EI and retrieve the necessary information from the EI to draw the GUI. All information will be readily available in the EiStateInfo-object, so one only needs to determine how to display it on the screen.

Customizing the GUI. A customized GUI-generator can retrieve all necessary information from the EiStateInfo-object. For example: if the user chooses to make a bid in an auction, the GUI-generator would read from the EiStateInfo-object that an Integer parameter must be set to represent the price the user wants to bid. The programmer of the GUI-generator should make sure that whenever a parameter of type Integer is required, the GUI displays an input-control that allows the user to introduce an integer value.

The fact that one can also define user-defined types in an EI adds a lot of flexibility. Suppose for example that one would like a user to record an audio file and send this in a message to another agent. Electronic Institutions do not support audio files by default. However, the institution designer may define a new type with the name 'Audio'. Once the user chooses to send a message that includes audio, the EiStateInfo-object will indicate that a parameter of type Audio is needed. A customized GUI-generator could then be implemented such that a microphone is activated whenever this type of parameter is required.

5.6   Case Study: PRAISE

We have used the P2P infrastructure in an application to music learning. As one-to-one teaching is very expensive we have built electronic institutions that support the interactions of communities of learners. We call each institution a 'lesson plan' where each scene in the institution represents a musical activity of students and teachers (upload songs, analyse progress, give feedback, etc.), see Fig. 7. In this use case, human interaction is facilitated by GENUINE, you can see an example of interface from the point of view of student Carles in Fig. 8 and the result of an automatic audio analysis in Fig. 9. For further details go to www.iiia.csic.es/praise.

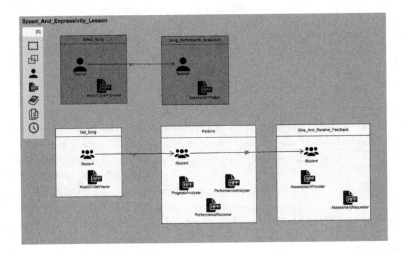

Fig. 7. An example of a lesson plan. Boxes represent scenes, arrows flow of participants and APPs represent web services.

5.7   Case Study: WeCurate

WeCurate is an image browser for collaboratively curating a virtual exhibition from a cultural image archive—group curation. WeCurate allows users to synchronously view media and enables negotiation about which images should be added to the group's image collection. Further, it accelerates the navigation of extensive museum databases and provides a platform for sociocultural experiences, combining the actions of autonomic agents and users to facilitate decision-making. WeCurate is tasked with establishing the users' presence in the shared

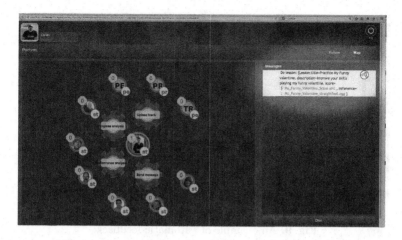

Fig. 8. A group of students within an activity to check their progress using automatic analysis tools.

experience by enabling communication around the deconstruction and appropriateness of the media, representing social proxies, and making agent and group members' actions manifest to everyone. In Figs. 10, 11 and 12 you can see the ad-hoc interface developed over P2P for WeCurate. For further details visit http://www.iiia.csic.es/ace/project.

6   On the Relationships Between Electronic Institutions and Environments

It is time to analyse the relationship between EIs and environments by considering how research on EIs has contributed to the challenges posed by research on environments for multi-agent systems. As mentioned in 1, since their inception, EIs have focused on computationally realising environments for multi-agent systems. With this aim, research on EIs has contributed with infrastructures for agent environment design [21], such as illustrated by the different infrastructures surveyed in this paper. EIs propose a particular software architecture for an agent environment [22] that distinguishes between the agents participating in the environment and the institutional agents (staff agents and governor agents) in charge of guaranteeing that the norms of the institution are satisfied. Thus, institutional agents in EIs are in charge of the responsibilities of an agent environment as detailed in [22] and they share the required synchronisation mechanisms to support social interactions according to norms.

Notice though, that research on EIs has not only focused on infrastructures for agent environment design. In a more general sense, research on EIs has strongly focused on tools that support the systematic engineering of agent environments, identified as one of the main challenges in environment engineering in [20].

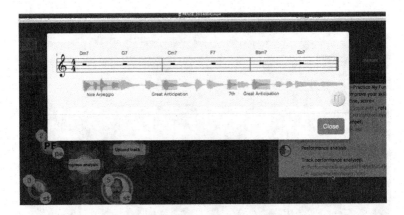

Fig. 9. An example of automatic feedback.

Fig. 10. The selection scene, which aims to gauge the interest level of users in the proposed image.

The infrastructures surveyed in this paper have tried to illustrate how EIs can help enact environments. Thus, 1G and 2G EIs help enact environments that are open to agent participation but whose rules are static. Next, 3G EIs allow to enact agent environments at run time. Moreover, EIs are enacted in the realm of the Agreement Technologies Environment (ATE). That means that an environment, ATE, can host agent environments that run as EIs. Finally, 4G EIs go even one step further, since they allow agents to *design* and *enact*

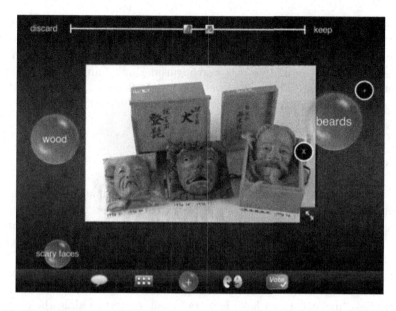

Fig. 11. The forum scene, which allows users to engage in a discussion about the image, once it has been deemed interesting in the selection scene.

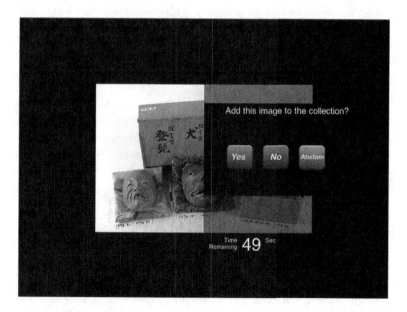

Fig. 12. The vote scene, where users can vote on whether they wish to store the image to their collection.

their own environments at run-time. Notice therefore that 3G EIs and 4G EIs share a commonality: there is an environment that allow agents to start their own environments. This makes us revisit the three levels of environment support discussed in [22]. We argue that it is worth considering a fourth level of support: *interaction design level*. This is the level of support offered to agents so that they can design themselves their own interactions, namely their own environments within the environment they are immersed in.

7   Conclusions

In this paper we have shown the evolution of the coordination infrastructures that we have employed for almost 20 years to engineer open environments as EIs. First, we have discussed that the first evolution of our coordination infrastructures was motivated by the need for supporting the development of EIs. Thereafter, our focus on new application domains (e.g. social networks, social computing, collaborative on-line learning) posed new challenging requirements that pushed the development of the next generation of coordination infrastructures for EIs. In short, there have been two main drivers guiding the evolution of EIs, namely:

- The need for designing and running *social environments*. We have pursued to increase openness to computationally realise environments where users can dynamically create and enact their own interaction environments. On the one hand, users are allowed to collaboratively design on-line the rules of their own interaction environments. On the other hand, the coordination infrastructure is ready to enact the decentralised design and execution of such interaction environments.
- The need to facilitate human interaction. The next decade will witness an increased amount of mixed societies where humans, devices, sensors and actuators will constitute an Internet of Things as the substrate of new applications like smart homes, service robotics or ambient intelligence. The simplification of the human interaction with co-ordination infrastructures like EIs is key for those applications.

These two needs have by no means been fully satisfied. Thus, future generations of coordination infrastructures for EIs will definitely focus on making progress along these two directions.

Acknowledgements. This paper has been partially funded by the following projects: TIN2012-38876-C02-01, PRAISE (FP7-318770), CollectiveMind (TEC2013-49430-EXP), ACE (Autonomic software engineering for online Cultural Experiences), and the Generalitat of Catalunya (2014 SGR 118).

References

1. Penya-Alba, T., Mikhaylov, B., Pujol-Gonzalez, M., Rosell, B., Cerquides, J., Rodríguez-Aguilar, J.A., Esteva, M., Fabregues, A., Madrenas, J., Sierra, C., Carrascosa, C., Julian, V., Rodrigo, M., Vassirani, M.: An environment to build and track agent-based business collaboration. In: Ossowski, S. (ed.) Agreement Technologies, vol. 8, pp. 611–624. Springer, Heidelberg (2013)
2. OSGi Alliance. Osgi. http://www.osgi.org. Accessed February 2015
3. Arcos, J.L., Esteva, M., Noriega, P., Rodríguez-Aguilar, J.A., Sierra, C.: Engineering open environments with electronic institutions. Eng. Appl. AI **18**(2), 191–204 (2005)
4. Arcos, J.L., Esteva, M., Noriega, P., Rodríguez-Aguilar, J.A., Sierra, C.: An integrated development environment for electronic institutions. In: Software Agent-Based Applications, Platforms and Development Kits, pp. 121–142. Birkhäuser, Basel (2005)
5. Argente, E., Botti, V., Carrascosa, C., Giret, A., Julian, V., Rebollo, M.: An abstract architecture for virtual organizations: the THOMAS approach. Knowl. Inf. Syst. **29**(2), 379–403 (2010)
6. Brito, I., Pinyol, I., Villatoro, D., Sabater-Mir, J.: Hiherei: human interaction within hybrid environments, Budapest, Hungary, pp. 1417–1418 (2009)
7. Castro, M., Druschel, P., Kermarrec, A.-M., Rowstron, A.: One ring to rule them all: service discovery and binding in structured peer-to-peer overlay networks. In: Proceedings of the 10th Workshop on ACM SIGOPS European Workshop, pp. 140–145. ACM (2002)
8. Cerquides, J., Endriss, U., Giovannucci, A., Rodríguez-Aguilar, J.A.: Bidding languages and winner determination for mixed multi-unit combinatorial auctions, pp. 1221–1226 (2007)
9. Cuni, G., Esteva, M., Garcia, P., Puertas, E., Sierra, C., Solchaga, T.: Masfit: Multi-agent system for fish trading. In: ECAI, vol. 16, p. 710 (2004)
10. Di Napoli, C., Sierra, C., Giordano, M., Norlega, P., Furnari, M.M.: A PVM implementation of the fishmarket multiagent system. In: Proceedings of the ISAI/IFIS 1996, Mexico-USA Collaboration in Intelligent Systems Technologies, pp. 68–76. IEEE (1996)
11. Rowstron, A., Druschel, P.: Pastry: scalable, decentralized object location, and routing for large-scale Peer-to-Peer systems. In: Guerraoui, R. (ed.) Middleware 2001. LNCS, vol. 2218, pp. 329–350. Springer, Heidelberg (2001)
12. Esteva, M., de la Cruz, D., Sierra, C.: ISLANDER: an electronic institutions editor. In: Proceedings of the First International Joint Conference on Autonomous Agents & Multiagent Systems, AAMAS 2002, Bologna, Italy, 15–19 July 2002, pp. 1045–1052 (2002)
13. Esteva, M., Rosell, B., Rodríguez-Aguilar, J.A., Arcos, J.L.: Ameli: an agent-based middleware for electronic institutions. In: Proceedings of AAMAS, pp. 236–243 (2004)
14. Fabregues, A., Madrenas-Ciurana, J.: SRM: a tool for supplier performance. In: Proceedings of the 8th International Conference on Autonomous Agents and Multiagent Systems, vol. 2, pp. 1375–1376. International Foundation for Autonomous Agents and Multiagent Systems (2009)
15. Geist, A., Beguelin, A., Dongarra, J., Jiang, W., Manchek, R., Sunderam, V.: PVM: Parallel Virtual Machine-A Users' Guide and Tutorial for Networked Parallel Computing. MIT Press, Cambridge (1994)

16. Noriega, P.: Agent-mediated auctions: the fishmarket metaphor. Ph.D. thesis Universitat Autònoma de Barcelona (1997). Number 8 in IIIA Monograph Series. IIIA (1999)
17. Platon, E., Mamei, M., Sabouret, N., Honiden, S., Van Dyke Parunak, H.: Mechanisms for environments in multi-agent systems: survey and opportunities. Auton. Agent. Multi-Agent Syst. **14**(1), 31–47 (2007)
18. Rodriguez-Aguilar, J.A., Noriega, P., Sierra, C., Padget, J.:. Fm96.5 a java-based electronic auction house. In: Second International Conference on the Practical Application of Intelligent Agents and Multi-Agent Technology: PAAMS 1997, pp. 207–224 (1997)
19. Rowstron, A., Kermarrec, A.-M., Castro, M., Druschel, P.: SCRIBE: the design of a large-scale event notification infrastructure. In: Crowcroft, J., Hofmann, M. (eds.) NGC 2001. LNCS, vol. 2233, pp. 30–43. Springer, Heidelberg (2001)
20. Valckenaers, P., Sauter, J., Sierra, C., Rodriguez-Aguilar, J.A.: Applications and environments for multi-agent systems. Auton. Agent. Multi-Agent Syst. **14**(1), 61–85 (2007)
21. Viroli, M., Holvoet, T., Ricci, A., Schelfthout, K., Zambonelli, F.: Infrastructures for the environment of multiagent systems. Auton. Agent. Multi-Agent Syst. **14**, 49–60 (2007)
22. Weyns, D., Omicini, A., Odell, J.: Environment as a first class abstraction in multiagent systems. Auton. Agent. Multi-Agent Syst. **14**(1), 5–30 (2007)

Author Index